S0-CRP-573

N.Y.S. Textbook Law
WHITESBORO CENTRAL
SCHOOL DISTRICT,
WHITESBORO, N.Y.

25

UNDERSTANDING AND USING APPLEWORKS™

Frank Short
Computer Coordinator
Brookfield Public Schools

West Publishing Company
St. Paul   New York   Los Angeles   San Francisco

To Julie, Michael, Lisa, and Bobby for their help, patience, love, and understanding

Credits: pp. 9, 10, 12, 13, 15, 17, 34, 46, 48, 50–53, 55, 67, 68, 78, 81, 82, 84, 87, 94, 102, 116, 119, 131, 163, 177, 179, 205 Courtesy of Apple Computer, Inc.

Copy Editor: Pamela S. McMurry
Cover Design: Bob Anderson, Artform Communications, Inc..

Apple® is a registered trademark of Apple Computer, Inc.
AppleWorks™ is a trademark of Apple Computer, Inc.

COPYRIGHT © 1986 by WEST PUBLISHING COMPANY
50 West Kellogg Boulevard
P.O. Box 6452
St. Paul, MN 55164-1003

All rights reserved

Printed in the United States of America

Library of Congress Cataloging-in-Publication Data

Short, Frank.
  Understanding and using appleworks.

  (The Microcomputing series)
  Includes index.
   1. AppleWorks (Computer program) 2. Business Data
processing. I. Title. II. Series.
HF5548.4.A68S54 1986   005.36'9   86-15877
ISBN 0-314-26023-4 (soft cover)
ISBN 0-314-31159-9 (hard cover)

CONTENTS

PUBLISHER'S NOTE

This book is part of THE MICROCOMPUTING SERIES. As such it is an endeavor unique both to West Educational Publishing and to the College Publishing Industry as a whole.

We are "breaking this new ground" because in talking with educators across the country, we found several different needs not easily met by just one publication. Those needs are:

1. To teach the principles or concepts of microcomputer use independent of running specific software programs,
2. To teach the skills of specific application software programs, and
3. To create a microcomputer curriculum flexible enough to handle changes in technology or courses with a minimum of change in the teaching materials used.

THE MICROCOMPUTING SERIES is an innovative attempt to meet those needs by closely integrating a machine independent overview of microcomputers (the core text) with a series of inexpensive, software specific, "hands on" workbooks. Although each text in the series can be used independently, they become especially effective when used together to provide both an understanding of how microcomputers work as well as experience using popular software packages.

We hope THE MICROCOMPUTING SERIES fits your needs and the needs of your students, and that you will adopt one or more of its components for use in your classes. We are also interested in hearing your reaction and suggestions concerning our series and encourage you to share your ideas with us through:

West Publishing Company
College Division
50 W. Kellogg Blvd.
P.O. Box 43526
St. Paul, MN 55164

ABOUT THE AUTHOR

Frank Short holds an M.S. degree from Western Connecticut State College in Mathematics Education and is working toward a Certificate of Advanced Study in Educational Technology at Fairfield University. He is the Computer Coordinator for the Brookfield, Connecticut, Public School System, where he has worked extensively with students and school personnel in the field of computers since 1971. He is responsible for the introduction and growth of computers in the Brookfield schools, where computer topics are now taught from Kindergarten to Continuing Adult Education.

Mr. Short also teaches a course in AppleWorks at Fairfield University. His teaching and consulting experiences have provided ample material for this book.

Other books by Mr. Short include IBM PC For Kids From 8 to 80, Howard W. Sams & Co., Inc., 1984, and IBM PC Jr. For Kids From 8 to 80, not yet published.

PREFACE

AppleWorks™, a product of Apple Computer, Inc., has been praised for its ease of use and versatility in both school and business applications. It recently has become the most sold, most popular software package in the microcomputer industry. Its applications for personal, school, and business use are apparently inexhaustible.

WHY THIS BOOK?

Understanding and Using AppleWorks™ originated as a guide for several AppleWorks courses and inservice programs taught in Brookfield and New Milford in 1985 and 1986. As of this writing there are several AppleWorks books available, but none specifically address the use of AppleWorks at the secondary level and none are appropriate as a text for a semester course. **Understanding and Using AppleWorks™** is such a book.

WHO SHOULD USE THIS BOOK?

You are part of the intended audience if you are learning or teaching AppleWorks in a vocational or academic environment. Examples and illustrations in the book are specifically designed for young adults of high school, or college age.

Using and Understanding AppleWorks™ may be used alone, with other books in the series (listed on the back cover), or to supplement any other book in a course where knowledge of AppleWorks is required.

The book may be used with AppleWorks versions 1.0 through 1.3. The figures in the book were produced with version 1.3.

HOW TO USE THIS BOOK

Understanding and Using AppleWorks is divided into three main parts: fundamental, intermediate, and advanced AppleWorks operations. The units in the first part should be covered in order, but the order is not critical for the units in the second and third parts. Each guided activity is designed for hands-on work. You will get the maximum benefit of the activity only when you sit at the computer and work through the lessons step by step. Some of the exercises ask you to modify the work that you have done in the guided activities. All of these exercises should be completed.

All of the units in parts 1 and 2 contain:

Learning Objectives: the knowledge and skills addressed in the unit.

Important Keystrokes and Commands the commands to be covered; a quick reference to the contents of the unit.

Guided Activities: a step-by-step, hands-on illustration of the operations discussed in the unit.

Computer Screens: full screen figures depicting the steps and results of most commands; a point of reference as you work through Guided Activities.

Checkpoints: questions to test your understanding of the Guided Activity and to reinforce your learning. Answers to checkpoints are in Appendix B.

Review Questions: an additional study tool.

End-of-Unit Exercises: further projects you can do to practice the skills and concepts you have developed.

Additional features of **Understanding and Using AppleWorks** are:

Applications: simulations of real-world situations to provide more opportunities to practice what you have learned so far.

Getting Started on Your Microcomputer (Appendix A) a reference for using the Apple IIe, and its keyboard, printer, and utility programs.

Quick Reference Charts: a handy list of all of the AppleWorks commands on the last pages of the book.

Data Disk: a disk that is available to instructors and contains both student files (starting points for some of the Guided Activities) and instructor files (solutions to the Applications and selected Unit Exercises as well as a test bank).

A NOTE OF THANKS ...

to the many people who assisted in the preparation of this manuscript.

to my wife, Julie, who gave up much of her time with me so that I might write, a special note for her help with encouragement, proofreading, and clarification.

to Rich Wohl, editor of **THE MICROCOMPUTING SERIES,** for the many positive, encouraging, and enlightening comments and suggestions.

to Trudi Abel for introducing me to West.

to Karen Watterson for allowing me to use **Understanding and Using Framework**® as a format guide and model for this text, and for numerous ideas for exercises and chapter questions.

to Mary Lou Noel, Mr. Wohl's assistant, for her help in keeping a very large amount of correspondence in order and to Sharon Walrath of West for her help with production questions.

to copy editor Pam McMurray who clarified and corrected innumerable paragraphs.

to reviewers Jim Campbell of Spokane School District, David Hunt of Manzanita Elementary School, Bari Kligerman of Greece Central School District, Blanch Kosche of Everett School District, Richard L. McCain of Montgomery County Public Schools, Cathy Radziemski of Grace Church School, Nancy Schornstein of SUNY College at Geneseo, and Sue Varnon of South East Missouri State University for the many excellent suggestions which have been implimented in the final manuscript.

to Dr. Fred Mis and Dr. John Schurdak of Fairfield University for their help in printing the laser copy of this manuscript.

to the following people, who have provided valuable suggestions and data: Karl Hermonat, Joseph Sapienza, Martin Sauer, Michael Short, and especially Jim Honeycutt of Saples High School and Fairfield University.

to others who helped proofread and who played the role of student-reader-learner to help clarify the lessons in the book: Holly Ann Gaeta, Andrew Goddard, Joyce Hermonat, Frank Meoli, Dorothy Miles, Virginia Morgan, Helen Rusanowsky, Jeff Tworek, Karen Ursitti, and Cathy Walker.

to the numerous students, teachers, and office personnel who have participated in AppleWorks courses at Brookfield and New Milford Public Schools, and at Fairfield University.

to Apple Computer, Inc. for extending the courtesy to reproduce AppleWorks screens.

TRADEMARK ACKNOWLEDGMENTS

Apple®, AppleWorks, ImageWriter, Uni-Disk, Duo-Disk®, Disk II®, Profile, ProDOS®, and LaserWriter are trademarks of Apple Computer, Inc.

Macintosh™ is a trademark of McIntosh Laboratory, Inc. and is used by Apple Computer, Inc. with its express permission.

Any other product names mentioned in this text are for identification purposes and may be trademarks of their respective companies.

Most of the manuscript for Understanding and Using AppleWorks was prepared with AppleWorks software on an enhanced Apple IIe computer with an extended memory card installed. It was transferred to a Macintosh Plus computer, reformatted and printed with an Apple LaserWriter printer to produce the text you see before you now. Screen images were transfered directly to the Macintosh and then modified with a graphics program.

1

FUNDAMENTALS OF APPLEWORKS OPERATIONS

UNIT

1

AN OVERVIEW OF APPLEWORKS

LEARNING OBJECTIVES

1. After completing this overview, you should know ...

    a. the three components of AppleWorks.

    b. the types of documents that each AppleWorks component can produce.

    c. why you use AppleWorks.

2. After completing this overview, you should be able to ...

    a. decide whether a document should be produced with the Word Processor, Data Base, or Spreadsheet.

    b. explain what an AppleWorks file is.

SUPPLIES NEEDED

Paper and pen or pencil for note taking and answering the review questions at the end of the chapter.

ASSIGNMENTS

REVIEW QUESTIONS

THE THREE PARTS OF APPLEWORKS

AppleWorks has three main components. These are the **Word Processor**, the **Spreadsheet**, and the **Data Base**. This unit discusses the uses of each component, how to decide which one to use for a given application, and how the parts interact or **integrate**.

THE WORD PROCESSOR

A word processor can be thought of as a tool that produces the same results as a typewriter. With a word processor, however, words are first typed onto a computer screen, a cathode ray tube (**CRT**). Revisions and corrections are made on the screen; then a printed copy is generated. The documents you can compose on a word processor include:

- letters
- college applications
- book reports
- term papers
- newspaper articles

```
                        Lounge
                          by
                       Laurie S.

     Anger, was the feeling expressed by many the
first few weeks of school.  They were not mad because of
scheduling errors, overcrowding or long lunch lines, but
because the lounge was closed.
     The lounge is the area between the library and room
103.  It is usually available during lunches and studies.  A
lot of students thought the lounge was closed because of
previous classes abusing it.  Just the opposite is true.
     The lounge was closed for safety reasons.  A broken air
conditioner was spread out over the benches waiting to be
fixed.  It took longer for this to be taken care of because
the town maintenance crew had to fix it, not High School
custodians.
     The lounge was not closed because of abuse.  Our
principal said that students have always kept the area clean
and used it at the proper times.
```

FIGURE 1-1. A Document Produced with a Word Processor.

After you learn some basic concepts and commands, you will be able to use the word processing tool as well as you use a typewriter. Shortly after that, you will be able to do things with the word processor that can not be done with a typewriter.

THE DATA BASE

A **data base** is a collection of information that is organized in some way. A telephone book is an example of a data base file. A printed data base such as the phone book is limited in that it is organized in only one fixed way. Our phone books, for example, are alphabetized by last name.

An AppleWorks electronic data base file can be rapidly re-organized any way you desire. An electronic phone book is a list that could be alphabetized by street address or even numerically by phone number. In addition, electrons can do the walking instead of your fingers; that is, the computer can find information for you on command -- by pressing a key on the keyboard.

Other examples of data bases include information you might keep in lists or on file cards:

- team rosters
- greeting card lists
- birthdays of friends
- subscriptions lists for yearbooks or newspapers
- information about items in a collection

Figure 1-2 is an example of a data base report. The information in the report is arranged like mailing labels. The style of the report is appropriately called **labels style** report.

```
Dorothy  Beneway
23  Brook  Road
Brookfield,  CT  06804

Claude  Wallace
47  Brook  Road
Brookfield,  CT  06804

Muriel  Gross
12  Eastbrook  Court
Brookfield,  CT  06804
```

FIGURE 1-2.   A Data Base Report.

THE SPREADSHEET

A **spreadsheet** consists of rows and columns of information, usually numbers, that may be added, averaged, multiplied, or treated in some mathematical way to obtain other numbers. A good example of a spreadsheet is your teacher's grade book. In a grade book, student names and grades are kept in columns of information. At the end of each marking period, the row of grades for a student is subjected to an arithmetic process that results in an average grade. At the completion of the course, each marking period grade is used in another arithmetic process to obtain a course average for each student.

Other examples of spreadsheets include:

- sports scores
- a log of miles and gallons used on a trip
- a payroll stub
- the income and expense report from a business

Figure 1-3 is an example of a spreadsheet report.

```
INCOME
        Part Time Job & Misc. Work

        January              $176.50

EXPENSES
        Clothes              $26.30
        Auto                 $38.54
        Lunches              $21.40
        Dates                $17.46
        Misc.                $12.34
                             =========
                             $116.04


BALANCE FOR SAVINGS
                             $60.46
```

FIGURE 1-3. A Spreadsheet Report.

YOUR FILES

Information that you enter into the Word Processor, the Data Base, or the Spreadsheet is called a **file**. For example, each of the AppleWorks documents given in Figures 1-1, 1-2 and 1-3 would be a separate file. Each file is identified by a unique name so that you (and the computer) can tell them apart. Files are stored in the computer or on a separate storage unit called a **disk.** Copies or duplicates of a file can be in both places.

INTEGRATED SOFTWARE

AppleWorks is an **integrated** program application. Several features are associated with integrated software. First, each component of AppleWorks uses the same keystroke commands for a task, wherever possible. For example, you use the exact same combination of keys to save the file you are working on, whether it is a Word Processing file, a Data Base file, or a Spreadsheet file. In other words, the command set is shared.

"Integrated" also means that you can quickly change from working on a Data Base file to a Spreadsheet file or to a Word Processing file.

Yet a third feature is that information can be "cut and pasted" from one file to another file quite easily. For example, a list generated in the Data Base can be "cut" from the Data Base file and "pasted" into a Word Processor file. Information can be shared between files electronically by issuing a few commands rather than by typing in all of the information a second or third time.

WHY YOU USE THE COMPUTER

I'm sure you have heard the term that "nothing is ever perfect". If everything and everyone were perfect, there would be no need for computers to keep track of things. Since nothing is ever perfect, computers sure do make life easier. Here are some examples of how.

1. You find that you have duplicated a word on the five page term paper that you just finished writing or typing. If you wanted to hand in a better paper, you would need to write or type the whole page over again. With the computer, a few keystrokes eliminate the word and close up the empty space. Another few keystrokes and the page is reprinted.

2. You have just organized the list of players for tomorrow's game. It's all neatly typed and ready for the coach. Suddenly there is a cheer from the locker room. The team's star player passed a make up test and can play after all. You're happy, but, you need to re-organize the list. The computer can do it in a matter of seconds.

3. You have just finished a very difficult math problem. It's a three part problem. The answer to part two depends on the answer to part one and the answer to part three depends on the correct answers to the two previous parts. You find that your answer is wrong; you made an error in the beginning of part one. Fortunately, you worked out all of the steps on the computer. Change one number in the first part of the problem and all of the steps are re-computed for you in almost the blink of an eye. Now you have it correct.

The changes and corrections that are part of the development of any document are far easier to do on a computer than they are to do with any other tool. They are so easy that some people consider writing, filing, and calculating with a computer to be fun.

REVIEW QUESTIONS

1. Name the three components of AppleWorks.

2. What is an AppleWorks file?

3. Why should you use a computer to write a term paper?

4. Why should you keep a list of yearbook subscribers in a computer file rather than on a sheet of paper?

5. Which AppleWorks component (Word Processor, Data Base, or Spreadsheet) would you use for the following applications:

   a. typing a letter to a pen pal;

   b. keeping a list of the movies and TV shows that you have recorded on your VCR;

   c. writing a term paper;

   d. keeping track of the funds collected and distributed by your Junior Achievement business organization;

   e. keeping a file of names and addresses of the members of your club;

   f. keeping an inventory of your team's sporting equipment and its condition.

UNIT

2 AN INTRODUCTION TO APPLEWORKS

LEARNING OBJECTIVES

1. After completing this unit, you should know ...

    a. why you prepare (format) a data disk.

    b. how a data disk is used.

    c. the meaning of a beep.

    d. what a cursor is and how AppleWorks two cursors are used.

    e. why you make a backup of your work.

    f. how to find information on the Help screens.

    g. why you follow a specific procedure for quitting Appleworks.

2. After completing this unit, you should be able to ...

    a. start AppleWorks on your computer.

    b. navigate through AppleWorks Menus and Help screens.

    c. prepare a disk to store data.

    d. add a word processor file to the Desktop from the disk.

    e. save a word processor file to the disk from the Desktop.

    f. quit AppleWorks correctly.

9

SUPPLIES NEEDED

1. An Apple IIe or IIc computer with at least 64K of memory (128K recommended), one disk drive (two recommended), and a printer.

2. A copy of the **AppleWorks Startup Disk** and a copy of the **AppleWorks Program Disk** (obtaine these from your instructor).

3. A write-protected copy of the **Understanding and Using AppleWorks Student Data Disk** that accompanies this book.

4. Two new unformatted (blank) disks with labels for each disk.

ASSIGNMENTS

1. START: Begin an AppleWorks session.

2. NAVIGATE: Move from one menu to another and back.

3. FORMAT: Create a data disk.

4. HELP: Explore Appleworks' Help Screens.

5. QUIT: End an AppleWorks session.

6. BACKUP: Copy a word processor file into the computer and store the file on your disks.

7. REVIEW QUESTIONS AND EXERCISES: Additional review and practice with the concepts presented in this chapter.

IMPORTANT KEYSTROKES AND COMMANDS

COMMAND/KEY	MEANING
Up-arrow	Move the cursor up one line.
Down-arrow	Move the cursor down one line.
Right-arrow	Move the cursor right one character.
Left-arrow	Move the cursor left one character.
Escape (Esc)	"Back out" of a selection or task.
Return	Complete a command. This key is used for most commands.
Shift	When shift is held down as a two symbol key is pressed, the character typed is the upper symbol on the key . Shift changes letter keys to capitals if it is held down as a letter key is pressed.
⌘	This key is used like a shift key to issue special Appleworks commands.

COMMAND/KEY	MEANING
&#63743;	This key works like ◕ in current versions of AppleWorks. Since this may change in future or modified versions of AppleWorks, you should use the ◕ key exclusively.
Delete	Erases one character to the left of the cursor.

STARTING APPLEWORKS

Starting AppleWorks soon will become an automatic task. As with any task that you must perform on a regular basis, you should follow the correct procedure from the start. Your first Guided Activity explains each step in the startup process. You should follow these steps carefully.

If you are not familiar with the Apple computer, read Appendix A before you work through the Guided Activity.

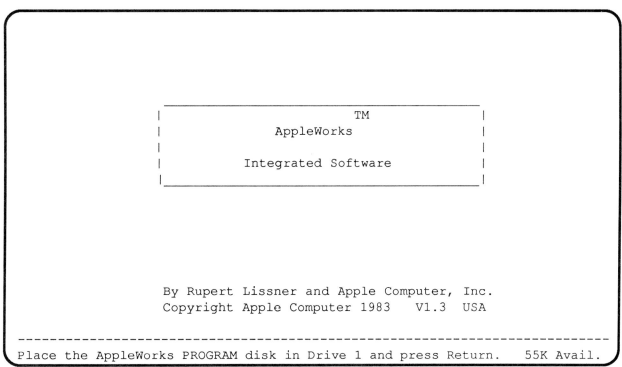

```
 _____
|                         TM                     |
|              AppleWorks                        |
|                                                |
|           Integrated Software                  |
|_____|




            By Rupert Lissner and Apple Computer,  Inc.
            Copyright Apple Computer 1983    V1.3   USA

-------------------------------------------------------------------------
Place the AppleWorks PROGRAM disk in Drive 1 and press Return.   55K Avail.
```

FIGURE 2-1 AppleWorks Start up Screen 1

GUIDED ACTIVITY: START

You need the following materials: a copy of the **AppleWorks Startup Disk** and a copy of the **AppleWorks Program** Disk. You should be sitting in front of your computer. The computer and monitor should be turned off. If there is a printer attached to your computer, it should also be turned off.

1. Insert the **AppleWorks Startup Disk** in drive 1. (Remember, to properly insert the disk, the oval cut out is away from you, and enters the disk drive first with the label up.)
2. Close the drive door.
3. Turn the monitor on.
4. Turn the computer on.

The red light on disk drive 1 comes on while information is loaded into the computer. After a few moments, your screen should look like the one shown in Figure 2-1.

5. Remove the **AppleWorks Startup Disk** from disk drive 1
6. Place the disk in its jacket.
7. Insert the **AppleWorks Program Disk** in drive 1 as the bottom line of your screen indicates.

(Some copies of AppleWorks have the Startup on one side and the Programs on the other. If you have this type of disk, you need to remove, flip, and re-insert the disk to follow steps 5, 6, and 7.)

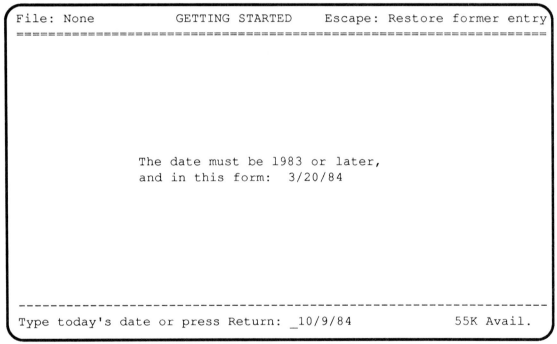

```
File: None            GETTING STARTED     Escape: Restore former entry
=====================================================================




                  The date must be 1983 or later,
                  and in this form:  3/20/84




--------------------------------------------------------------------
Type today's date or press Return: _10/9/84              55K Avail.
```

FIGURE 2-2 Start up Screen 2, Date Entry.

8. Close the door on the disk drive.
9. Press the <RETURN> key.

NOTE: The keys that you press are shown in capital letters using a special type style as in step 9 above. The keys are also enclosed in angle brackets < >. (You do NOT type the brackets) If you need to press a key because of an unusual problem or if you need to decide to press a key, the key is not capitalized, and is not enclosed in brackets, but, the key is printed in the special type style. In other words, don't press the keys shown in lower case unless you carefully decide that you should. In addition, other tasks that you need to perform are printed on indented lines as are the nine steps shown above. (The steps are not always numbered.) The indentation is done throughout the book to make it easier to pick out the instructions you must perform or the keys that you must press.

Your screen should now look like the one shown in figure 2-2.

TROUBLESHOOTING:

    Problem: Your screen still looks like figure 2-1.

    Correction: Try reinserting the Program Disk. Make sure the disk door is completely closed and press Return again. If you still have problems, tell your instructor or the computer room monitor.

Notice the box blinking on the first digit in the date. (Your date will be different; it may even be the current date. The box always blinks on the first digit in the date, no matter what date is shown.) The blinking box is called the **edit** or **overstrike** cursor. When new information is entered at this cursor point, the old information is replaced by the new.

In order to continue, you must enter a date in the form requested. If you wish to enter August 12, 1987, for example, you would type: 8/12/87. As you type, each character in the new date erases a character in the old date. You can press the space bar to erase any additional characters that remain from the old date. If you type the wrong character, use a left or right arrow key at the lower right corner of the keyboard to move the cursor over the incorrect character. Then type the correct character. If the date showing is correct, you need only press Return.

GUIDED ACTIVITY: START   (continued)

    10. Type: today's date   Enter the date as explained in the paragraph above.
    11. Press: <RETURN>   Notice the different type style for the word RETURN at the left. Keys you press are in this style of type and are enclosed in angle brackets.

TROUBLESHOOTING:

    Problem: The computer beeps.

    Correction: If you enter the date in an incorrect format or if you move the cursor too far to the left or right, the computer will beep at you. The beep is the Apple's way of saying that you've asked it to do something it cannot do or it doesn't understand. The beep does not mean that any of the information you have entered is altered in any way. Take your time and enter the date correctly; this step is important, since each file you save is dated with the date entered here.

Problem: The following message appears on your screen:

```
Your copy of the AppleWorks PROGRAM disk
must be in Drive 1.  The write-protect
notch must be uncovered.
```

Correction: You have one of the following two problems. Either you have placed the original AppleWorks program disk in Drive 1 or you have placed a tab over the write-protect notch. In the first case, remove the original AppleWorks and insert your copy in Drive 1. In the second case, remove the disk from the drive, carefully remove the paper tab from the notch, discard the tab, and reinsert the disk in Drive 1. Once you have made the appropriate correction, press the Space Bar to move back to the date screen (Figure 2-2). Then press Return to accept the date showing on the screen.

You have completed the startup procedure and now have AppleWorks' first menu screen before you.

```
Disk: Disk 1 (Slot 6)                 MAIN MENU
_____

    _____
   |     Main Menu             |_____
   |                           |                                      |
   |                           |                                      |
   |     1.   Add files to the Desktop                                |
   |                                                                  |
   |     2.   Work with one of the files on the Desktop               |
   |                                                                  |
   |     3.   Save Desktop files to disk                              |
   |                                                                  |
   |     4.   Remove files from the Desktop                           |
   |                                                                  |
   |     5.   Other Activities                                        |
   |                                                                  |
   |     6.   Quit                                                    |
   |                                                                  |
   |_____|


_____
Type number, or use arrows, then press Return 5        ⌂-? for Help
```

FIGURE 2-3. - Main Menu.

THE MENUS

AppleWorks allows you to select what you want to do from lists of things that can be done. These lists are known as **menus**. The menu in Figure 2-3 should now be on your screen. It is AppleWorks **Main Menu.**

The first Main Menu item, `1. Add files to the Desktop`, is highlighted. This task will be your usual selection when you first start AppleWorks. If you wished to add files now, you would press Return and move to the Add Files Menu. You don't want to do this just yet, as you still have some first-time tasks to perform. (If you have already pressed Return and moved to the Add Files Menu, press the Escape (Esc) key now to go back to the Main Menu.)

Notice the type style for the menu item, `Add files to the Desktop`. Information that you are to look for on your display appears in this type style.

GUIDED ACTIVITY: NAVIGATION

There are two ways to change the highlighted menu selection. One way is to use the up or down arrow key. The other way to highlight a menu item is to type the number that appears in front of the item. This Guided Activity lets you practice both methods. Which one you use as you continue with AppleWorks is entirely up to you.

The commands that you use in this Guided Activity are presented in a table. The table lists what you are to type and the reason that you type it. As you press each key, you should check the screen to observe that the reason given for typing a key is correct, and that your computer displays the expected results.

WHAT YOU TYPE	WHY YOU TYPE IT
<DOWN-ARROW>	Press and release this key to highlight item 2.
<DOWN-ARROW>	Press and release this key to highlight item 3.
<UP-ARROW>	To highlight Item 2 again.
<UP-ARROW>	To highlight Item 1.
<UP-ARROW>	To highlight item 6.
Hold <DOWN-ARROW>	To rapidly move the highlight bar down the list.
Release <DOWN-ARROW>	To stop the highlighting movement.
1	To highlight **Add files to the Desktop.**
<RETURN>	To display the **Add Files Menu.**
<ESCAPE> (ESC)	To return to the **Main Menu.**
6	To highlight **Quit.** Notice that 6 appears at the bottom of the screen.
<DELETE>	To remove the 6 on the bottom line.
5	To highlight **Other Activities.**
<RETURN>	To display the **Other Activities Menu.**

The **OTHER ACTIVITIES Menu** shown in Figure 2-4 should appear on your screen. If it does not, Escape to the Main Menu and select item 5 by repeating the last two steps on the list above. (Remember, since Escape is typed in lower case, you only need to press it if you have the problem indicated at the beginning of the sentence. Lower case means that you decide if the key must be pressed.)

```
Disk: Disk 1 (Slot 6)           OTHER ACTIVITIES            Escape: Main Menu
_____

  _____
 |      Main Menu           |_____
 |                          |                                        |
 |   |    Other Activities     |_____|__
 |   |                                                           |
 |   |     1.   Change current disk drive or ProDOS prefix       |
 |   |                                                           |
 |   |     2.   List all files on the current disk drive         |
 |   |                                                           |
 |   |     3.   Create a subdirectory                            |
 |   |                                                           |
 |   |     4.   Delete files from disk                           |
 |   |                                                           |
 |   |     5.   Format a blank disk                              |
 |   |                                                           |
 |   |     6.   Select standard location of data disk            |
 |__|                                                            |
     |     7.   Specify information about your printer(s)        |
     |_____|

_____
Type number, or use arrows, then press Return 6              55K Avail.
```

FIGURE 2-4   Other Activities Menu

The Main Menu branches to other menus or to specific tasks that you wish AppleWorks to perform. The menus branch like a tree. Branches lead to other branches or to a leaf -- the branches are other menus and the leaves are specific programs or tasks to perform. A combination of keys is needed to move from one menu to the next. Only one key is needed to return to the main menu. No matter where you are, whether on a menu branch or performing a task such as word processing, pressing the **Escape** key (Esc) one or more times brings you back to this Main Menu. Remember the function of the Escape key and you'll never get lost.

WHAT YOU'VE LEARNED

- When the highlight reaches the end of the list, it **wraps around** to the other end automatically.

- Holding a key down places the key in auto repeat mode. The character or action repeats rapidly.

- A brief touch and release is sufficient for typing one character.

- The Return key signals a move to the next screen.

- The Escape key returns you to the Main Menu.

- The Delete key erases a character to the left of the cursor.

- The cursor has a second shape, a dash rather than a box.

The dash is another cursor. It is the **insert cursor**. Like the overstrike box cursor you used when you entered the date, it informs you where the information you type will appear on the screen.

Look at the Other Activities Menu (Figure 2-4).. Notice that there appear to be two file folders displayed. The Other Activities folder overlaps the Main Menu folder. You can tell at a glance where this menu is in relation to the Main Menu. In addition, the top and bottom lines of all AppleWorks screens contain brief information about where you are and what you are able to do. The top line of this screen informs you that you are working with OTHER ACTIVITIES, that the disk drive used to store your files is Drive 1, and that when you press Escape, you'll return to the Main Menu. The bottom line of the screen has a brief message describing how to select a menu item and tells you that there are 55,000 character storage locations (55K) available on the Desktop for your files. (Computers without extended memory cards show 10,000 character storage locations (10K) available. These computers have only 64K of memory available for both the program and files.)

Your first task is to set a **standard location** for your data disk. The standard location is the one that appears at the top of the screen. It indicates where AppleWorks expects to find your data disk. When you set the standard location, you make it the automatic or **default** display that AppleWorks uses at startup.

1. Press 6   **Standard location of data disk** is highlighted.
2. Press <RETURN> The **STANDARD DATA DISK** Menu appears.

The Standard Data Disk Menu is shown in Figure 2-5. (If you have other disks attached to your computer, your display will be different.)

Notice that you now see three file folders on the screen.

```
┌──────────────────────────────────────────────────────────────────────────┐
│  Disk: Disk 1 (Slot 6)            STANDARD DATA DISK          Escape: Erase entry
│  ──────────────────────────────────────────────────────────────────────
│      ┌─────────────────────────┬──────────────────────────────────────┐
│      │     Main Menu           │_____│
│      │  ┌──────────────────────┴─────┬──────────────────────────────┐ │
│      │  │    Other Activities        │_____│_│
│      │  │  ┌─────────────────────────┴───┬────────────────────────┐  │
│      │  │  │   Standard Data Disk        │_____│  │
│      │  │  │                                                      │  │
│      │  │  │                                                      │  │
│      │  │  │                                                      │  │
│      │  │  │                                                      │  │
│      │  │  │      Disk drives you can use:                        │  │
│      │  │  │                                                      │  │
│      │  │  │      1.   Disk 1 (Slot 6)                            │  │
│      │  │  │      2.   Disk 2 (Slot 6)                            │  │
│      │  │  │      3.   ProDOS directory                           │  │
│      │  │  │                                                      │  │
│      │  └──│                                                      │  │
│      │     │                                                      │  │
│      └─────│                                                      │  │
│            │                                                      │  │
│            └──────────────────────────────────────────────────────┘  │
│  ──────────────────────────────────────────────────────────────────────
│  Type number, or use arrows, then press Return  2            55K Avail.
└──────────────────────────────────────────────────────────────────────────┘
```

FIGURE 2-5. Standard Data Disk Menu.

If you have only one disk drive, press Return to select Drive 1.

If you have two disk drives,

        Press **2**   To highlight Drive 2.
        Press **<RETURN>**   To complete the selection.

(This book does not discuss the ProFile hard disk system. See your AppleWorks Reference Manual, appendix A: "Using AppleWorks with a ProFile". Follow the instructions for one disk drive users until you install your hard disk.)

When you complete the disk drive selection, the computer returns to the **Other Activities Menu**. The upper left corner of the display shows which disk drive you selected for your files.

The computer remembers the data disk drive number on the AppleWorks disk, so it will use the same data disk location the next time you start AppleWorks. You will not need to set the standard data disk location again unless it is reset by another person using this copy of the program disk or if you use a computer with a different number of disk drives.

✓   CHECKPOINT

What key do you press to return to the Main Menu? Press the key to verify your answer.

Feel free to explore other menus. Remember that you can always find your way back to the Main Menu by pressing Escape one or more times.

You have one last task before you use AppleWorks. You must prepare a data disk for saving your files.

CREATING A DATA DISK

The information that you type into AppleWorks' Word Processor, Data Base or Spreadsheet must be saved on a disk called a **data disk**. One disk can hold several files. The number of files it can hold depends on the size of the files. For example, one standard 5 1/4" floppy disk can store:

- about 34 two-page reports (Standard pages of 8 1/2 by 11 inches paper.)
- about 17 four-page papers
- your budget for the next four years
- about 1,400 names and addresses
              or
- various combinations of the above.

(A 3.5 inch disk holds about six times this amount of information. A 10-megabyte hard disk holds about seventy times this amount.)

As you work with AppleWorks and find more and more uses for it, you'll need additional data disks to store your work. The process of creating these data disks is called **formatting**. In common terms, a new disk can be compared to a newly paved parking lot. Formatting the disk is like marking parking lines on the pavement. Once it's done, cars or computer information can be stored in an orderly manner. The electronic complexities of what is done are not important to understand. What is important is that formatting must be done in order to use the disk to store files.

GUIDED ACTIVITY: FORMAT

Create a data disk for your files by following the instructions below. AppleWorks' Main Menu should appear on your display. You should have two blank disks and two disk labels for this exercise.

WHAT YOU TYPE	WHY YOU TYPE IT
5 <RETURN>	To display the **OTHER ACTIVITIES** Menu.
5 <RETURN>	To display the **DISK FORMATTER** Menu (see Figure 2-6).

AWD   To enter AWD as the electronic name of your disk. (AWD
                             stands for AppleWorks Data Disk.)
<RETURN>   To complete the name entry.

```
Disk: Disk 2 (Slot 6)            DISK FORMATTER          Escape: Erase entry
_____

  _____
 |     Main Menu             |_____
 |   _____                                       |
 |  |     Other Activities          |_____|__
 |  |   _____                                    |
 |  |  |     Disk formatter              |_____|__
 |  |  |                                                                        |
 |  |  |                                                                        |
 |  |  |     The formatter will use the disk drive                             |
 |  |  |     shown on the top line of the screen.                              |
 |  |  |                                                                        |
 |  |  |     A disk name consists of up to 15 letters,                         |
 |  |  |     numbers, and periods.  The first character                        |
 |  |  |     must be a letter.                                                 |
 |  |  |                                                                        |
 |  |  |                                                                        |
 |__|  |                                                                        |
    |  |                                                                        |
    |__|                                                                        |
       |_____|

Type a disk name:   AWD                                         55K Avail.
```

FIGURE 2-6. DISK FORMATTER Screen.

TROUBLESHOOTING:

Problem: You make a typing error when you type AWD.

Correction: Press Delete to erase one character to the left.

Problem: You wish to create your own disk name.

Correction: Here are some hints to help you do this correctly. No spaces can be used in the
              name. Symbol characters other than a period are not allowed either. If you use
              an illegal character as part of the name, the computer beeps and erases the
              incorrect name when you press Return. You then must type in a corrected name
              and press Return. The name can be typed in capital or lower case letters,
              however the computer converts all lower case letters to upper case when it
              names the disk.

GUIDED ACTIVITY: FORMAT (continued)

After you have entered a correct name and pressed Return, the computer responds:

```
The disk to be formatted should
be in the disk drive NOW.
```

Before placing a disk in the disk drive, write the following on the two disk labels with a felt tip pen:

on the first: AppleWorks
                   Data Disk
                   Primary   (This means it is your original disk.)
                   your name

on the second: AppleWorks
                   Data Disk
                   BACKUP
                   your name

Remove each label from its backing and place it on an empty disk.

Note where the label is on the AppleWorks disks as a guide for the location of the label. Do not cover the notch, the circular opening or the oval opening of the disk.

Insert the new blank disk labeled **AppleWorks Data Disk Primary** into disk drive 2.
Close the drive door.
Press the <SPACE BAR>.

The word Formatting appears on the screen and the disk drive operates during the formatting process. (The grinding noise is normal.) The message **Successfully formatted** appears on the screen when formatting is complete.

When the message appears, press the <SPACE BAR>.

You should now see the Disk Formatter menu in Figure 2-6. The disk name you used is at the bottom of the screen in capital letters, and the cursor is blinking at the beginning of the name.

The electronic name for the backup disk for the Data Disk should indicate that it is a backup for that disk, so let's insert B.U. at the beginning of the name, AWD. (The B.U. indicates Backup.)

WHAT YOU TYPE	WHY YOU TYPE IT
B.U.	To add B.U. to the beginning of the name. The name appears as `B.U.AWD`. The B.U. characters are automatically prefixed to the name because the insert cursor is used.
<RETURN>	To accept the name. (You need not move the cursor to the end of the name.)

Remove the Primary Data Disk, the one you just formatted, from the disk drive.
Insert the **AppleWorks Data Disk BACKUP** in the drive indicated at the top left corner of the screen.
Close the drive door.
Press the <SPACE BAR>.

When the second disk is successfully formatted, press the <ESCAPE> key <u>twice</u> to return to the Main Menu.

TROUBLESHOOTING:

Problem: Messages other than `Successfully formatted` may appear.

Correction: Possible messages and their corrections are shown in the following table.

MESSAGE	CORRECTION
`Disk has write protect tab`	A write-protected disk can not be formatted. Remove the tab from the disk and try again. (You may have the disk in upside-down or in another incorrect orientation. Make sure that the disk is inserted correctly and the disk door is fully closed.)
`Unable to find the disk`	Either the disk door is not closed properly, or the disk drive is not operating properly. Remove the disk, reinsert it, and close the door. If you have two drives, try to format with the other drive. You need to change the drive to Drive 1 in order to do so. (Use `Other Activities` menu item #1 `Change current disk drive or ProDOS prefix` to do this.)
`Disk is ProDOS/SOS volume /APPLEWORKS`	(`/APPLEWORKS` may be different on your screen.) The disk contains information. You have a disk that either you or someone else has already copied information onto. If you are certain that the information on the disk is useless, type the letters y e s to answer yes to the question `OK to`

destroy contents?. Otherwise obtain another blank disk, label it, and put the used disk aside.

You are finished with all of the preparation work.

HELP SCREENS

There are several help screens available in AppleWorks. The screens contain information to help you use the current section of the program. The Guided Activity below lets you explore a Help Screen. Some of the information that you discover will be of use to you in the Guided Activity: BACKUP later in this unit.

GUIDED ACTIVITY: HELP

The Main Menu should appear on your display. If it does not, press Escape until it does appear.

WHAT YOU TYPE	WHY YOU TYPE IT
Hold down ⌘	To use the Open-Apple key in combination with another key, hold Open-Apple down while you press and release the other key.
?	To give the Open-Apple Question-Mark command. You do not need to shift to get the question mark. The ⌘ key acts as a shift key. When you release the question mark, the Help Screen appears.
Release the ⌘ key.	To complete the command.

You have given the AppleWorks command ⌘-?. This command displays the Help Screen for the Main Menu. Notice the message at the bottom left.

✓ CHECKPOINT

What is the message in the bottom left corner of the Help Screen?

Let's use the arrows to see the remainder of Help.

WHAT YOU TYPE	WHY YOU TYPE IT
<DOWN-ARROW>	To move one line down the list. The new line appears at the bottom of the display and the top line disappears from the top of the display.
Hold <DOWN-ARROW>	To move rapidly down the list.
Release <DOWN-ARROW>	To stop the scrolling.
Hold <UP-ARROW>	To move rapidly up the list.
Release <UP-ARROW>	To stop the scrolling.
<ESCAPE>	To leave Help and return to the Main Menu.

WHAT YOU'VE LEARNED

- The ⌘ key is used like a shift key. You hold it down while you press and release another key.

- The dash (-) in the ⌘-? command is not typed.

- The ⌘-? combination displays a Help Screen.

- The Help Screens contain a lot of information.

✓ CHECKPOINT

Use the Help screen to determine what key you press to remove the character preceding the cursor. What is this key?

What is the key combination you use to save a file?

QUITTING APPLEWORKS

Never quit AppleWorks by turning off the computer in the middle of the program.

You can quit any program by turning off the computer but don't do it with AppleWorks. AppleWorks keeps track of everything you do with it. When you follow its "Quit" procedure, it tells you in plain English if you have left a job partially completed and it suggests ways to store your progress. PLEASE follow the procedure outlined below when you quit AppleWorks. When AppleWorks reminds you that you forgot to save the ten-page report you just typed, you'll be glad you did.

GUIDED ACTIVITY: QUIT

Practice the proper method of quitting AppleWorks.

WHAT YOU TYPE	WHY YOU TYPE IT
Escape (one or more times)	To display the Main Menu. (Remember, Escape written in lower case letters means that you may not need to press this key. If the Main Menu is already showing in your display, don't press the key.)
6	To highlight **6. Quit**.
<RETURN>	To select the highlighted menu item.

The following message appears at the bottom of the screen:

```
Do you really want to do this?   No   Yes
```

WHAT YOU TYPE	WHY YOU TYPE IT
<RIGHT-ARROW>	To highlight the word **Yes**.
<RETURN>	To select the highlighted item.

The disk light goes on for a moment and the screen display changes to:

```
ENTER PREFIX (PRESS 'RETURN' TO ACCEPT)
/APPLEWORKS/
```

At this point, you may turn the computer and monitor off.

Practice the startup and quitting procedure until you are comfortable doing it. Remember, if the computer is off, insert the AppleWorks Startup Disk in Drive #1, close the drive door, and then turn on the monitor and computer.

You do not need to turn the computer off to start AppleWorks. When the computer is on, follow this procedure:

1. Insert the Startup Disk in drive #1 and close the drive door.
2. Press the <CONTROL> key, the ⌘ key, and the <RESET> key together.

The three key combination is called a **warm start**. The computer responds exactly as if you had turned it off and then turned it on; that is, everything in its memory is cleared and information is loaded into the computer from the disk in drive #1. The warm start, Control-⌘-Reset, saves wear on the computer's on-off switch. Use it to start AppleWorks whenever you find that the computer has been left on.

Quit AppleWorks, turn off the computer and the monitor, and return the AppleWorks disks to your instructor.

You have completed an AppleWorks session.

SAVING FILES

Every file that you create in AppleWorks should be stored on your data disk. This process is called saving your files or just **save**. Storage in the computer's memory is temporary. If the computer is turned off, if it loses power, or if you "Quit" AppleWorks, any file stored in memory is lost.

Files stored on the disk are more permanent. They remain on the disk even when power to the computer is cut off. However, disks can be lost or damaged and it is good practice to store a file on more than one disk. It only takes a few seconds to save the file a second time and it is well worth the trouble should you lose the first copy. The duplicate saving process is so important to computer people that it has been given its own name, **backing up**.

At the end of your work session on the computer, you would save the file you're working with on your disk. To back up, you would remove the original disk, replace it with another disk, and save the file again. You then have your work on two disks. The second disk can be yours, your friend's or your instructor's. It is a fast, simple step that may save you hours of work.

When you back up a disk, you protect against the loss or failure of that disk. Some of the ways that you can cause a disk to fail are: 1. store it in a notebook (this squeezes the jacket so that the disk cannot turn), 2. leave it in the car (the heat or cold may damage it), 3. leave it on the computer monitor (the magnet in some monitors is strong enough to erase a disk) or 4. bring it to the library (some library security devices are magnetic and can erase disks).

Backing up is so important that you can even backup the work in the computer. Save your work every 15 minutes or so and you have two copies as you go along, one on the disk, and another in the computer.

The next Guided Activity shows you how to copy a file from the disk into the computer. This action has several names: **open** a file, **load** a file or **add a file to the Desktop**. (More on this in the next unit.) After the file is loaded, you'll save it on your primary disk. You'll learn how to make sure that the file is indeed on the disk, and then how to save a copy of the file on your backup disk.

GUIDED ACTIVITY: BACKUP

"If it is going to fail, it fails when you need it the most", Murphy's Law.
"The best protection against failure is a backup copy of your work", Short's Law.

(All guided activities in this book assume a two disk drive system. Special notes for one disk drive systems are given in this activity only.)

1. Gather your materials at the computer. You need five disks:
   AppleWorks Startup
   AppleWorks Programs
   Understanding and Using AppleWorks Student Data Disk
   Your two data disks which you have formatted and labeled.

2. Startup AppleWorks and proceed to the Main Menu.

3. Insert the Student Data Disk into drive 2 and close the drive door. (One disk drive users do not insert the disk at this time.)

4. From the Main Menu, follow this sequence of commands:

WHAT YOU TYPE	WHY YOU TYPE IT
<RETURN>	To select **Add files to the Desktop.**
<RETURN>	To select **Get files from current disk.**

(If you have one drive, AppleWorks asks that you put your data disk in drive 1. Remove the Program disk and insert the Student Files Disk then press Return to continue.)

WHAT YOU TYPE	WHY YOU TYPE IT
Down-arrow	To highlight the program **Activity 1 File.** (Remember, the lower case commands mean that you might need to press this key several times or, perhaps, not at all. You need to decide based on the information on your display. If you press the key too many times, press Up-arrow to move up the list.)
<RETURN>	To load the program.

(One drive users will be prompted to remove the data disk and re-insert the AppleWorks Program Disk. Do so when you see the message at the bottom of the screen and then press Return.)

5. Remove the Student Data disk from the computer if you have not already done so and return it to the computer room monitor. You'll no longer need it.

A copy of the file is now in the memory of your computer. Your instructor has a copy of the file on the Student Data Disk that you just returned. Your only copy at this moment is in the computer; you see it before you on your display.

6. If you have two disk drives, put your Primary Data Disk in drive 2.
7. Give the **save** command as shown below.

WHAT YOU TYPE	WHY YOU TYPE IT
Hold Ⅽ	To start an Open-Apple command..
Press and Release S	To save the file on your disk.
Release the Ⅽ key.	To complete the Open-Apple-S command.

(If you have one disk drive, put your Primary Data Disk in drive 1 when the you are prompted to do so on the bottom line of the screen.)

You now have the file saved on your primary disk. (One disk drive users will be asked soon to insert the AppleWorks Program disk into drive 1. Watch the bottom line of the screen and do this when you are prompted.)

✓ **CHECKPOINT**

The combination of keys you used to save the file is referred to as Ⅽ-S. Where have you found this information before?

8. Remove your Primary Data Disk from the disk drive.
9. Insert your Backup Data Disk in the empty drive and close the drive door.

WHAT YOU TYPE	WHY YOU TYPE IT
Ⅽ-S	To save the file on your Backup Data Disk. (Remember, to type Ⅽ-S, press and hold Ⅽ, press and release S, and then release Ⅽ.)

You have saved the file again on a separate disk, your backup. If backups are this easy to make, you should never leave the computer without one.

10. If you have two disk drives, remove your Backup and replace it with your Primary Data Disk. It is good practice to leave your Primary Data Disk in the drive so that you do not unintentionally save the most current copy of the file on the backup.

You now see the document in the display but, you cannot see the document on the disk. How do you know that it really saved? 1. You saw the red light on the disk drive come on, indicating that the disk was working. 2. AppleWorks displayed a message that it was carefully saving your file. 3. AppleWorks did not give you any error messages saying that it did not save the file. If you are still not convinced that the file saved correctly, you can list all of the files on your disk. Here's how:

WHAT YOU TYPE	WHY YOU TYPE IT
<ESCAPE>	To return to the Main Menu.
5	To highlight **Other Activities**.
<RETURN>	To select the highlighted item.
2 <RETURN>	To select **List all files on the current disk drive**.

The list of files appears on your display. You see the file name, Activity 1 File, in the list. This is another indication that the file is indeed saved on your disk.

✓   **CHECKPOINT**

The upper right corner of the display indicates what key to press to return to the Other Activities Menu. What key is this?

Press the key to confirm your answer. The upper right corner of the display now indicates what key to press to return to the Main Menu. What key is this?

GUIDED ACTIVITY: BACKUP (continued)

At this moment, all three of your copies of the Activity 1 File document are identical (you have one in the computer, one on your Primary Data Disk, and one on your Backup Data Disk). If you make a change in your computer copy of the document, you need to save the file again to change the copy on your disk. What happens if you make a change and then you forget to save the change on your disk? Let's make a small change in the document to find out.

WHAT YOU TYPE	WHY YOU TYPE IT
2 <RETURN>	To select **Work with one of the files on the Desktop**.
your name	To enter your own name into the document.
<RETURN>	To move `Guided Activity: Backup` down one line.
<RETURN>	To insert a blank line.
<ESCAPE>	To return to the Main Menu.
6 <RETURN>	To start the quit AppleWorks process. Remember, you did not save the changes you made in the file.
Y	To answer `Yes` to the question `Do you really want to do this?`

AppleWorks informs you that you have made changes to the file "Activity 1 File". It suggests that you `Save the file on your current disk`.

Because you followed the correct procedure to quit, you are prevented from accidentally throwing away the valuable information (your name) that you have just added to the file.

WHAT YOU TYPE	WHY YOU TYPE IT
<RETURN>	To save the file on the current disk.
<RETURN>	To let the new information replace the old.

All of the information in the file Activity 1 File, including your name, is saved on the disk. The copy of the file with your name replaces the copy of the file that did not include your name. When the save is completed the quit message shown below appears.

```
ENTER PREFIX (PRESS 'RETURN' TO ACCEPT)
/APPLEWORKS/
```

You can now turn the computer off. You have updated the changes you have made to the file on your Primary Data Disk only. Your backup file does not include your name and the blank line you added. The exercise in this unit discusses this problem; so, do not make any changes to your disks.

REVIEW QUESTIONS

1. Before you turn the computer on to start AppleWorks, what disk do you place in drive 1?

2. What does "standard location of the data disk" mean?

3. Where on the screen do you find information about the Escape key?

4. Why does the computer sometimes beep at you?

5. In general, what is the ○ key used for?

6. Explain two ways that you can highlight and select the Main Menu item
   2. Work with one of the files on the Desktop.

7. What keys do you press in order to get AppleWorks' Help Screen? How can you remember these keys?

8. What key do you press to exit from the Help Screen?

9. What is your data disk used for?

10. Why did you prepare two data disks?

11. How did you backup your file on a second data disk?

12. Why did you backup your file on a second data disk?

13. What does AppleWorks do if you quit without saving the latest version of your file?

14. Which data disk should you use to save the <u>last</u> version of your file. Why use that disk?

EXERCISES

NOTE: The lesson of this exercise is very important. You are going to erase all of the information on your Primary Data Disk. You are then going to restore all of the information from your backup. If you are careful about how you treat your data disks, you should not lose information that you store on them. If you ever do, this exercise should help you to understand how to recover from the loss. Start this exercise with the computer turned off and your two data disks prepared as explained in this unit.

1.   Start AppleWorks, enter the date and display the Main Menu.
2.   Display the Other Activities Menu. (Select #5 from the Main Menu.)
3.   List the files on your Primary Data Disk. (Select #2 from the Other Activities Menu.)

   a.   Is the file, Activity 1 File, still on your disk?

4. Format your Primary Data Disk.

WHAT YOU TYPE	WHY YOU TYPE IT
5 <RETURN>	To display the **Disk Formatter Menu** .
AWD	To enter AWD as the electronic name of your disk. (AWD stands for AppleWorks Data Disk.)
<RETURN>	To complete the name entry.
<SPACE BAR>	To start the disk formatting process.
YES	To respond **YES** to the instruction: **Type YES to destroy the contents**.
<RETURN>	To complete the YES response.
<ESCAPE>	To return to the Other Activities Menu.

   b.   Is the file, Activity 1 File, still on the disk? How can you be sure if it is or is not on your disk?

5. Replace your Primary Data Disk with your Backup Data Disk.

6. Add the file, Activity 1 File, to the Desktop from your Backup Disk.

7. Replace your Backup Data Disk with your Primary Data Disk.

8. Use ⌂-S to save the file on your Primary Data Disk.

    c. What is different about the file that you just saved and the one that was lost from the Primary Disk?

    d. Explain how you would make the file in the computer the same as the one that you lost.

    e. Why should you NOT format a disk that contains information?

    f. What lesson(s) did you learn from this exercise?

The answers to these questions are in Appendix B. Make sure that you understand these answers before you proceed to the next unit.

UNIT

3

GETTING STARTED WITH THE WORD PROCESSOR

LEARNING OBJECTIVES

1. After completing this unit, you should know ...

   a. text appearance can be easily modified after it has been entered.

   b. how printer commands change the text.

   c. what keys and commands have multiple uses.

   d. why you can make the same change in the text using a variety of methods.

   e. how special words help you remember AppleWorks commands.

2. After completing this unit, you should be able to ...

   a. create a new document with the Word Processor.

   b. enter and edit text in the document.

   c. move the cursor through the document to any location.

   d. control centering and justification in the document.

   e. save your document.

   f. print your document.

ASSIGNMENTS

1. OPEN: Add a new document to the Desktop for the word processor.

2. LOUNGE: Create a school newspaper story.

3. PRINT: Generate a paper copy of the story.

4. NAVIGATE: Move the cursor through a document.

5. EDIT: Change and correct the Lounge story.

6. FORMAT: Control centering, justification, and character (type) size.

7. MODIFY AND SAVE: Change the story again and save the changes onto your disks.

8. REVIEW QUESTIONS AND EXERCISES: Additional review and practice with editing, formatting, and printing.

IMPORTANT KEYSTROKES AND COMMANDS

COMMAND/KEY(S)	MEANING
CURSOR MOVEMENT -	
Up or Down arrow	Move the cursor up or down a line.
Right or Left arrow	Move the cursor right or left a character.
○ Up or Down arrow	Move the cursor up or down one screen.
○ Right or Left arrow	Move the cursor right or left a word.
○ 1 to 9	Move the cursor proportionally through the text.
DISK COMMANDS -	
○-S	Save a file.
EDITING COMMANDS -	
○-E	Edit/insert cursor change.
○-D	Delete text.
○-Z	Zoom in/out.
PRINTING OPTIONS -	
○-O	Options display.
CN	Center text lines.
UJ	Unjustified text.
CI	Characters per Inch.

THE DESKTOP

The files that you copy into the computer from a disk and the files that you make from scratch are stored in the random access memory (**RAM**) of the computer. AppleWorks refers to this memory as a **Desktop**. Although it is not a real desktop, it is similar to a standard desktop in several ways. It gets full: you can put no more than twelve files on it at one time (if the files are large, you will not be able to get that many on the Desktop). You can work with only one Desktop file at a time. Information can be moved from one file to another and files can be moved onto and off of the Desktop at will.

Unlike a traditional desktop, the computer's Desktop is instantly cleaned off and everything is lost if the computer's power is somehow cut off.

Floppy Disk

Files stored
on the disk
are not part
of the Desk-
top. They
are copies
of Desktop
files.

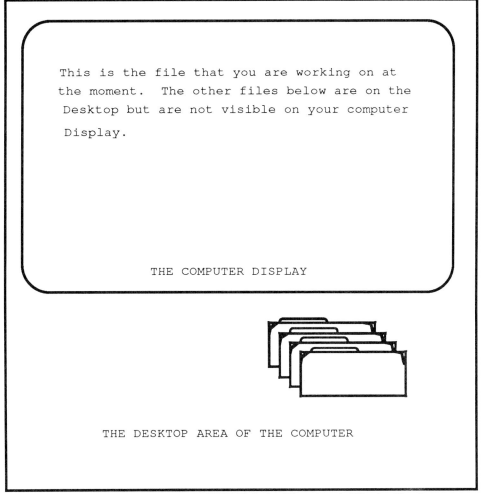

```
This is the file that you are working on at
the moment.  The other files below are on the
Desktop but are not visible on your computer
Display.




                THE COMPUTER DISPLAY




         THE DESKTOP AREA OF THE COMPUTER
```

FIGURE 3-1. The AppleWorks Desktop.

Before you can work with any file, you must electronically place it on the Desktop. Where you can add to it, review it, change it, or print it. At the conclusion of your work with the file, you store the file on a disk and remove it from the Desktop.

Figure 3-1 is a pictorial representation of the computer Desktop. Note that only one file is visible on the computer screen, even though up to twelve files can be on the Desktop at one time.

ADDING A WORD PROCESSING FILE TO THE DESKTOP

The first step in Word Processing a new document is to **open** a new file on the Desktop. This process is also known as **add a file to the Desktop**. The document that you'll be adding in this case is created from scratch; that is,you must type it into the computer. The Guided Activity below shows you how to open a new file so that you can type a document into the Word Processor.

GUIDED ACTIVITY: OPEN

Start up AppleWorks as described in Unit 1. Begin at the Main Menu. Your copy of the AppleWorks Program Disk is now in Drive 1 and your "AppleWorks Data Disk #1 Primary" is in Drive 2. Keep your "AppleWorks Data Disk #1 Backup" near for use later in the unit. You won't need it until you start AppleWorks again.

WHAT YOU TYPE	WHY YOU TYPE IT
1	To highlight **1. Add files to the Desktop.**
<RETURN>	To select the highlighted item. The **ADD FILES Menu** shown in Figure 3-2 appears.

WHAT YOU TYPE	WHY YOU TYPE IT
3	To highlight **Word Processor.**
<RETURN>	To select the highlighted item. The **WORD PROCESSOR Menu** appears. See Figure 3-3.

```
Disk: Disk 2 (Slot 6)              ADD FILES            Escape: Erase entry
_____

    _____
   |                             |_____
   |   Main Menu                 |                                           |
   |    _____                                         |
   |   |                         |_____|__
   |   |   Add Files             |                                           |  |
   |   |                         |                                           |  |
   |   |      Get files from:                                                |  |
   |   |                                                                     |  |
   |   |      1.  The current disk: Disk 2 (Slot 6)                          |  |
   |   |      2.  A different disk                                           |  |
   |   |                                                                     |  |
   |   |      Make a new file for the:                                       |  |
   |   |                                                                     |  |
   |   |      3.  Word Processor                                             |  |
   |   |      4.  Data Base                                                  |  |
   |   |      5.  Spreadsheet                                                |  |
   |___|                                                                     |  |
       |_____|
_____
Type number, or use arrows, then press Return  3              55K Avail.
```

FIGURE 3-2.   ADD FILES Menu..

```
Disk: Disk 2 (Slot 6)            WORD PROCESSOR          Escape: Erase entry
_____

    _____
   |                             |_____
   |   Main Menu                 |                                           |
   |    _____                                         |
   |   |   Add Files             |_____|__
   |   |    _____                                      |  |
   |   |   |   Word Processor     |_____|__
   |   |   |                      |                                           |  |
   |   |   |   Make a new file:                                               |  |
   |   |   |                                                                  |  |
   |   |   |   1.  From scratch                                               |  |
   |   |   |                                                                  |  |
   |   |   |   2.  From a text (ASCII) file                                   |  |
   |___|   |                                                                  |  |
       |___|                                                                  |  |
           |_____|
_____
Type number, or use arrows, then press Return  1              55K Avail.
```

FIGURE 3-3.   Word Processor Menu.

The same name is used to identify the file on the screen and on the disk. The name can contain up to fifteen characters that can be upper- or lowercase letters, digits, spaces, or periods. The name must start with a letter.

WHAT YOU TYPE	WHY YOU TYPE IT
1 <RETURN>	To highlight and select **From Scratch.**
Lounge	To enter the word "Lounge" as the name for your new file.
<RETURN>	To complete the name entry.

The screen now displays a blank Word Processor page, like the one shown in Figure 3-4.

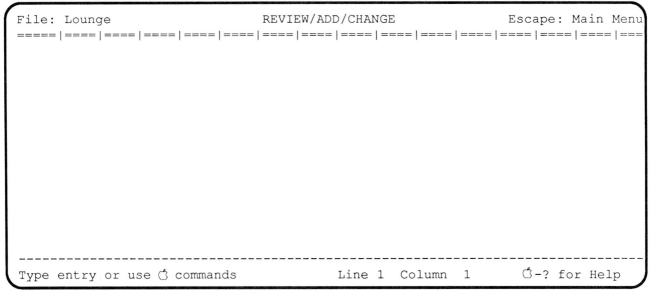

FIGURE 3-4. Blank Word Processing Screen.

The top and bottom lines of the screen give you a great deal of information. Take a moment to examine the screen and compare it to the list below.

- The file name is **Lounge** (top left).
- The computer is set to **REVIEW/ADD/CHANGE** this file (top center).
- Pressing **Escape** returns you to the **Main Menu** (top right).
- You are expected to **Type** your **entry** (the text of your document) **or use** one of the Ó **commands** (bottom left).
- The cursor is located on **Line 1** in **Column 1** (bottom center).
- Holding down the Ó key and pressing the question mark key (?) displays the Help Screen (bottom right). (Note: On older IIe's the Ó symbol appears as a capital A in a white box.)

Once you open a document you do not need to create it again. It remains in the computer's memory, on the Desktop, until you tell the computer to remove it, or until you quit AppleWorks. Even if you cannot see the document on your display, it is on the Desktop.

✓   CHECKPOINT

> Press <ESCAPE> to return to the Main Menu. There is now a message on the screen telling you what key to press to return to the file "Lounge". What is the message and where does it appear on the screen?

You have created a word processing document and now you are ready to type in text.

ENTERING TEXT

Your first document is a one page story that might have been written for the school newspaper. You type the story and then make some changes and corrections to it. You are prompted from time to time in this Guided Activity to save your work. Remember, saving your work periodically is similar to backing up; you make a duplicate copy of the work on the Desktop on your primary disk.

GUIDED ACTIVITY: LOUNGE

Your display should show the blank word processor screen shown in Figure 3-4. If this is not displayed on your monitor, press Escape until you see the Main Menu; then select item 2 Work with one of the files on the Desktop, and press Return. (The complete text of the story appears in a box on the next page.)

WHAT YOU TYPE	WHY YOU TYPE IT
<CAPS LOCK>	To make all of the letters you type capitals. The Caps Lock Key should be in the down position. If it is not, press the key one more time.
LOUNGE	To enter the title.
<RETURN>	To move down to line two. Return ends short lines.
<CAPS LOCK>	To release the caps lock. The Caps Lock Key is now in the up position.
by <RETURN>	To enter the word "by" and move down a line.
Press and hold <SHIFT>	To make the next letter a capital.
L	L and shift together produce the capital letter.
Release <SHIFT>	To enter lower case letters.
aurie S. <RETURN>	To finish the name and move down to the next line.
<RETURN>	To enter a blank line.
<TAB>	To indent the paragraph.

TROUBLESHOOTING:

Problem: You see extra letters in your document or your text scrolls off of the top of the screen. (If it does this, you see nothing of what you have typed.)

Correction: Some people have a problem with the light touch of the computer's keyboard. They are typing a key even when they do not mean to. To observe an example of their problem, hold the Return key down, (if you hold a key down, it automatically repeats) the text disappears off of the top of the screen. Text is not lost when it scrolls off the top of the screen; it moves up to make room for additional lines added at the bottom. To remove the extra blank lines (or any extra characters), press the Delete key several times until you are one line below Laurie S. To avoid the problem in the future, keep your finger pressure on the keys as light as possible.

WHAT YOU'VE LEARNED:

- Caps Lock is used to change all the letters typed to capitals.
- Shift is held down as a letter is typed to make that single letter a capital.
- Return is pressed to end a paragraph. When you press Return at the beginning of a line, you create a blank line.
- Tab is used to indent a paragraph.

GUIDED ACTIVITY: LOUNGE (continued)

WHAT YOU TYPE
_____

It seems that every year when we return from summer

You have reached the end of the line, but not the end of the paragraph. **Do not press Return.** Watch the screen as you slowly type the next word.

WHAT YOU TYPE
_____

vacation

When you type "a", the word moves automatically to the next line. (If it didn't, your line doesn't exactly match the one shown or you may have had an AppleWorks expert change your margins.) This feature is called word wraparound. Word wraparound is a common word processing feature. Do not try to defeat it by pressing Return yourself. If you do, you may create some strange printing problems. Press Return only at the end of paragraphs or when you want to insert a blank line.

The rule that you need to follow as you type your rough draft is: **Only press Return at the end of a paragraph or short line..** Look over the complete text; then, type away as fast as you can. Your objective is to enter the story into the computer. There are errors in the text; enter them as they appear.

You need not be concerned about any additional errors that you make. Your next task will be corrections. (If you'd like to correct your errors as you type, remember that the Delete key erases one character to the left of the cursor each time you press it. Feel free to use or not use the Delete key as you prefer.)

Finish typing the text of the story as it is shown below.

```
LOUNGE
b y
Laurie  S.


     It  seems  that  every  year  when  we  return  from  summer
vacation  there  have  been  some  changes  made.
     Anger!   The  feeling  that  was  felt  by  many  the  first  few
weeks  of  school.   They  were  not  mad  because  of  overcrowding
or  long  lunch  lines,  but  because  the  lounge  was  closed.
     The  lounge  is  the  area  outside  in  between  the  library
and  room  103.   It  is  available  during  lunches  and  studies.
A  lot  of  students  thought  the  lounge  was  closed  because  of
previous  classes  abusing  the  privelege  of  it.   Just  the
opposite  is  true.
     The  lounge  was  closed  for  safety  reasons.   A  broken  air
conditioner  was  spread  out  over  the  benches  waiting  to  be
fixed.   It  took  longer  for  this  to  be  taken  care  of  because
the  town  maintenance  had  to  fix  it,  not  High  School
custodians.
     The  lounge  was  not  closed  because  of  abuse.   Our
principal  said  that  students  have  always  kept  the  area  clean
and  used  it  at  the  proper  times.
```

When you are finished move on to the next section, where you will carefully preserve the work you did.

✔ CHECKPOINT

At this moment, you have only one electronic copy of the story that you just typed. Where is that copy of the story?

SAVING YOUR DOCUMENT

If the power to your computer were interrupted at this very moment, all of the typing you have just finished would be lost. The only copy of your work is on the Desktop stored in the computer's random access memory (RAM). However, if you record a duplicate of the work on your disk, you then have a copy that is not as easily lost. Let's do this.

WHAT YOU TYPE	WHY YOU TYPE IT
-S	To save the document showing in the display. (Remember, -S is an abbreviation for the instructions: Hold the  key down then press and release the S key. Finally, release .)

The text disappears from the screen. Don't worry, it is still in the computer's memory. The **SAVE FILES Menu** appears. The top file folder on the screen shows that the computer is "Carefully saving your file". For a moment you are given the chance to press Escape to cancel the save. **Don't press Escape** (if you do, your file is not saved). After a few seconds the disk save is complete and your document reappears. The cursor returns to the same location it was in before you saved (it should be at the end of the story).

TROUBLESHOOTING:

Problem: The message **Can't write on disk at Drive 2** appears.

Correction: Make sure that your file data disk is in the drive and that the drive door is closed properly. Press the space bar to continue, and try to save again with -S.

Problem: The letter S (or s) is typed on the screen.

Correction: Remember that you need to hold down the  button while you press and release the S.

Problem: The computer displays the message: **Place your DATA disk in Drive 1** at the bottom of the screen.

Correction: If you only have one drive, remove the AppleWorks Program disk from Drive 1 and replace it with your Primary Data Disk. Leave this disk in Drive 1 until AppleWorks prompts you to re-insert the AppleWorks Program disk.
If you have two drives and you are prompted to place your data disk in Drive 1, you need to select the standard location of the data disk as explained in Unit 2.

Problem: The Main Menu is displayed. (You pressed Escape and you should not have.)

Correction: Select option 2. Work with one of the files on the Desktop. When you press Return, you again see your document on the screen. Save the document again with ⌘-S. (Pressing Escape stops the save so your file may not have saved correctly the first time.)

Let's discuss what happened when you saved your file. Lounge now exists in two places, in the computer and on the disk. The copy in the computer is identical to the one on the disk. If the computer lost power at this very moment, the copy of the document in the computer' memory would be lost, but the copy on the disk would not. You have just made a backup of the text.

Now you will change one of the copies of the text.

WHAT YOU TYPE	WHY YOU TYPE IT
<RETURN>	To get a blank line at the end of your document (you may need to press it twice to get the blank line).
The End	To type this line into the document.
<RETURN>	To move the cursor down to the start of the next line.

The copy of the text in the computer is now different from the copy of the text on the disk.

✓ CHECKPOINT

How does the text in the computer differ from the text saved on the disk?

What happens if you lose power now? The copy of the document in the computer is lost, but the incomplete copy on the disk is not lost. Once the power is restored and AppleWorks is re-started, a copy of the text can be loaded from the disk. When the blank line and "The End" are re-typed, the complete text is once more in the computer.

A wise computer operator saves his or her work after every fifteen minutes or so. The saving process takes only a few seconds and can prevent hours of re-typing. Start the habit now, press:

⌘-S   (Remember, this is an abbreviation for the instructions: Hold the ⌘ key down then press and release the S key. Finally, release ⌘.)

The complete text in the computer (including "The End") replaces the text previously stored on the disk. The copy on the disk is **updated**. The computer copy and the disk copy of the story are again identical. The two copies will remain identical until you modify, correct, or otherwise change the text in the computer.

PRINTING TEXT

Its exciting to see the work you have done in printed form. Let's get right to it.

GUIDED ACTIVITY: PRINT

Make sure that you have a printer attached to your computer before you begin this activity. If you do not have a printer on your computer, wait until one is available and use that machine for this activity.

It is a good habit to save your document before you print. (You just did this.) If you do not have a printer attached to your computer and you mistakenly try to print, AppleWorks may continue to send the document to a non-existent printer and ignore your commands. If there is a problem with the printer attached to your computer, the same thing may happen. If AppleWorks ignores you, your only choice for correction may be to turn the computer off and restart AppleWorks (before you do this, check with your instructor). Of course, if you turn the computer off, you lose any work that you have not saved.

WHAT YOU TYPE	WHY YOU TYPE IT
⌘-P	To start the printing process.

The bottom line of the screen displays the question:

Print from? Beginning   This   page   Cursor

The most frequently selected option, print from the **Beginning**, is highlighted. The other options, **This page** and **Cursor**, allow you to start printing with the page containing the text where the cursor is blinking or from the cursor position. All three options print to the end of the file. These options are helpful when you are editing a large document and you wish to print only a portion of it.

WHAT YOU TYPE	WHY YOU TYPE IT
<RETURN>	To select **Print from (the) beginning.**

The computer displays the PRINT MENU, a list of locations where the file may be printed. This list is displayed in Figure 3-5. (Your list is different if you have another printer or more than one printer.)

WHAT YOU TYPE	WHY YOU TYPE IT
1	To highlight the line for your printer. (The number and the name may be different for your computer system. Your instructor should inform you of any differences.)
<RETURN>.	To select the highlighted printer.

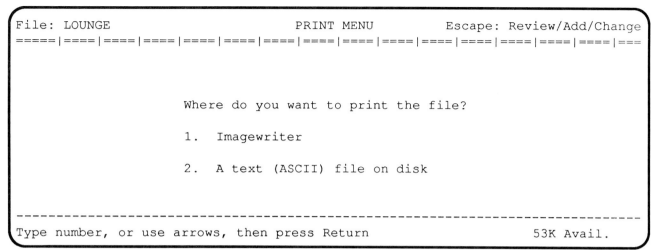

```
File: LOUNGE                    PRINT MENU        Escape: Review/Add/Change
=====|====|====|====|====|====|====|====|====|====|====|====|====|====|====|===



                    Where do you want to print the file?

                    1.   Imagewriter

                    2.   A text (ASCII) file on disk


         ----------------------------------------------------------------
Type number, or use arrows, then press Return              53K Avail.
```

FIGURE 3-5.   Print Menu.

The last question to answer before printing is "How many copies?" The **default** answer, the one that is used when you just press Return, is "1". Any number from 1 through the number showing on the screen is an acceptable answers to this question.

Make sure that the printer is turned on and properly connected, paper is correctly loaded, and the printer "select" ("on line" on some printers) light is lit. If you are not certain of any of these steps, ask your instructor for help.

WHAT YOU TYPE	WHY YOU TYPE IT
<RETURN>	To accept the default answer 1 and start printing.

Save this copy of your printout to compare with other printouts of this file.

✓ CHECKPOINT

While the document is printing, a message about two keys is displayed. What are the two keys and what do they do?

MAKING CHANGES

There are several corrections that the newspaper advisor and the author wish to make. The corrections involve insertion or deletion of a few letters or words. Let's make those corrections, but first you'll need some practice moving the cursor to different locations in the document.

GUIDED ACTIVITY: NAVIGATION

At the start of this activity, the Lounge story is displayed. The cursor is located at the end of the document.

WHAT YOU TYPE	WHY YOU TYPE IT
<UP-ARROW>	To move the cursor up one line.
⌂-<UP-ARROW>	To move the cursor to the top of the screen.
⌂-<UP-ARROW>	To move the cursor up another screen.
<RIGHT-ARROW>	To move the cursor right one character.
⌂-<RIGHT-ARROW>	To move the cursor right one word.
Hold ⌂-<RIGHT-ARROW>	To rapidly move the cursor to the right one word at a time.

Practice the cursor movements by moving to a specific letter in a specific word. Move the cursor to the letter "E" in the word "End".

WHAT YOU TYPE	WHY YOU TYPE IT
⌂-<DOWN-ARROW>	To move the cursor to the very bottom of the document. (If the cursor is not at the bottom of the text, type this command a second time.)
⌂-<LEFT-ARROW> 3 times	To move the cursor to the "E". (If the cursor is to the right of the word, type the command one more time.)

AppleWorks also provides another way of moving through the text. Consider the text divided into eight roughly equal sized pieces. Open-Apple-1 moves the cursor to the start of the first piece. Open-Apple-2 moves the cursor to the start of the second piece, and so on through Open-Apple-8, the start of the eighth and last piece. Open-Apple-9 moves the cursor to the very end of the text. The document you have before you is small and therefore has relatively small eighths, but you can still observe the cursor movement using the Open-Apple commands. Try the following sequence.

WHAT YOU TYPE	WHY YOU TYPE IT
⌂-9	To move to the end of the text. The text moves up to allow information to be added.
⌂-6	The cursor moves to the beginning of the sixth segment of text. The text moves up so that this segment starts at the middle of the screen.
⌂-1	The cursor moves to the top of the text.

INSERTING

The underline cursor that is blinking now is called the **insert cursor.** When this cursor appears, it is possible to insert text anywhere in the document. You have already inserted text. You inserted the words "The End" at the bottom of the document. To insert text in other locations, you would move the cursor to the location and then type.

GUIDED ACTIVITY: EDIT

Laurie's advisor pointed out that in the past some students were upset with scheduling errors, so they decided to insert the words "scheduling errors", before "overcrowding" in the first paragraph.

The first step to take is move the cursor to the letter "o" in the word "overcrowding." The arrow keys are used to do this. There are several combinations of up, down, right, and left arrows that move to this location. You're on your own -

Move the cursor to the "o" in "overcrowding".

WHAT YOU TYPE	WHY YOU TYPE IT
scheduling errors,	To insert the words and comma into the text.
<SPACE BAR>	To insert a blank space between the comma and the "o".

The insertion is complete and the paragraph now reads:

```
      Anger!  The feeling that was felt by many the first
few weeks of school.  They were not mad because of
scheduling errors, overcrowding or long lunch lines, but
because the lounge was closed.
```

OVERSTRIKING

Some changes involve typing over old text to replace it with new text. Correcting the spelling of "privelege" by overstriking the first "e" with an "i" is an example of this type of change.

Move the cursor to the incorrect character, the first "e" in "privelege".

WHAT YOU TYPE	WHY YOU TYPE IT
⌘-E	To change from the insert cursor to the **overstrike** or **edit cursor.** (It doesn't matter if you use a capital or lowercase "E" for the ⌘-E command.) The edit cursor now appears as a blinking box.
i	To replace the "e" with "i".

It is a good idea to turn off the edit cursor when you finish using it. If you don't, you may find yourself typing over text that you do not wish to change.

WHAT YOU TYPE	WHY YOU TYPE IT
⌘-E	To change back to the insert cursor.

Let's practice the edit cursor one more time. Change the beginning of the second paragraph to read " Anger, the feeling ... "

Move the cursor to the "!" in "Anger!"

WHAT YOU TYPE	WHY YOU TYPE IT
⌘-E	To "turn on" the edit cursor.
, <SPACE BAR> t	To replace the exclamation and two spaces with a comma, a space, and the letter t.
⌘-E	To change to the insert cursor.

I'm sure you noticed that the job is not finished. The text reads: "`Anger, tThe ...`". Correcting this leads us to the next section.

DELETING LETTERS

There is nothing new to learn here. A letter is deleted by moving to the right of the letter and pressing the Delete key.

GUIDED ACTIVITY: EDIT (continued)

The insert cursor is blinking on the letter "T" in "tThe".

WHAT YOU TYPE	WHY YOU TYPE IT
<RIGHT-ARROW>	To move to the right of the capital "T".
<DELETE>	To delete the "T".

Notice that you could have changed the "e" in "privelege" to an "i" by deleting the "e" and then inserting the "i". Similarily, you could have used the Delete key to delete "! T" and then finished that change by inserting ", t". The method that you select is entirely up to you.

Now you will look at another way to delete words or any large block of text.

DELETING WORDS AND PARAGRAPHS

Many times whole words, sentences, or even whole paragraphs need to be removed from a document. For example, the phrase "... abusing the privilege of it." is poor English. It is possible to delete the phrase using the Delete key, hovever, the delete command is much faster for large blocks of text. Practice this command by change the phrase above to "... abusing it."

GUIDED ACTIVITY: EDIT (continued)

Remove "the privilege of" as follows:

> Move the cursor to the letter "t" in the word "the".

WHAT YOU TYPE	WHY YOU TYPE IT
⌂-D	To give the **Delete Text** command. (It doesn't matter if you use a capital or lower case "D").

Several things happen when you issue the ⌂-D command.

- A small block appears at the end of each paragraph and at the beginning of each blank line. This block marks every place where you pressed Return. It is called a **return blot** and looks like a little checkerboard.
- The message at the top center of the screen changes to DELETE TEXT.
- The bottom line displays the message: Use cursor moves to highlight block, then press Return.
- The cursor on the "t" changes to a solid rectangle and stops blinking.
- The amount of available memory in K (1000's) is displayed in the lower right corner.

It should be obvious that something different is happening.

> Press the <RIGHT-ARROW> key.

The highlighted text is now "th".

> Press the <RIGHT-ARROW> three more times.

The highlighted block is now "the p". You are highlighting the text that you want AppleWorks to delete when you press Return. The highlighting extends to the right or left of the initial cursor position. Therefore, the cursor needs to start at the beginning or at the end of the text to be deleted.

> Highlight the unwanted text, "the privilege of".
> Press the <RIGHT-ARROW> key one more time to highlight the space after "of".

The words "the privilege of " and the space after the word "of" should now be highlighted. The space after "of" needs to be deleted so that there is only one space remaining between the words "abusing" and "it".

Once the block of text to be deleted is correctly highlighted, press <RETURN>.

The highlighted text is then removed, the empty space is closed, the Return blots disappear, and the screen messages turn to normal.

Make sure that the text you highlight is the text that you really want to delete. Once text is deleted the only way to bring it back into the document is to re-type it. You can stop the delete process without deleting any text by pressing the Escape key.

The document would read much better without the first paragraph. Let's take it out.

GUIDED ACTIVITY: EDIT (continued)

Move the cursor to the first space in the first line of the paragraph that starts "   It seems that every year ..."

WHAT YOU TYPE	WHY YOU TYPE IT
⌒-D	To start the delete process.
<DOWN-ARROW> twice	To highlight the paragraph and one space.
<LEFT-ARROW>	To move back to the end of the paragraph.
<RETURN>	The paragraph disappears and the text closes up.

THE HELP SCREENS

By now most students learning AppleWorks for the first time are wondering how they are going remember all of the commands. If you think about it for a moment, you will soon realize that you only need to remember some word processing terminology for the things you want to do. A process is usually invoked by holding down the Open-Apple key and pressing the first letter of the key word. For example, deleting text is invoked with Open-Apple-D and changing to the edit cursor is invoked with Open-Apple-E. In case you forget, however, there is always help available.

The bottom right corner of the screen reminds you that holding down the Open-Apple key and pressing the question mark (?) key displays the Help Screens. (? for help is one of the exceptions to the rule given in the last paragraph.)

WHAT YOU TYPE	WHY YOU TYPE IT
⌒-?	To display the Word Processor Help Screen.

You have used three of the Open-Apple commands so far: Open-Apple-D to delete; Open-Apple-E to change to the edit cursor and Open-Apple-S to save the file. Look for these commands on the Help Screen. Notice that this Help screen is different from the one that you viewed from the Main Menu.

The list of Open-Apple commands is too long to fit on one screen.

> To see the rest of the list, press the <DOWN-ARROW> key.

Each time you press it the list scrolls up the screen.

> <u>Hold down</u> the <DOWN-ARROW> key and the list scrolls up rapidly.
> <u>Release</u> the key and the scrolling stops.
> The <UP-ARROW> key scrolls in the reverse direction.
> To return to the text, press the <ESCAPE> key once.

The Help Screens do not give you complete information on the use of an Open-Apple command. They only list the keys needed to start the command. When you issue an Open-Apple command for a multistep operation, the computer leads you through the process step by step.

✓ CHECKPOINT

> Two of the three Open-Apple Commands you have used so far in this chapter appear on the Main Menu Help Screen and are not repeated on the Word Processor Help Screen. What are those commands?

EXERCISE 3.1

Change the second paragraph of the document by deleting the words "outside in" in the first line and inserting the word "usually" in the second sentence. When you are finished, the paragraph should read:

```
        The lounge is the area between the library and room 103.
It is usually available during lunches and studies.
```

Add the word "crew" to the sentence in the third paragraph to make it read:

```
     It took longer for this to be taken care of because the town
maintenance crew had to fix it, not High School custodians.
```

Change the first sentence in the story to read:

> Anger, that was the feeling expressed by many the
> first few weeks of school.

CENTERING TEXT

Let's make a few enhancements to the text. It would be nice if the title and byline (by Laurie S.) were centered. Centering as well as several other enhancements are considered **printing option** changes, also as **format** changes. **Formatting** changes the way the text appears on the printed page. Make a format change by following the next Guided Activity.

(Formatting text is not the same as formatting a disk. Formatting a disk means arranging the electrons on the disk so that information can be saved by a particular brand of computer. Formatting text means arranging words in a document in a visually pleasing form. The idea common to the two operations is that something is organized or ordered in some way.)

GUIDED ACTIVITY: FORMAT

Two steps are need to enter printing options into a word processing file. First, locate the cursor at the spot where the option is to start. (Locating the cursor by moving around the text one character or even one line at a time seems rather slow. Remember, pressing and holding the Open-Apple key while you press an arrow key increases the cursor's movement.)

Move the cursor to the "L" in the word "Lounge" at the beginning of the document.

The second step in setting up a printer option is to insert the option:

WHAT YOU TYPE	WHY YOU TYPE IT
⌘-O	To start the printer options entry.

The bottom half of the screen changes to display the printer options. This screen is shown in Figure 3–6.

There is a lot of information in this table. For now, look at the highlighted line. AppleWorks uses three types of justification: **justified right margin**, **unjustified right margin**, and **centered**. For example, except for this paragraph, the paragraphs in this book are justified right margin (the right edge is lined up); this paragraph is unjustified right margin (the right edge is not lined up). The titles under the figures in this book are centered.

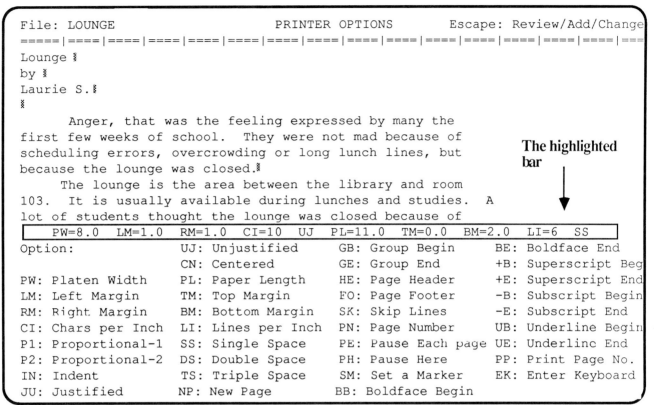

FIGURE 3-6. Lounge Story and Printer Options.

Near the center of the line the characters "UJ" appear. This indicates that the text is unjustified, that is, the right edge is ragged. Change the justification to centered.

WHAT YOU TYPE	WHY YOU TYPE IT
CN <RETURN>	To center the text line-by-line on the screen.

CN is the code for centering. This code is listed in the second column, second item down. The following message appears in the text to indicate where the centering begins.

```
-------Centered
```

Press <ESCAPE> to exit the printer options.

Now that you can see the entire screen, it is even more apparent that each line is centered. You only wanted the top three lines centered, so let's continue.

Unjustified Text

After you pressed Escape, the `-------Centered` message and the blots showing carriage return locations disappeared. It is obvious when you look at the text on the screen that each line is centered but it would be helpful to be able to see the printer messages.

GUIDED ACTIVITY: FORMAT (continued)

When you make editing changes in the text, it is often helpful to be able to see the return blots and the printer commands. The printer commands are always in the document; even if you can not see them. You use the zoom command to make them visible or invisible.

What You Type	Why You Type It
⌘-Z	To zoom in on the text. The blots and the `-------Centered` message appear.
⌘-Z	To zoom out. The blots and message disappear.

Correct the centering problem as follows:

What You Type	Why You Type It
⌘-Z	To zoom in.
ARROWS	To move the cursor to the blot under Laurie's name.
⌘-O	To display the printer options (be sure to type the letter "O" not the digit zero (0)). (Note that the center of the highlight line now reads CN.)
UJ <RETURN>	To change to unjustified text (unjustified text is not centered).
<ESCAPE>	To exit the printer options.

Your screen should now match the one shown in Figure 3-7.

What You Type	Why You Type It
⌘-Z	To zoom out and turn off the blots.

By the way, if you experiment with justified text, keep in mind that the justification shows only on the printed copy. AppleWorks does not show justified text on the screen.

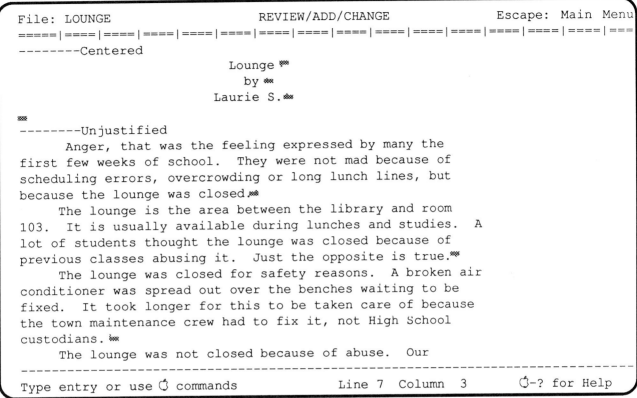

FIGURE 3-7. Display Showing Centered and Unjustified Messages.

BACKING UP

You have made many changes to the text you typed in at the beginning of the chapter. It is time to save again, since the copy of your document on the disk does not have the most recent changes.

Issue the ⌘-S command to save onto the disk the text now in the computer.

Once the computer has saved the file, you again have two identical copies of it, one in the computer and the other on the disk. You'll turn the computer off and take a break in a moment. When you do that, the computer copy of the file is lost and only the disk copy remains leaving you with only one copy of your file. In other words, no backup of the work you have done will exist. The solution to this dilemma is to save the file on a second disk.

Remove the file disk labeled **AppleWorks Data Disk #1 Primary** from Drive 2.
Insert the file disk labeled **AppleWorks Data Disk #1 Backup** in Drive 2.
Give the ⌘-S command to save the file again.
When the save process is complete, remove **AppleWorks Files Disk #1 Backup** from Drive 2.
Reinsert **AppleWorks Files Disk #1 Primary**.
Your backup disk should now be placed in its safe storage place.

In a very short time you made a third copy of your file. You now have a copy in the computer, a copy on your primary disk, and a copy on your backup disk. You should follow the procedure outlined above at the end of every work session. Making a backup before you quit should be an automatic habit.

GUIDED ACTIVITY: FORMAT (continued)

As you continue to work, you change the Desktop copy of the file again. Center "The End" in the last line of the story.

WHAT YOU TYPE	WHY YOU TYPE IT
Arrows	To position the cursor on the beginning of the line "The End". (The lowercase letters mean that you need to decide which arrow keys to press and how many times to press them.)
⌂-O	To display the printer options.
CN <RETURN>	To center the text from this point down.
<ESCAPE>	To exit the printer options and return to the text.

Now that you have made a change, think about the three copies of your file. The computer copy does not match either disk copy, but the two disk copies are still identical. Save your file (⌂-S). Now the computer copy and the primary disk copy are identical. The backup copy is one generation behind and no longer reflects your most recent changes. Save the file on the backup disk once at the end of your work session. Save frequently on the Primary Data Disk.

TYPE SIZE

Several character sizes ranging from four characters per inch (large letters) to twenty-four characters per inch (small letters) are available in AppleWorks. The character sizes that you can use depend on your printer. For example, the Apple Imagewriter printer uses 5, 8, 9, 10, 12, 15, or 17 characters per inch. Most modern printers offer at least three character sizes. Ten, twelve, and five characters per inch are the most common.

GUIDED ACTIVITY: FORMAT (continued)

The different character sizes appear on the printout only. The type size remains constant on the screen. The screen display does adjust to show approximately what words fit on a printed line. Try this example:

WHAT YOU TYPE	WHY YOU TYPE IT
⌂-1	To return to the beginning of the text.
⌂-O	To select the printer options.

```
CI <RETURN>              To change Characters per Inch.
5  <RETURN>              To get 5 characters per inch.
<ESCAPE>                 To exit the printer options.
```

The display changes to the one shown in Figure 3-8 to reflect the 5 characters per inch printout. (You may need to zoom in to match the display exactly.)

```
File: LOUNGE                    REVIEW/ADD/CHANGE              Escape: Main Menu
=====|====|====|====|====|====|====|====|====|====|====|====|====|====|====|===
--------Chars per Inch: 5 chars
--------Centered
          Lounge▓
            by ▓
         Laurie S.▓
▓
--------Unjustified
       Anger, that was the
feeling expressed by many the
first few weeks of school.
They were not mad because of
scheduling errors,
overcrowding or long lunch
lines, but because the lounge
was closed.▓
       The lounge is the area
between the library and room
103.  It is usually available
during lunches and studies.  A
lot of students thought the
-------------------------------------------------------------------------
Type entry or use Ở commands            Line 1  Column  1       Ở-? for Help
```

FIGURE 3-8. Lounge Story - 5 Characters per Inch.

✓ __CHECKPOINT__

The copy of the document on the Desktop now has some information that is not on either disk copy. What is that information?

QUITTING THE WORD PROCESSOR

You've just made another change in the text that is not reflected on the disk copy of the file, but don't save just yet.

> <ESCAPE> back to the Main Menu.
> Highlight option **6. Quit** and press <RETURN>.
> Respond **Yes** to the question **Do you really want to do this?** by pressing **Y**.

AppleWorks detects that you have a file with changes (a new character per inch value) that you are about to lose. It takes you through a series of questions to determine exactly what you wish to do with the changes that you made to the file.

The first screen you encounter is shown in Figure 3-9.

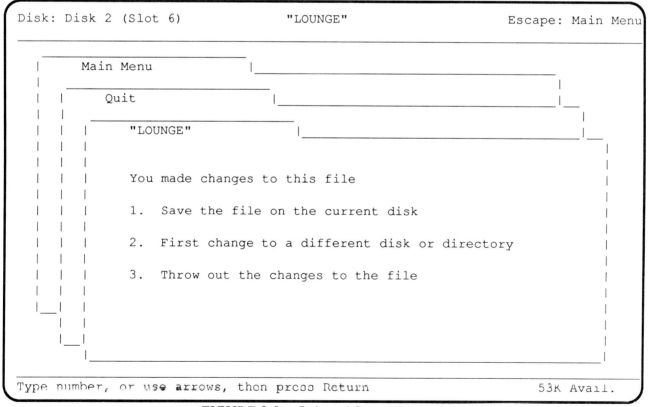

```
Disk: Disk 2 (Slot 6)              "LOUNGE"              Escape: Main Menu
_____
  |      Main Menu          |_____
  |    _____                                  |
  |   |     Quit            |_____|__
  |   |   _____                                   |
  |   |  |   "LOUNGE"        |_____|__
  |   |  |                                                        |
  |   |  |                                                        |
  |   |  |   You made changes to this file                        |
  |   |  |                                                        |
  |   |  |   1.   Save the file on the current disk               |
  |   |  |                                                        |
  |   |  |   2.   First change to a different disk or directory   |
  |   |  |                                                        |
  |   |  |   3.   Throw out the changes to the file               |
  |   |  |                                                        |
  |__|  |                                                        |
     |  |                                                        |
     |__|_____|
_____
Type number, or use arrows, then press Return          53K Avail.
```

FIGURE 3-9.   Quit and Save Menu.

The first and third options seem obvious. If you select option 1, you save the file with the final changes. After the file has been saved again, the disk copy of the file matches the Desktop copy. If you select option 3, the changes that you made since you last saved the file are lost (there may be times when you may wish to discard changes). For example, you are not satisfied with the changes you made so you throw them out. Later, you would restart your work with the last copy of the file saved.

Option 2 is used by people with more than two disk drives, a 3.5 inch disk drive, or with a hard disk system. (Option 2 can also be used to change back to disk Drive 2 if the standard disk location has somehow been switched to another drive.)

> Highlight option **1. Save the file on the current disk.**
> Press <RETURN>.

The menu shown in Figure 3-10 appears.

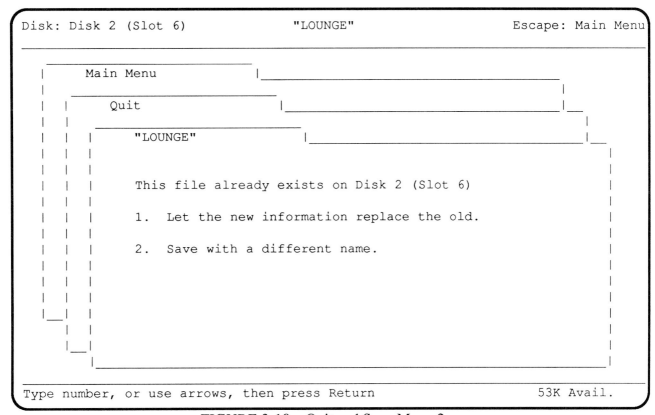

```
Disk: Disk 2 (Slot 6)              "LOUNGE"              Escape: Main Menu
 _____

     _____
    |      Main Menu              |_____
    |   _____|                                   |
    |  |     Quit               |_____|    |__
    |  |   _____|                                 |      |
    |  |  |    "LOUNGE"        |_____|     |__    |
    |  |  |                                                         |     |
    |  |  |                                                         |     |
    |  |  |    This file already exists on Disk 2 (Slot 6)          |     |
    |  |  |                                                         |     |
    |  |  |    1.  Let the new information replace the old.          |     |
    |  |  |                                                         |     |
    |  |  |    2.  Save with a different name.                       |     |
    |  |  |                                                         |     |
    |  |  |                                                         |     |
    |  |  |                                                         |     |
    |__|  |                                                         |     |
       |  |                                                         |     |
       |__|_____|     |
          |_____|

 _____
 Type number, or use arrows, then press Return              53K Avail.
```

FIGURE 3-10.   Quit and Save Menu 2.

Option 1. Let the new information replace the old is the usual choice here. (It is the automatic or **default** choice used when you issue the Open-Apple-S command.)

> Press <RETURN> to select option 1.

(If you wished to reflect on the changes you made since you last saved your file, you might select option 2 here. The computer then asks for a new name for your file. The "old" version is on the disk with the original name and the "new", latest, corrected version is stored with the new name. At some future time you can review both versions, either on the screen or on paper, and decide which to keep.)

AppleWorks makes every attempt to save you from error. It can only do this if you follow the proper procedure when you quit. Never turn off AppleWorks in the middle of the program. Always Escape to the Main Menu and select option 6." Quit." The keystrokes again are:

WHAT YOU TYPE	WHY YOU TYPE IT
<ESCAPE>	To display the Main Menu.
6 <RETURN>	To select **Quit**.
Y	To answer yes to **Do you really want to do this?**

This is a good time to take a break if you wish and if it is ok with your instructor. Don't forget to turn off the computer and the monitor, straighten up your work area, and return materials.

RETRIEVING PREVIOUSLY STORED TEXT

Many times when you start an AppleWorks session, you want to continue working with a file that you have already saved on the disk. Therefore, your first step after getting started is to add the file to the Desktop from the disk. (Since you are going to print your file in this section, you should use a computer that has a printer attached. If that is not possible, you can repeat this Guided Activity on a machine with a printer at a later time.)

Start AppleWorks.
Enter the date and proceed to the Main Menu.
Insert your Primary Data Disk, labeled **AppleWorks Data Disk #1 Primary,** into Drive 2.

WHAT YOU TYPE	WHY YOU TYPE IT
<RETURN>	To select **Add files to the Desktop.**
<RETURN>	To select **Get files from: The current disk: Drive 2.** The **APPLEWORKS FILES** Menu appears in the display as shown in Figure 3-11.

Important information to note on this display includes:

• The name of the disk volume is AWD (AppleWorks Data). This is the name you used when you formatted the disk. (Your backup disk should not be in the drive now. Remember that the backup disk is not always as current as the primary and should not be used to load a file. See the following troubleshooting section if B.U. is part of the disk name; you inadvertently inserted the wrong disk.)

- The amount of space available to store additional information on the disk is 132K. This number decreases by the size of the file as you add more files to the disk.
- `Lounge` and `Activity 1 File` are the only files on the disk. They are Word Processor files that take approximately 2,000 characters (2K) and 1,000 (1K) of space, respectively. (AppleWorks rounds up to the nearest thousand.)
- The date the file was last saved is displayed. (If you have a clock accessory installed in your computer, the time the file was last saved is also displayed.)

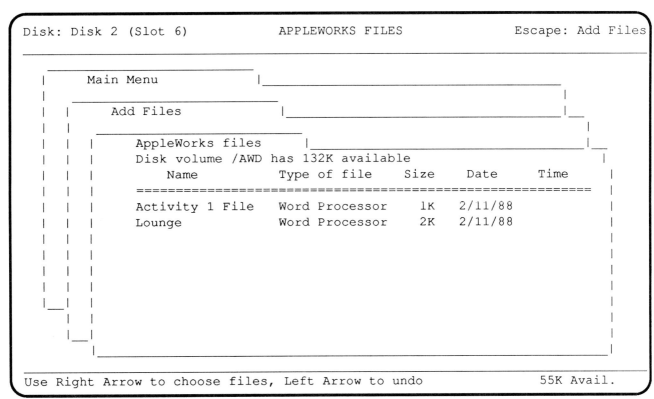

FIGURE 3-11.   AppleWorks Files Menu.

TROUBLESHOOTING:

Problem: The "APPLEWORKS FILES" menu display indicates that the backup disk is in the disk drive ("B.U.AWD" appears as the disk name).

Correction: Press the Escape key to return to the "ADD FILES" menu. Remove the backup disk from the drive. Insert the primary disk in the drive and close the drive door. Press Return to select the option **Get files from: The current disk: Drive 2.**

Problem: The message **Getting errors trying to read the directory at Drive 2** appears.

Correction: First be sure that you are using an AppleWorks file disk. Make sure that the disk is in the drive and the drive door is properly closed. Then press Return to try again. If the problem persists, you have either a bad disk or a bad disk drive. To narrow down the problem, select `Try a different location`, and then select `Drive 1`. Place your data disk in Drive 1 and press `Return`. If the files list appears you know that your disk is ok and your drive may need repair. If the same error message appears the disk and/or Drive may be damaged. A bad disk drive can destroy a disk; do not test the drive out with your backup. It's time to seek expert help from your instructor or from the computer room monitor.

To select a file to add to the Desktop from the list of files displayed, you would use the up and down arrow keys to highlight the file's name and press Return. Files are listed alphabetically within file types; that is, word processing files are listed alphabetically, followed by data base files alphabetically, and then spreadsheet files alphabetically.

Highlight **Lounge** and press <RETURN>

The file is copied from the disk into the computer's memory. A copy of the file remains on the disk; at this point the disk copy is identical to the Desktop copy.

Print the file again to observe the effect of the changes that you made.

Once you have done it a few times, printing a Word Processor file from the beginning is a snap. Make sure that your printer is ready and then follow the five step sequence of keystrokes:

WHAT YOU TYPE	WHY YOU TYPE IT
⌂-S	To save the file.
⌂-P	To start the printing process.
<RETURN>	To select **Print from** (the) **beginning.**
<RETURN>	To select the previously selected printer. (Until you quit, AppleWorks remembers which printer to use.)
<RETURN>	To select 1 copy.

"Lounge" is then printed. The print out, as it appears on some printers, is shown in Figure 3-12.

```
              Lounge
                by
            Laurie S.

     Anger, that was the
feeling expressed by many the
first few weeks of school.
They were not mad because of
scheduling errors,
overcrowding or long lunch
lines, but because the lounge
was closed.
     The lounge is the area
between the library and room
103.  It is usually available
```

FIGURE 3-12.   Partial Story Printout.

TROUBLESHOOTING:

Problem:	The story does not print in five-character-per-inch-type.
Correction:	Not all printers are capable of printing all type sizes. Custom printers need special codes entered into the "Add A Printer" option to be able to print sizes other than ten characters per inch. If AppleWorks cannot determine how to apply a special printer command to your printer, it ignores the command. If your printer prints ten characters per inch across the full page, AppleWorks did not have the five-character-per-inch-command for your printer. If ten characters per inch are printed across only half the page, AppleWorks was probably given incorrect information about printing five characters per inch on your printer. See appendix C for more information on printers.

GUIDED ACTIVITY: MODIFY AND SAVE

Proper practice makes near perfect so let's practice some of the lessons and concepts that you learned in this unit. In this Guided Activity you modify Lounge by: changing back to 10 characters per inch and centering "The End". You also reprint the document, and re-save the file on both the primary and backup disks. Finally, you end you work session by quitting AppleWorks.

Modify the story.

WHAT YOU TYPE	WHY YOU TYPE IT
⌂-Z	To display the Return Blots and printer commands.
⌂-1	To move to the beginning of the file.
Down-Arrow	If the cursor is not already on the 5 character per inch message, move it there with this key.
⌂-D	To highlight the 5 character per inch printer message.
<RETURN>	To delete the 5 characters per inch printer command. Characters per inch return to the default setting, 10.
<ESCAPE>	To return to text display.
⌂-9	To move to the end of the text.
<UP-ARROW>	To move to the "T" in "The End".
⌂-O	To display printer options.
CN <RETURN>	To center "The End"
<ESCAPE>	To return to the text display.

Reprint the story.

Make sure your printer is on and selected.
Make sure your Primary Data Disk is in drive 2.

WHAT YOU TYPE	WHY YOU TYPE IT
⌂-S	To save the file on the primary disk.
⌂-P	To start the printing process.
<RETURN>	To select **Print from** (the) **beginning.**
<RETURN>	To select the highlighted printer.
<RETURN>	To select 1 copy.

Re-save the story on the backup disk.

Remove the Primary Data Disk.
Insert the Backup Data Disk.

WHAT YOU TYPE	WHY YOU TYPE IT
⌂-S	To save the file on the backup disk.

Remove the Backup Data Disk.
Insert the Primary Data Disk.

Quit AppleWorks.

What You Type	Why You Type It
<ESCAPE>	To display the Main Menu.
6 <RETURN>	To highlight and select **6. Quit.**
Y	To select **Yes.**

The standard message appears and you are finished using AppleWorks for this session.

✓ CHECKPOINT

When you quit this time, you were not asked to save your file. Why not?

REVIEW QUESTIONS

1. Why would you change a document after you have typed it into the computer?

2. Why does the display change when you change the print option from 10 characters per inch to 5 characters per inch?

3. You sometimes hold the Open-Apple key down when you press other keys. Why do you do this?

4. You save your work onto the disk after each ten minutes of typing. Why do you do this?

5. You wish to change one five letter word to another five letter word. Which cursor mode, insert or overstrike, would you best use to do this? Why that mode?

6. How do you insert a blank line?

7. It is helpful to remember special words for Open-Apple commands. What special words should you remember for the following commands?

   a. ⌂-S
   b. ⌂-E
   c. ⌂-D
   d. ⌂-Z
   e. ⌂-O
   f. ⌂-?

8. You always remove the Backup Data Disk and replace it with the Primary Data Disk after you backup your documents. Why do you do this?

EXERCISES

3.2 Load the file "Sayings" from the Student Data Disk. Save the file on your Primary Data Disk.
   a. Make corrections in the file so that the corrected file reads:

>   Frank Short   (Replace the words **Your Name** with your own name.)
>
>   A stitch in time saves nine. (Change **mine** to nine.)
>   (Delete the paragraph not printed here.)
>   If wishes were horses, then everyone would ride. (Change **walk** to ride.)
>
>   Every cloud has a silver lining.   (Insert this line.)
>
>   AppleWorks is awesome.   (Change **really great** to awesome.)
>
>   All good things must come to an end. Therefore, this is the
>   end of this exercise.   (Change **IS** to is. Add two spaces before
>   Therefore.)

   b. Save the file on both your Primary and Backup Data Disks.
   c. Print a copy of the file as it now exists.
   d. Center you name. Do not center the remaining lines in the file.
   e. Print the file a second time. Turn both printouts of your file into your instructor.

   Your instructor may ask you at some future date to display a copy of this file on your screen. The display should show the last copy that you printed.

3.3 Write a one page paper discussing some of the uses you may have for the AppleWorks Word Processor. Produce the paper using AppleWorks. Make any revisions to your first printout that your instructor suggests. Print a final draft. Turn in your first printout and your final draft for grading.

3.4 Research the programs that are available for AppleWorks by looking through computer magazine and newspaper ads. Produce a summary of your findings with AppleWorks Word Processor. Make any revisions to your first printout that your instructor suggests. Print a final draft. Turn in your first printout and your final draft for grading.

3.5 Poetry is sometimes printed using centered lines of text. Produce a poem with centered lines using AppleWorks Word Processor. Provide a printout for your instructor. Here is a very short sample:

```
        A poet sure
   would have much bliss
      with centering
         as nice
         as this.
```

3.6 EXPERIMENT: Load the document "Character Sizes" from the Student Data Disk. Run the program on the printer attached to your computer. Examine the printout to determine what type sizes are available on your printer.

APPLICATION

A SATURDAY'S BOAT RIDE

THE SCENARIO

You have been assigned to write a short story for your English class. It is the first story of the year and your teacher requested that it be only one page in length. You decide to write the story using the AppleWorks' Word Processor. The Understanding and Using Appleworks Student Data Disk contains the original draft of the story. It is reproduced here with suggested corrections.

~Center~

SeaLea
Corrected by →Insert your name here.

It was ~~s~~Saturday and the~~ir~~ re ~~is~~ was no school. Anne, Larry,

Bob, Lynn, Chris, Jennifer, Jamie, Henry, John, Ken, and I

were ~~are~~ going to go across Long Island Sound on my boat. We

drove down to the docks, in the early morning to start our adventure.

When we arrived, it was 10 o'clock A.M. ~~and~~ ~~w~~We walked

down to the ~~the~~ peir where my ship lay. Ken and I jumpﬆed on board

first. I unlock ed the cabin while he lowered ~~let~~ the life lines ~~down~~

on the starboard side to let everyone else on. Chris, and

Jennifer had seen her before but the others had never seen

my vessel, SeaLea. One by one, the y came below to see the

69

cabin. John an~~d~~ Ken couldn't believe their eyes at the sight of the ~~large vessel~~ *thirty footer.* Jamie started up the motor and ~~B~~ob and I got the sails ready. I gra~~b~~ed the wheel. John and Henry handled the lines at the bow and stern as we ~~prepared~~ ~~to shove~~ *cast* off. I decided to put up the small jib because the wind was really blowin~~g~~ hard - about 30 miles per hour over the clear water. *¶* The boat sailed at a good ten ~~k~~ots. It only took us an hour to get ~~there~~ *to Port Jefferson* with that *strong* wind. Most of the time, it takes about two hours.

We stayed in the New York port for a while; then we decided to start head~~ed~~ *ing* back to ~~Captin Cove~~, my marin~~a~~ *at Captain's Cove.* I let several of my guests take the wheel in the open waters of the ~~S~~ound, as we ~~headed~~ *were going* home at a slower pace th~~a~~n we had ~~come over at~~. *coming out.* I~~t~~ took close to three hours to make the trip back. Everyone enjoyed the slow lazy ride.

"Hey, let's go, let's go. It's time ~~to go to~~ *for* class," Larry said. *¶* "Huh," I slowly replied. "Where did *the* SeaLea go?" *¶* "Come on, he said, "~~Y~~ou~~r~~ daydreaming adventure is over. It's tim~~e~~ for English and the ~~T~~all ~~S~~ea ~~T~~ails." *¶* Well," I thought, "there is s~~o~~me more great sailing com~~i~~ng up soon."

YOUR TASK

Load the story, Boat Ride, from the Student Data Disk. Save the story on your disk. Make the corrections that are indicated in the text above. Save the corrected copy of the story on your disk. Please make sure that your name is typed on the page and all of your corrections are complete; then print out the corrected copy. Remove the pin feed holes and throw them in the trash. Submit the corrected copy with pages separated and stapled together to your instructor.

UNIT
4

GETTING STARTED WITH THE DATA BASE

LEARNING OBJECTIVES

1. After completing this unit, you should know ...

   a. what a data base is.

   b. when and how a data base file can be used to organize information.

   c. why an electronic data base is used.

   d. the definitions of record, field, category, labels format, tables format, and sorting.

2. After completing this unit, you should be able to ...

   a. use an existing data base file.

   b. modify an existing data base file by adding and deleting records.

   c. modify an existing data base file by changing records.

   d. select a portion of a file for a report.

   e. sort a data base file.

   f. print a data base report in tables format.

   g. design and print a data base report in labels format.

71

ASSIGNMENTS

1. OPEN: Add a data base file to the Desktop from a disk.

2. RENAME: Change the name of a data base file.

3. CURSOR: Move the cursor through the categories and records of a data base file.

4. ADD: Add a record.

5. MODIFY: Modify records.

6. ARRANGE: Organize the file alphabetically and/or numerically.

7. PRINT: Select and print records.

8. RULES: Select a portion of the file using the rules command.

9. LABELS: Design the printer format for a labels report.

10. REVIEW QUESTIONS AND EXERCISES: Additional review and practice with editing records and printing layouts.

IMPORTANT KEYSTROKES AND COMMANDS

The first group of Data Base Commands is for moving the cursor and entering information into a data base file. Notice that several of the commands are identical to those used in the Word Processor. The similarity in commands is part of the integrated feature of AppleWorks.

COMMAND/KEY(S)	MEANING
Left-arrow	Move the cursor left one character within a category.
Right-arrow	Move the cursor right one character within a category.
Up-arrow	Move the cursor one category up the list.
Down-arrow	Move the cursor one category down the list.
⌘-Up-arrow	Move the cursor up one screen.
⌘-Down-arrow	Move the cursor down one screen.
⌘-1 to 9	Move the cursor proportionally through the file.
Tab	Move the cursor down a category in single record layout. Move a column right in multiple record layout or from the last column in a line to the first column in the next line.
⌘-Tab	Move the cursor up a category in single record layout. Move a column left in multiple record layout or from the first column in a line to the last column in the previous line.
Control-Y	Delete the characters on the line to the right of the cursor.
⌘-Y	Same as Control-Y.

Ú-N	Change the name of a file or category. Insert or delete categories.
Ú-S	Save a file, its records, custom layouts, and reports to the disk.

The following commands are used in designing a report format and in printing reports:

COMMAND/KEY(S)	MEANING
Ú-P	Proceed to Report Format menu from Review/Add/Change or print a report from the report format display.
Left, Right arrows	Cursor movement from one category to another.
Ú-Left-arrow	Change the size of a category column in the tables format or move a category to the left in the labels format.
Ú-Right-arrow	Change the size of a category column in the tables format or move a category to the right in the labels format.
Ú-<	Change the position of a category in the tables format or display the previous record in labels format.
Ú->	Change the position of a category in the tables format or display the next record in labels format.
Ú-A	Arrange the file in alphabetical, numerical, or chronological order.
Ú-D	Delete a category from the report.
Ú-I	Insert a previously deleted category into the report. Insert a blank line in a labels format report.
Ú-N	Change the name or title of a report.
Ú-R	Change the record selection rules.
Ú-V	View the category name and the category information in a labels style report.
Ú-Z	Zoom in or out to show records or category names in labels or tables format.

INTRODUCTORY CONCEPTS

The Data Base in AppleWorks is a tool for keeping information of the type that might be stored in lists or on file cards. A computer list is far more versatile than one kept on paper or on three-by-five cards. It is also more fun and easier to use. In this unit, we'll use a yearbook subscription list to learn some data base commands and concepts.

Think of a data base file as a set of three-by-five cards. Each card in the set contains specific information about one thing from a collection of many things. The collection could be names and addresses of people in your club, on your team, or going on a trip or it could be a collection of books, video tapes, baseball cards, music, stamps, coins, and so forth. Similar information is recorded on each card. You determine what that information is and how it is to be arranged (its layout) on the card. Similarily, you determine what information is to be stored and how it is to be arranged in the electronic data base file.

To insure that everyone working with your three-by-five-card data base file is consistent in recording information, you would have a form printed on each card to identify the information to be entered on blanks in the form. You do the same thing with an electronic data base file.

Once cards are completed for items in the collection, they can be ordered in some meaningful way and used. A sample three-by-five-card data base file is shown in Figure 4-1. These cards can be ordered by name so that an amount paid can be quickly found, by homeroom for help in organizing the yearbook delivery, or in any other convient way.

All of the cards stored together for a particular collection are called a **file**. The file is named to reflect its contents. Names such as: Yearbook Sales, Name and Address File, Book List, or Tape Collection specify the contents and are appropriate file names. The individual cards are referred to as **records**. Each record contains one or more pieces of information called a **category** or categories. (Another name for a category is a **field**.) For example, in the card file in Figure 4-1, each record (card) in the file (box of cards) contains the categories (pieces of information): last name, first name, homeroom, date ordered, the amount charged, and the amount paid.

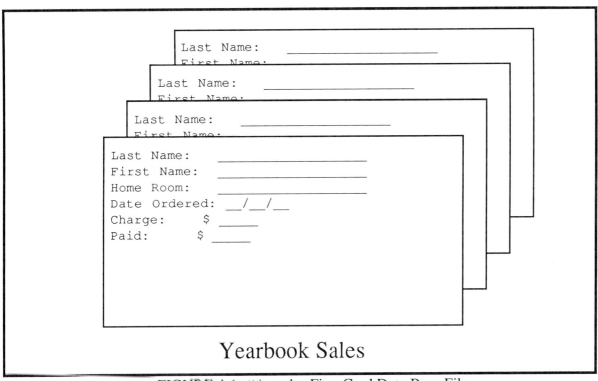

FIGURE 4-1. Three-by-Five-Card Data Base File.

USING AN EXISTING DATA BASE FILE

The data base file for this chapter has already been created for you. To use it, you first add the file to the Desktop from the Student Data Disk.

GUIDED ACTIVITY: OPEN

If AppleWorks is not running on your computer, start AppleWorks.
Insert the Student Data Disk that accompanies this text in Drive 2.

WHAT YOU TYPE	WHY YOU TYPE IT
<RETURN>	To select **Add files to the Desktop.**
<RETURN>	To select **Get files from the current disk.**
Down-arrow (Several times)	To highlight **Original YrBk.**
<RETURN>	To load the file.

The Original YrBk file appears on the screen as shown in Figure 4-2.

```
File: Original YrBk          REVIEW/ADD/CHANGE          Escape: Main Menu

Selection: All records


Last Name  First Name Home Room Date Ordered Charge Paid
==========================================================================
Cuber      Andrea     21        Nov 87       20     20
Fallon     Lisa       21        Nov 87       20     10
Fallon     Julie      21        Nov 87       20     0
Gross      Muriel     21        Nov 87       20     15
Keller     Flora      21        Nov 87       20     10
Scully     -          21        Nov 87       20     20
Adamski    Cynthia    111       Jan 88       24     15
Burd       Samuel     111       Nov 87       20     20
Ferris     Frank      111       Nov 87       20     10
Ferry      Dona       111       Nov 87       20     20
Lohmann    Mary       111       Nov 87       20     10
Wallace    Claude     111       Nov 87       20     10
Beneway    Dorothy    112       Nov 87       20     20
Carlson    Robert     112       Jan 88       24     24
Fishman    Ann        112       Jan 88       24     24
--------------------------------------------------------------------------
Type entry or use Ú commands                            Ú-? for Help
```

FIGURE 4-2.   Yearbook File Loaded from Student Files Disk.

Return the Student Data Disk to the teacher or computer room monitor.
Insert your Primary Data Disk in drive #2.

The first tasks are to save the file, to change the file name to make a working copy of the file; and then to save the working file on your disk. Make sure that your Primary Data Disk is in Drive 2 then follow this command sequence.

GUIDED ACTIVITY: RENAME

WHAT YOU TYPE	WHY YOU TYPE IT
⌘-S	To save the file **Original YrBk** on your disk.
⌘-N	To start the name change.
CONTROL-Y	To erase (Yank out) the old name.
Yearbook Sales	To indicate the name for your working copy of the file.
<RETURN>	To complete the name change.
<ESCAPE>	To return to the data display.
⌘-S	To save the file **Yearbook Sales** on your disk.

✓ **CHECKPOINT**

How many copies of the Yearbook Sales file are on your disk? What is (are) the file name(s)?

What is the name of the file on your Desktop?

Why did you make a separate working copy of the file?

THE SCREEN LAYOUTS

The data base file can appear on the screen in two different formats, as the **multiple record list** that you see when the file first appears (Figure 4-2) or in a **single record** format (Figure 4-3).

Switching from one layout form to the other is done with the **zoom** command Open-Apple-Z. Zooming out displays the multiple record layout and zooming in displays the single record form.

WHAT YOU TYPE	WHY YOU TYPE IT
⌘-Z	To zoom in and display the single record layout.

The single record layout is shown in Figure 4-3.

```
┌─────────────────────────────────────────────────────────────────────────────┐
│  File: Yearbook Sales              REVIEW/ADD/CHANGE            Escape: Main Menu │
│                                                                                  │
│  Selection: All records                                                          │
│                                                                                  │
│                                                                                  │
│  Record 1 of 17                                                                  │
│  ============================================================================   │
│  Last Name: Cuber                                                                │
│  First Name: Andrea                                                              │
│  Home Room: 21                                                                   │
│  Date Ordered: Nov 87                                                            │
│  Charge: 20                                                                      │
│  Paid: 20                                                                        │
│                                                                                  │
│                                                                                  │
│                                                                                  │
│                                                                                  │
│  -----------------------------------------------------------------------------  │
│  Type entry or use ⌂ commands                                    ⌂-? for Help    │
└─────────────────────────────────────────────────────────────────────────────┘
```

FIGURE 4-3.   Single Record Format Display.

MOVING THE CURSOR

Whenever you wish to change a category, see a record that does not appear in the display or add records or categories, you must move the cursor. In addition, you sometimes need to move the cursor within the contents of one category. Moving from one category to another is accomplished using the Tab or Open-Apple-Tab keys. Moving from one record to another is accomplished with the up-arrow, down-arrow, Open-Apple-up-arrow, Open-Apple-down-arrow or Open-Apple-1 to Apen-Apple-9 keys. The left- and right-arrow keys move the cursor left and right within one category.

MULTIPLE RECORD LAYOUT MOVEMENT

Cursor movement is similar in the two types of screen displays. There is enough of a difference that we will examine each type of display separately in the Guided Activity that follows.

GUIDED ACTIVITY: CURSOR

Let's experiment with the arrow keys.

Give the ⌂-Z command to display the multiple record layout as shown previously in Figure 4–2.

WHAT YOU TYPE	WHY YOU TYPE IT
<RIGHT-ARROW> four times	To move the cursor right within the category.
<LEFT-ARROW>	To move the cursor left within the category.

Observe that the cursor does not move across the screen from one category to the next.

Up and down-arrow keys move the cursor up and down one record at a time. Try it.

WHAT YOU TYPE	WHY YOU TYPE IT
<DOWN-ARROW>	To move down one record (line).
<UP-ARROW> key	To move up one record (line).

Observe the cursor movement. It stays within one column as you move it up or down.

Open-Apple-up-arrow and Open-Apple-down-arrow move the cursor up a screen or down a screen.

Try the Open-Apple moves on your own.

To move right or left across the categories of a record, use the Tab and Open-Apple-Tab keys.

WHAT YOU TYPE	WHY YOU TYPE IT
<TAB> six times	To move the cursor to the right from one category to the next.

Observe that the cursor drops to the first category in the next line when you Tab from the last category in a line.

WHAT YOU TYPE	WHY YOU TYPE IT
⌂-TAB six times	To move the cursor left from one category to the next.

Observe that the cursor moves up to the last category on the line above when you Open-Apple-Tab from the first category on a line. Tab and Open-Apple-Tab do not cause the cursor to jump from the very last record up to the first or from the first down to the last; there is another set of commands to do this.

Consider the file divided into eight roughly equal pieces. Open-Apple-1 moves the cursor to the start of the first piece. Open-Apple-2 moves the cursor to the start of the second piece and so on through

Open-Apple-8, the start of the eighth and last piece. Open-Apple-9 moves the cursor to the very end of the file. Observe the cursor movement using the Open-Apple-Number commands.

What You Type	Why You Type It
⌂-1	To move the cursor to the top of the file.
⌂-9	To move the cursor to the bottom of the file.
⌂-5	To move the cursor to the middle of the file.

Remember that ⌂-1 through ⌂-9 work this same way in the Word Processor. This is a very helpful feature, having commands that do the same thing in more than one application. Notice that there is a slight difference; the cursor always moves to the top or the bottom of the screen in the Data Base, not to the center as it does in the Word Processor.

TROUBLESHOOTING:

Problem: The cursor does not move when you expect it to.

Correction: Press Escape. You may have made a change in the category. Escape cancels the change and allows the cursor movements again.

SINGLE RECORD LAYOUT MOVEMENT

Cursor movement in the single record layout is similar to cursor movement in the multiple record layout. The few differences are explained in the remainder of the Guided Activity.

GUIDED ACTIVITY: CURSOR   (continued)

What You Type	Why You Type It
⌂-1	To move to the top of the list.
⌂-Z	To zoom in and display a single record.

You now see record 1 of 17 as shown previously in Figure 4-3.

What You Type	Why You Type It
<RIGHT-ARROW> five times	To move to the end of the name **Cuber**.
<RIGHT-ARROW>	To attempt to move past the end of the name Cuber. The computer beeps to indicate that you cannot do this.
<LEFT-ARROW> twice	To move left within the category. There is no beep.
<DOWN-ARROW> six times	To move down to the second record.
X	To change the name to **XFallon**.

<DOWN-ARROW>	To attempt to move down to the next category. The computer beeps and the cursor does not move.
<ESCAPE>	To restore the former entry, `Fallon`. This process removes the `X` from the name.

TROUBLESHOOTING:

Problem: You find that the Main Menu has appeared on your screen.

Correction: You have missed a step; you did not enter the x. Press Escape to return to the file; move the cursor to the name Fallon in record 2 of 17 and start again from X. Notice the message in the upper right corner after you type the X is **Escape: Restore former entry**. This means that when you press Escape, you should not return to the Main Menu.

WHAT YOU TYPE	WHY YOU TYPE IT
<DOWN-ARROW>	To determine that the cursor now moves as expected.
<TAB>	To observe that Tab moves to the next category. This time, however, the movement is down the list rather than to the right.
<TAB> six times	To move to the next record.
⌘-TAB	To move to the previous category. This time the movement is up rather than left.
⌘-DOWN-ARROW four times	To move ahead four records. Record 7 now appears in the display.
⌘-UP-ARROW	To move back one record. Record 6 now appears in the display.
⌘-1	To move to the top of the file, the first record.
⌘-9	To move to the end of the file, the last record.
⌘-5	To move to the middle record, record 9.

WHAT YOU'VE LEARNED

- The arrow keys move the cursor in a way that is very similar to the way the arrow keys work in the Word Processor.
- The cursor does not move from category to category if a change is made.
- Escape is used to remove an incorrect change and allow the cursor to move again.

✓   CHECKPOINT

Give the ⌘-Z command to display the multiple record layout.

Indicate the movement the cursor takes in the multiple record layout for each of the following commands. (You should be able to do this from memory.)

1. ⌘-1

2. ⌘-9

3. <UP-ARROW>

4. <DOWN-ARROW>

5. ⌘-DOWN-ARROW

6. ⌘-UP-ARROW

7. <TAB>

8. ⌘-TAB

9. <RIGHT-ARROW>

10. <LEFT-ARROW>

MODIFYING RECORDS

Working with a data base often involves making changes. New records must be inserted, existing ones corrected, and old ones removed. For the Yearbook Sales data base file, a new record is inserted each time a yearbook is sold; an existing record is corrected each time someone pays the balance due on their yearbook; and a record is removed when someone decides that they no longer wish to buy a book. The following sections help you to make some modifications to your data base.

INSERTING RECORDS

Let's add some additional information into the data base file on your Desktop. Greg Peerson of Homeroom 111 purchased a yearbook in January for $24 (the book was offered at a discount to early buyers). Greg paid the full amount. Add a record to the file to reflect this activity.

GUIDED ACTIVITY: ADD

WHAT YOU TYPE	WHY YOU TYPE IT
⌘-9	To move to the last record in the file.
If necessary, ⌘-Z	To display single records.
<DOWN-ARROW>	Until the following message appears on the screen.

```
You are now past the last record
of your file and can now start
typing new records at the end.
```

Y	To answer Yes to the question **Do you really want to do this?**

A blank form for record 18 appears. Type in the first three categories of the record as shown below.

WHAT YOU TYPE		WHY YOU TYPE IT
Peerson	<RETURN>	To enter the last name.
Greg	<RETURN>	To enter the first name.
111	<RETURN>	To enter the homeroom.

Notice that you must press Return after each category entry. Return indicates that the entry is complete and that the cursor is to advance to the next category.

Categories that contain the words "Date" or "Time" in their name receive special treatment. Dates and times are stored in a consistent format so that these categories can be arranged chronologically. You may enter dates in a variety of ways; AppleWorks will convert them to its special format automatically. The date entries 9/10/89, 9-10-89, and September 10, 1989 are all converted to Sep 10 89 when you press Return. If part of the date is missing, the part that is entered is converted to the standard format if it is possible.

Finish entering the last three categories of the record.

WHAT YOU TYPE		WHY YOU TYPE IT
1/88		To enter the date.
<RETURN>		To complete the date entry. AppleWorks converts the date to Jan 88.
24	<RETURN>	To enter the Charge amount.
24	<RETURN>	To enter the Paid amount.

When you press Return at the end of the last entry, you are given a new blank form to fill in for the next entry.

✓ CHECKPOINT

The screen display indicates the mode that you are using in the center of the top line. What is this mode?

What key do you press to leave this mode and return to Review/Add/Change mode?

DELETING A CHARACTER

If you dectect any errors that you have made before you press Return, you would, of course, use the Delete key together with the left- and right-arrows to correct them. If you detect an error after you press Return, the error correction is a little more involved.

GUIDED ACTIVITY: MODIFY

The student's name is really Pearson. We'll correct this by deleting the second "e" and inserting an "a". Here are the precise steps to follow:

WHAT YOU TYPE	WHY YOU TYPE IT
<ESCAPE>	To return from Insert Mode to Review/Add/Change.
⌂-DOWN-ARROW	To move the cursor to the new record. The cursor blinks on the "P" in "Peerson".
<RIGHT-ARROW> 3 times	To move the cursor right. The cursor blinks on the "r".
<DELETE>	To delete the "e".
a	To insert the "a".

(Notice the message in the upper right corner. **Escape** now means that you can cancel any changes you have made and restore the former entry. You may do this any time before you press Return.)

When you edit the information in a category, you must tell AppleWorks when you are finished. Try using the <TAB>, ⌂-TAB, <UP-ARROW>, or <DOWN-ARROW> key. The computer beeps because you are not allowed to leave the category until you indicate your editing is complete.

WHAT YOU TYPE	WHY YOU TYPE IT
<RETURN>	To indicate that you have completed your changes. The cursor advances to the next category.

The restrictions placed on cursor movement in the Data Base take a while for most people to get accustomed to; this is especially true after using the Word Processor which has unrestrained cursor movement. You'll find the beep occurs frequently when you first start to revise Data Base records. It almost always means: press Return in order to continue. (When you work on the Data Base in the company of other beginners, the frequent beeps demonstrate that getting accustomed to cursor movement restrictions is a universal problem.)

DELETING A WORD

The method used to delete a word is exactly the same as the method used to delete a letter. Move the cursor to the category line, move to the right of the unwanted information, and press Delete until the unwanted information is removed.

DELETING A RECORD

To delete an entire record, you would give the Open-Apple-D command when the record is in view on the single record screen or when the cursor is on the record line in the multiple record display. In the single record layout, you are asked if this is the record that you wish to delete, and AppleWorks continues to ask this question for each record in the file. In the single record layout, press Escape to end the delete process. In the multiple record layout, the record that you are about to delete is highlighted. You may delete several records at a time by highlighting additional records. Press Return to delete the highlighted record(s) or press Escape to leave the record(s) in the file.

In the Data Base, Open-Apple-D is used only to delete an entire record; it cannot be used to delete a category, a part of a category or a part of a record. Once a record is deleted, there is no easy way to restore it.

CHANGING A CATEGORY ENTRY

Open-Apple-Y can be used to delete all of the characters to the right of the cursor in a category. Let's use it to change "Dorothy Beneway" to "Dot Beneway". First, you would remove "rothy" from the name "Dorothy", and then you would add the "t".

GUIDED ACTIVITY: MODIFY   (continued)

Move the cursor to the category line containing the name, `Dorothy`.
Move the cursor to the `r`.

WHAT YOU TYPE	WHY YOU TYPE IT
⌘-Y	To delete `rothy`.
t <RETURN>	To finish the change.

REPLACING A CATEGORY ENTRY

There are four methods that can be used to replace an entry for a category. It does not matter which method you use.

1. Use Open-Apple-D to delete the entire record. All of the information must then be reentered for each category in the record. This is method certainly impractical, especially if the record contains a large amount of information.

2. Use the right arrow to move the cursor to the right end of the category containing the unwanted information ; then press and hold the Delete key until the information is erased. (Open-Apple-left-arrow and Open-Apple-right-arrow do not move the cursor a full word as they do in the Word Processor. This should not be a problem since the categories are at most 76 characters long and the cursor can be moved rapidly by holding down the left or right arrow key.) Then type the new entry.

3. Change to the edit cursor by issuing the Open-Apple-E command and overtype the old information with the new information. If the new entry is shorter than the old entry, the remaining characters can be overtyped with spaces (the extra spaces are removed from the end of the category when you press Return) or they can be deleted using the Open-Apple-Y keys. Remember to change back to the insert cursor by giving the Open-Apple-E command a second time after you finish typing the new entry.

4. Position the cursor at the beginning of the unwanted category and remove it with Open-Apple-Y (or Control-Y). Then type the new information.

GUIDED ACTIVITY: MODIFY   (continued)

The following yearbook sales activities have occurred:

1. Julie Fallon has decided that since her sister is buying a yearbook, she will not buy one.
2. Robert Carlson requested that his name be changed to Bob.
3. & 4. Karl Hermonat and Charles Herrick have paid in full.

You are to change the Yearbook Sales file to reflect this activity. Here's what you need to do:

WHAT YOU TYPE	WHY YOU TYPE IT

1.

☐-Z	To display the Multiple Record Layout.
<ARROWS>/<TAB>	To move to the row containing Julie's record.
☐-D	To highlight the unwanted record.
<RETURN>	To delete the record.

2.

<ARROWS>/<TAB>	To move to the category containing the name Robert .
☐-Y	To delete Robert.
Bob <RETURN>	To insert the name Bob.

3.

<ARROWS>/<TAB>	To move to the 15 in Karl Hermonat's row.
☐-Y	To remove the 15.
24 <RETURN>	To insert the 24.

4.

<ARROWS>/<TAB>	To move to the 10 in Charles Herrick's row.
20	To insert the 20.
⌘-Y	To remove the 10.
<RETURN>	To complete the change.

✓ CHECKPOINT

Notice that the order of the commands is reversed in cases 3 and 4 above. The process of changing the data with Open-Apple-Y works equally well either way. What exactly does Open-Apple-Y do?

SORTING AND SEARCHING THE DATA BASE FILE

The record for Greg Pearson that you added at the end of the file is not in alphabetical or room order. AppleWorks can quickly arrange the file by number, by date, or alphabetically either forward or backward. All you need to do is move the cursor to any record in the column the arrangement is based on, give the Open-Apple-A command, and select the type of arrangement. Let's do some examples.

ARRANGING ONE CATEGORY

Arrange the file alphabetically by last name.

GUIDED ACTIVITY: ARRANGE

WHAT YOU TYPE	WHY YOU TYPE IT
If needed, ⌘-Z	To display the multiple record layout.
<TAB> or ⌘-TAB	To move the cursor to the **Last Name** column. You may need to give this command more than once. The cursor can be on any record (line) in the Last Name column.
⌘-A	To arrange the records by this category.
<RETURN>	To select the arrangement order **From A to Z**.

After a moment, the multiple record display appears with the records in alphabetical order.

Arrange the file alphabetically by first name.

WHAT YOU TYPE	WHY YOU TYPE IT
<TAB>	To move the cursor to the **First Name** column.
⌂-A	To arrange the records by First Name.
<RETURN>	To select the arrangement A to Z.

The record with the blank First Name now appears at the top of the list. Blanks are always sorted to the top of an A to Z arrangement. An easy way to determine if any blanks have been left in a file is to arrange the file from A to Z in each category. Any blanks are readily apparent at the top of the column.

Scully's first name is Barbara. Please enter it.

Notice that the last names are no longer in alphabetical order, but the correct first and last name pairs are still together.

ARRANGING MORE THAN ONE CATEGORY

It is occasionly necessary to arrange a file in more than one category. For example, if this file should be alphabetical by homeroom an arrangement needs to be done on both the homeroom and the last name categories.

WHAT YOU TYPE	WHY YOU TYPE IT
<TAB>	To move to the Home Room column.
⌂-A	To arrange this category.
3 <RETURN>	To select the arrangement low number to high number.

Note that the rooms are in order, the first names are in alphabetical order by room and the last names are out of order.

Arranging one column always disturbs the arrangement in the other columns. The disruption is not totally chaotic, however, as you can see from the first names in the last sort. Our goal is still to have the students listed alphabetically by homeroom. The solution, alphabetize the list and then arrange it by homeroom.

UNGUIDED ACTIVITY: ARRANGE (continued)

Do the last steps in this activity on your own.

1. Save your Yearbook Sales file.

2. Arrange your Yearbook Sales file alphabetically by homeroom.

3. Compare your results with Figure 4-4.

✓   **CHECKPOINT**

In order to complete the steps above, you used the ⌨-A command. How many times did you need to use this command? What column or columns were arranged by this command and in what order were they arranged?

```
File: Yearbook Sales            REVIEW/ADD/CHANGE           Escape: Main Menu

Selection: All records


Last Name   First Name Home Room Date Ordered Charge Paid
================================================================================
Cuber       Andrea      21        Nov 87        20     20
Fallon      Lisa        21        Nov 87        20     10
Gross       Muriel      21        Nov 87        20     15
Keller      Flora       21        Nov 87        20     10
Scully      Barbara     21        Nov 87        20     20
Adamski     Cynthia     111       Jan 88        24     15
Burd        Samuel      111       Nov 87        20     20
Ferris      Frank       111       Nov 87        20     10
Ferry       Dona        111       Nov 87        20     20
Lohmann     Mary        111       Nov 87        20     10
Pearson     Greg        111       Jan 88        24     24
Wallace     Claude      111       Nov 87        20     10
Beneway     Dot         112       Nov 87        20     20
Carlson     Bob         112       Jan 88        24     24
Fishman     Ann         112       Jan 88        24     24
-----------------------------------------------------------------------------
Type entry or use ⌨ commands                          ⌨ -? for Help
```

FIGURE 4-4.   Yearbook Sales - Alphabetically by Homeroom.

Quit AppleWorks for now.

HIGHLIGHT option 6. "Quit," press <RETURN> and press Y.
Make sure that you SAVE the latest version of your file.
Turn off your computer, monitor, and printer, and take a break.

PRINTING THE DATA BASE FILE

Printing a data base file is a little more involved than printing a word processing file. Since the printer controls are not embedded in the records of a data base file, a separate printing process is needed. This process is called **creating a report format**.

The report format defines how a file is to be printed, what categories are to appear on the report, and where they are to appear. Up to eight different report formats can be created for each file. The Yearbook Sales file, for example, can have a report that lists only the names of subscribers, a report that prints labels to identify the books when they arrive, a report that lists the amounts due for collection, and so on. Each report can contain as many or as few of the categories in the file as you wish.

Reports can be generated in one of two formats, a **tables** format or a **labels** format. Figures 4-5 and 4-6 show sample reports in each of these formats.

```
File:     Yearbook Sales                          Page   1
Report:  Sample Tables                   January 26, 1988
Last Name  First Name  Home Room  Date Ordered  Charge   Paid
---------- ----------  ---------  ------------  -------  -----
Cuber      Andrea      21         Nov 87          20       20
Fallon     Lisa        21         Nov 87          20       10
Gross      Muriel      21         Nov 87          20       15
Keller     Flora       21         Nov 87          20       10
Scully     Barbara     21         Nov 87          20       20
Adamski    Cynthia     111        Jan 88          24       15
Burd       Samuel      111        Nov 87          20       20
Ferris     Frank       111        Nov 87          20       10
Ferry      Dona        111        Nov 87          20       20
Lohmann    Mary        111        Nov 87          20       10
Pearson    Greg        111        Jan 88          24       24
Wallace    Claude      111        Nov 87          20       10
Beneway    Dot         112        Nov 87          20       20
Carlson    Robert      112        Jan 88          24       24
Fishman    Ann         112        Jan 88          24       24
Hermonat   Karl        112        Jan 88          24       15
Herrick    Charles     112        Nov 87          20       10
```

FIGURE 4-5.   Yearbook Sales: Tables Format.

As you can tell from Figures 4-5 and 4-6, the tables format looks like the multiple record screen layout and the labels format resembles the single record screen layout. A file can have either or both styles of reports generated.

Notice the following features of the reports shown in the figures:

For the tables format in Figure 4-5:

- The report heading indicates the file used to produce the report, Yearbook Sales, and the name of the report, Sample Tables.
- The heading includes the date and page number. The date is written out in full; it need not appear in the data base standard date notation.
- Each column has the category name at the top of the column. (This is the same category name that appears on the screen. It was entered when the file was created.)
- The names are in alphabetical order.

```
File:    Yearbook Sales                    Page   1
Report: Sample Labels           January 26, 1988
Selection: Home Room equals 21

Home Room: 21
Cuber
Andrea
Nov 87

Home Room: 21
Fallon
Lisa
Nov 87

Home Room: 21
Gross
Muriel
Nov 87

Home Room: 21
Keller
Flora
Nov 87

Home Room: 21
Scully
Barbara
Nov 87
```

FIGURE 4-6. Yearbook Sales: Labels Format.

In the labels format in Figure 4-6:

- The file used to produce the report, "Yearbook Sales", and the name of the report, "Sample Labels", are listed in the report heading.
- There is a blank line between each record.
- The category "Home Room" is identified with a category name. It is the only category identified this way.
- The "Charge" and "Paid" categories are not printed on the report.
- Only homeroom 21 is printed.

PRINTING TABLE FORMATS

Let's modify and create reports in each of the two formats. We'll start with a tables format. (If you saved your file correctly at the end of your last computer session, it should be arranged alphabetically by homeroom. If it is not arranged this way, change it.)

GUIDED ACTIVITY: PRINT

Start AppleWorks.
Add the file, Yearbook Sales, to the Desktop from your Primary Data Disk.

When the file appears in the display, issue the command ⌘-P to start the report-printing process.

The Report Menu shown in Figure 4-7 appears.

```
File: Yearbook Sales               REPORT MENU          Escape: Review/Add/Change
Report: None


===============================================================================

                    1.   Get a report format
                    2.   Create a new "tables" format
                    3.   Create a new "labels" format
                    4.   Duplicate an existing format
                    5.   Erase a format


-------------------------------------------------------------------------------
Type number, or use arrows, then press Return                      51K Avail.
```

FIGURE 4-7.   Data Base Report Menu.

WHAT YOU TYPE	WHY YOU TYPE IT
<RETURN>	To select Item 1. **Get a report format.**
<RETURN>	To select the report **Full File List.**

The Report Format screen shown in Figure 4-8 now appears.

```
File: Yearbook Sales           REPORT FORMAT              Escape: Report  Menu
Report: Full File List
Selection: All records


==============================================================================
--> or <--   Move cursor                  Ć-J  Right justify this category
 >  Ć  <     Switch category positions     Ć-K  Define a calculated category
--> Ć <--    Change column width           Ć-N  Change report name and/or title
Ć-A  Arrange (sort) on this category       Ć-O  Printer options
Ć-D  Delete this category                  Ć-P  Print the report
Ć-G  Add/remove group totals               Ć-R  Change record selection rules
Ć-I  Insert a prev. deleted category       Ć-T  Add/remove category totals
------------------------------------------------------------------------------


Last Name  First Name Home Room Date Ordered Charge   Paid  L
-A--------  -B-------- -C------- -D---------- -E------ -F--- e
Cuber      Andrea     21        Nov 87       20       20    n
Fallon     Lisa       21        Nov 87       20       10    5
Gross      Muriel     21        Nov 87       20       15    9


------------------------------------------------------------------------------
Use options shown above to change report format               51K Avail.
```

FIGURE 4-8.   "Tables" Report Format Screen.

There is a great deal of useful information on this screen. The top third of the screen displays the file name, the section of the program you are using and the operation performed by pressing Escape. It also displays the report name and the note, "Selection: All records," indicating that the report will show all records when it is printed. (There will be more information about Selection given later in this Unit.)

The middle of the screen displays the Open-Apple commands that can be used in creating the report.

The bottom third displays the first few lines of the report. The columns are lettered for convenience; the letters do not appear in the printed report. The total number of characters printed across the page, including the spaces between the columns, is indicated by the vertical message Len59 (Length 59) after the last column.

GUIDED ACTIVITY: PRINT   (continued)

Make sure that you have a printer attached to your computer and that it is ready.

Here are the remaining commands needed to print a predefined report starting from the display in Figure 4-8.

WHAT YOU TYPE	WHY YOU TYPE IT
⌂-P	To start the print process.
Arrows <RETURN>	To select your printer. (Remember, Arrows in lowercase letters means that you must decide which arrow key(s) to press and how many times to press it(them).)
(today's date) <RETURN>	To enter the date.
<RETURN>	To select 1 copy and start the printing.

When you follow these steps your printer should print a report similar to the one in Figure 4-5. (Your title and date are different.)

MOVING CATEGORIES

Now you will change the report to print the categories in the order: Home Room, First Name, Last Name. Make sure that the Report Format screen shows in your display and proceed with:

WHAT YOU TYPE	WHY YOU TYPE IT
<RIGHT-ARROW> twice	To move the cursor to the Home Room column.
Hold ⌂ and press the	To move the Home Room column to the left. (You do not
LESS THAN key (<) twice	need to shift for the less than symbol.)
Release ⌂	

Now move the First Name column to the left of the Last Name column.

WHAT YOU TYPE	WHY YOU TYPE IT
<RIGHT-ARROW> twice	To move the cursor to the First Name column.
⌂-< (Open-Apple-Less-Than)	To move the First Name column left one column.

REMOVING AND INSERTING CATEGORIES

Let's eliminate the Charge and Paid columns from the report.

WHAT YOU TYPE	WHY YOU TYPE IT
<RIGHT-ARROW>	To move the cursor to the Charge category.
⌘-D	To delete the Charge category. This deletes the category from the report; it does not delete it from the file.
⌘-D	To delete the Paid category.

Your screen display should now match the one shown in Figure 4-9.

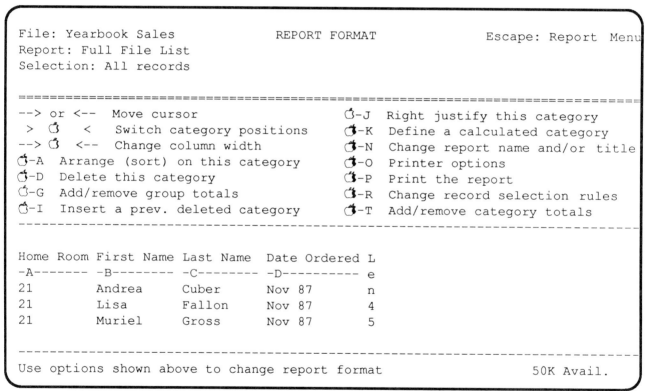

```
File: Yearbook Sales          REPORT FORMAT            Escape: Report  Menu
Report: Full File List
Selection: All records


========================================================================
--> or <--  Move cursor              ⌘-J  Right justify this category
 >  ⌘  <    Switch category positions ⌘-K  Define a calculated category
--> ⌘  <--  Change column width       ⌘-N  Change report name and/or title
⌘-A  Arrange (sort) on this category  ⌘-O  Printer options
⌘-D  Delete this category             ⌘-P  Print the report
⌘-G  Add/remove group totals          ⌘-R  Change record selection rules
⌘-I  Insert a prev. deleted category  ⌘-T  Add/remove category totals
------------------------------------------------------------------------


Home Room First Name Last Name  Date Ordered L
-A------- -B--------- -C--------  -D---------- e
21         Andrea      Cuber       Nov 87       n
21         Lisa        Fallon      Nov 87       4
21         Muriel      Gross       Nov 87       5


------------------------------------------------------------------------
Use options shown above to change report format         50K Avail.
```

FIGURE 4-9.   Yearbook Sales: Report Format.

Let's experiment. Delete the Home Room category from the report.

WHAT YOU TYPE	WHY YOU TYPE IT
Left-arrow	To move the cursor back to the first column.
⌘-D	To delete the Home Room category.

UNGUIDED ACTIVITY: PRINT

> Print the report on the screen to observe how it looks with the revised layout.
> If your instructor requests, print out a copy of the report to hand in.

The report is really more useful when Home Room is listed, so let's go back and revise the report again.

> Move the cursor into the first column, the location for this insertion.

WHAT YOU TYPE	WHY YOU TYPE IT
⌘-I	To insert a previously deleted category (be sure you type the letter I not the number 1).

A list of deleted categories appears in alphabetical order.

> Highlight **Home Room** and press <RETURN>.

The Home Room column is returned to the report at the cursor position. It is inserted in a standard column width of twelve characters. Reduce the width of the column.

WHAT YOU TYPE	WHY YOU TYPE IT
⌘-LEFT-ARROW three times	To reduce the Home Room column to 9 characters wide.

SELECTION RULES

Now it's collection time and you want a list of those who have not yet paid the full amount for the yearbook. A change in the **record selection rules** does this. You set a rule to limit the records that are displayed.

GUIDED ACTIVITY: RULES

Before you can set the rule, you need to determine what the rule must be so that only the records that interest you are displayed. Since people who owe money have paid less than $20, you will use the rule: Paid is less than 20.

WHAT YOU TYPE	WHY YOU TYPE IT
⌘-R	To start the rules process.
Arrows	To highlight **Paid**.
<RETURN>	To enter "Paid" into the rule.
Arrows	To highlight **is less than**.
<RETURN>	To enter "is less than" into the rule.
20	To give the comparison information.
<RETURN>	To enter "20" into the rule.

The third line from the top of the screen notes your changes; it reads: `Selection: Paid is less than 20.` (The words "and" and "or" also appear on the screen. Ignore them for now; their meaning is discussed in a later unit, Mastering the Data Base.)

WHAT YOU TYPE	WHY YOU TYPE IT
<ESCAPE>	To return to the Report Format screen.
⌘-P	To start the print process.
Arrows	To select the `screen` for this report.
Today's date <RETURN>	To enter today's date.

Only seven names should be listed. Notice that the selection works even though the Paid category is not displayed on the report. Remember, even if you remove a category from a report, it still remains in the file so that it can be printed on other reports or observed on the screen.

Follow the screen prompts; press the <SPACE BAR> to return to the Report Format display.

✓ CHECKPOINT

Write a rule that prints only the names Hermonat and Herrick. Use the computer to display the list of rule verbs (equals, is greater than, etc.) if you need help.

Remove the selection restriction:

WHAT YOU TYPE	WHY YOU TYPE IT
⌘-R	To enter a rule.
Y	To answer **Yes** to the question `Select all records?` This selects the rule `All records`.

PRINTING LABEL FORMATS

Records that contain more than fifteen or twenty average sized categories or that contain several long categories cannot be printed on one line of a tables report. A **labels** format report is used for such a file or for printing reports in mailing label style. In labels format, the categories can be printed on more than one line; in fact, up to fifteen lines can be used for each record.

GUIDED ACTIVITY: LABELS

Create a new labels report to generate labels that can be affixed to the yearbooks when they arrive. The information on the label should be: Home Room, First Name, and Last Name. The labels will help insure that each student who bought and paid for a book will recieve one.

WHAT YOU TYPE	WHY YOU TYPE IT
<ESCAPE>	To return to the REPORT MENU.
3 <RETURN>	To select **Create a new 'labels' format**.
Hand Out Labels	To enter the report name.
<RETURN>	To complete the name and display the format layout screen.

The labels Report Format display and the corresponding Help Screen are shown in Figures 4-10 and 4-11, respectively.

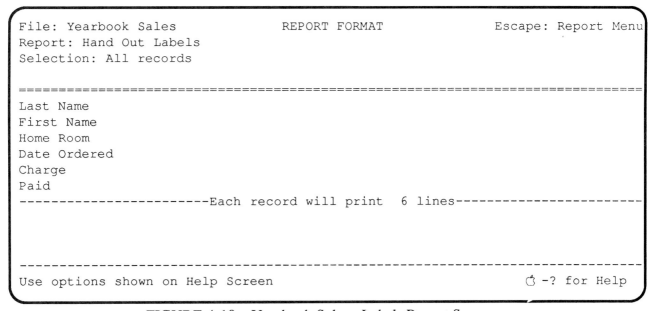

```
File: Yearbook Sales           REPORT FORMAT           Escape: Report Menu
Report: Hand Out Labels
Selection: All records


===============================================================================
Last Name
First Name
Home Room
Date Ordered
Charge
Paid
-----------------------Each record will print  6 lines---------------------



-------------------------------------------------------------------------------
Use options shown on Help Screen                          ⌀ -? for Help
```

FIGURE 4-10. Yearbook Sales - Labels Report Screen.

```
File: Yearbook Sales                HELP                  Escape: Report  Format
Report: Hand Out Labels
Selection: All records



=================================================================================
                 -->   <--    Move cursor location
                 Ú-arrows     Move category location
                   > Ú <       Next or previous record
                 Ú-1...Ú-9     Go to beginning...end of file
                 Ú-A          Arrange (sort) on this category
                 Ú-D          Delete this spacing line or category
                 Ú-I          Insert a spacing line or
                              a previously deleted category
                 Ú-J          Left justify this category
                 Ú-N          Change report name and/or title
                 Ú-O          Printer options
                 Ú-P          Print the report
                 Ú-R          Change record selection rules
                 Ú-V          Print category name AND entry
                 Ú-Z          Zoom between category names, entries
---------------------------------------------------------------------------------
Press Space Bar to continue                                        50K Avail.
```

FIGURE 4-11.   "Labels" Report Format Help Screen.

MOVING CATEGORIES

Now you need to rearrange the categories. Each label will consist of three lines. For example,

```
Home Room: 21
Andrea Cuber
(blank line)
```

GUIDED ACTIVITY: LABELS (continued)

WHAT YOU TYPE	WHY YOU TYPE IT
Arrows	To move the cursor so that it blinks under the L in "Last Name."
Ú-RIGHT-ARROW twelve times	To move the Last Name category right 12 positions.
Ú-DOWN-ARROW	To move the Last Name category down a line.
Ú-J	To **left justify** the last name on the printout.

Arrows	To move the cursor to the H in "Home Room".
⌘-RIGHT-ARROW twice	To move the Home Room category right 2 positions.
⌘-UP-ARROW twice	To move the Home Room category up 2 positions.
⌘-LEFT-ARROW twice	To move the Home Room category left 2 positions.
⌘-V	To **view** the category name and the category information together on the printout.

The justify option in the Last Name category tells AppleWorks to print only one space between the first name and the last. AppleWorks makes all of the adjustments necessary for long or short first names.

The zoom command shows the information in the categories rather than the category names.

> Issue the ⌘-Z command to zoom in on the category information.
> ⌘-Z again zooms out to display the category names.

Note that the Home Room category remains the same in the two displays since the category name and the category entry are both in view.

You can review the order that the file will be printed in.

> Make sure the category entries show in the display. (If they do not, give the ⌘-Z command.)
> Hold down the ⌘ key and the GREATER THAN key (>). (You do not need to shift.)

The entries appear in the display in the order that they would be printed. To move back through the records, you would use Open-Apple and <.

REMOVING AND INSERTING CATEGORIES

The only categories that are needed on the labels are: Home Room, First Name, and Last Name.

> Move the cursor down to the `Date Ordered` line. The cursor must blink on the "D".

WHAT YOU TYPE	WHY YOU TYPE IT
⌘-D	To delete the `Date Ordered` category from the report.

A blank line appears in place of the category name.

WHAT YOU TYPE	WHY YOU TYPE IT
⌘-D	To delete the blank line.
⌘-D four times	To delete the Charge and Paid categories and the resulting blank lines.

TROUBLESHOOTING

> Problem: The category cannot be deleted from the screen.

> Solution: Make sure that the cursor is positioned on the first letter of the category before you issue the Open-Apple-D command.

SELECTION RULES

Books are not to be given out to those who have not paid in full so no labels will be printed for these people. Since each person who owes a balance has paid less than $20, a selection rule to print labels only for those who have paid the full amount is: Paid is greater than 19.

GUIDED ACTIVITY: LABELS   (continued)

Enter the selection rule given above and print the labels report.

WHAT YOU TYPE	WHY YOU TYPE IT
⌘-R	To start the rule selection.
6 <RETURN>	To select `Paid`.
2 <RETURN>	To select `is greater than`.
19 <RETURN>	To enter the comparison information.
<ESCAPE>	To end the rule.
⌘-P	To start the print process.
(a number) <RETURN>	To select your printer.
(the date) <RETURN>	To enter today's date.
<RETURN>	To select 1 copy.

✓ **CHECKPOINT**

How do you reset the rules to select all records again?

SAVING THE REPORTS

⌘-S saves the file and the reports that you have created. Any custom screen layouts, reports and report selection rules are considered a part of the file. They are automatically saved when the file is saved.

Use ⌘-S to save the file on your Primary Data Disk.

This is a good time to back up your file.

> Remove your Primary Data Disk from the drive.
> Insert your Backup Data Disk in the drive.
> Give the Ⓒ-S command.
> After the red light goes out, remove your Backup and re-insert your Primary.

Here are some space-saving hints. Reports, custom layouts, and selection rules require space on the Desktop and on the disk. This space reduces the room on the Desktop for records. For example, the reports written for the sample file for this chapter take up approximately the same amount of room as 40 records. If you have a problem fitting the last few records into the file on the desktop, delete the least needed report from the file, and try adding the records again.

Many reports can be created from slight modifications of other reports. It is not necessary nor is it a prudent use of disk and Desktop storage to save all of the report variations.

Here's a time-saving hint. Protect yourself by saving the file and renaming it before you make a major change. Then, if the change doesn't work out to your satisfaction, you can always reload the original file and start again.

A WORD OF CAUTION:

> If you make an error such as attempting to print a report when there are no printers connected to your computer, AppleWorks may hang (get stuck). The only way to fix this condition is to restart AppleWorks. This means that your file will be lost. To protect yourself, always save your file before you print.

I ignored this caution in this Unit for two reasons. One, when you save a Data Base file, AppleWorks returns to the Review/Add/Change display. This can be very confusing to someone who is just starting to use the program. Two, if you do have a problem and you lose information, the original file is safely stored on the Student Data Disk. (If you did lose information, consider it a valuable lesson in the school of hard knocks; a lesson you probably will not forget - **Save your file before you print.**)

REVIEW QUESTIONS

1. In a general way, explain how a data base can be used to organize information.

2. Define:
   a. Record
   b. Category
   c. Field
   d. Labels Format
   e. Tables Format
   f. Sorting

3. Most AppleWorks commands are easy to remember if you attach the letter used in the command to a key word that describes what the command does. For example, the statement that Open-Apple-S makes a copy of your Desktop file on the disk would prompt you to think of the key word **Save**. Give the key words for the following AppleWorks commands:

   a. Open-Apple-A (sorts a file into an order that you specify).
   b. Open-Apple-D (removes a record from your file or a category from your report).
   c. Open-Apple-I (returns a previously removed item back into a report).
   d. Open-Apple-N (changes the title of your report or file).
   e.   Open-Apple-P (makes a copy of a report on paper).
   f. Open-Apple-R (selects only a portion of the file for a report).
   g. Open-Apple-Y (erases information from the cursor position to the end of the line).
   h. Open-Apple-Z (lets you have a close look at one record in a file or it lets you pull back and look at several records at one time).

4. The multiple record screen appears on your display; the computer beeps when you press the Tab key. List some possible problems and the corresponding corrections.

5. The multiple record layout appears in your display. What steps do you take to display only those students who are not in homeroom 111.

EXERCISES

4.1 Change the Yearbook Sales file to include the following activity:

   a Frank Ferris is moving and no longer wants a book. His deposit is refunded and you are to delete him from the file.

   b. Mary Lohmann paid her $10 balance. Change her paid amount to 20.

   c. Donna Ferry's name is spelled incorrectly. Add the second "n" to correct the spelling.

   d. Bob Carlson's mom requested that his name be listed as Robert. Change his first name back to Robert.

   e. Herb King from Room 21 bought a book in January of 1988. He paid $15 as a deposit against the $24 charge. Add a record for Herb.

   Print a report titled Changes that shows all of the changes you made from the list above. Circle all of your changes before you hand your report in.

4.2 Arrange the file in order, alphabetically by Date Ordered. All of the November orders should be listed alphabetically followed by all of the January orders listed alphabetically. Print the file showing all of the information in the file in a tables style report.

Reprint the file showing only the November orders. Note: You can modify an existing tables report for this problem.

4.3 Create and print a report to match the one shown in Figure 4-6. (Note that only records for homeroom 21 are printed.)

5 GETTING STARTED WITH THE SPREADSHEET

LEARNING OBJECTIVES

1. After completing this unit, you should know ...

    a. what the AppleWorks Spreadsheet is.

    b. when and how a spreadsheet could be used to organize information.

    c. why an electronic spreadsheet is used.

    d. the definitions of: cell, row, column, value, label, and pointing.

    e. why you use the pointing method for entering formulas.

2. After completing this unit, you should be able to ...

    a. create a spreadsheet and move the cell locator around it quickly.

    b. enter values, labels and formulas into cells.

    c. format the contents of Spreadsheet cells.

    d. copy the contents of one cell into other cells.

    e. print a spreadsheet.

    f. view, print, and verify the formulas in a spreadsheet.

    g. use a spreadsheet to monitor your income and expense for a week.

ASSIGNMENTS

1. OPEN: Add a spreadsheet file to the Desktop.

2. MOVE: Moving in a spreadsheet.

3. ENTER: Enter information into a cell.

4. FORMAT: Change value and label formats in a spreadsheet.

5. FORMULAS: Entering formulas into a spreadsheet.

6. BLANK: Remove unwanted information from a block of cells.

7. INCOME 1: Build a spreadsheet for earnings and spending.
   INCOME 2: Add formulas to the income spreadsheet using the copy command.
   INCOME 3: Title a spreadsheet.

8. SUM: Sum the values in a column.

9. REVIEW QUESTIONS AND EXERCISES: Additional review and practice with building spreadsheets.

IMPORTANT COMMANDS AND FORMULAS

COMMAND/KEYS	MEANING
Ć-B	Blank information from one or more cells.
Ć-C	Copy labels, values, or formulas from one or more cells to one or more cells.
Ć-F	Find a cell and move to it.
Ć-H	Make a hard copy of the screen on the printer.
Ć-L	Change the layout of one or more cells.
Ć-P	Print the Spreadsheet.
Ć-U	Edit the information in a cell.
Ć-V	Set Standard Values.
Ć-Z	Zoom in to show the formulas in the spreadsheet.
Ć-?	Examine Standard Values for the Spreadsheet.

FORMULA	MEANING
@AVG	Average the values in indicated cells.
@SUM	Total the values in indicated cells.

INTRODUCTORY CONCEPTS

The Spreadsheet is AppleWorks' math application. Adding, subtracting, multiplying, dividing, and using other, more involved math calculations is a snap with the Spreadsheet. Once you have mastered it, math problems can be easily organized, analyzed, modified, and printed.

Electronic spreadsheets are made up of blocks of information called **cells**. The cells are arranged across **rows** and down **columns**. Words, numbers, or formulas can be entered into each cell. The word entries are called **labels**, and the number and formula entries are called **values**. In a properly created spreadsheet, any change you make in a value quickly (and usually automatically) changes any calculation based on that value. For example, with the correct spreadsheet you can rapidly answer questions such as, If I get a raise in my part-time job and I bank some of that money, how much will I accumulate with interest in a year and a half? To get the correct spreadsheet, you need to enter the formulas and numbers for the problem you wish to do.

The first projects on this application keep the math as simple as possible so you can concentrate on using the Spreadsheet. The most difficult project in this unit involves some calculations you might do if you earn and spend money. Let's put a spreadsheet (also called a **worksheet**) on the Desktop and explore some of its features.

ADDING A SPREADSHEET FILE TO THE DESKTOP

The method that you use to set up a Spreadsheet file on the Desktop is similar to the one used to set up a Word Processing file or a Data Base file. (Another plus for integrated software.)

GUIDED ACTIVITY: OPEN

> Start at AppleWorks' Main Menu.
> Select option **1. Add files to the Desktop.** (Remember, select means that you highlight the option and then press <RETURN>.)
> Select `Make a new file for the:` **5. Spreadsheet.**

At this point you are presented with three choices:

```
Make a new file:
1.  From scratch
2.  From a DIF (TM) file
3.  From a VisiCalc (R) file
```

Briefly, the choices, in reverse order, are: 3. transfer a file from a Visicalc spreadsheet into an AppleWorks Spreadsheet; 2. transfer a Data Interchange Format (DIF) file created by another spreadsheet or data base program into AppleWorks Spreadsheet, or 1, enter all of the information for the new spreadsheet yourself from scratch. (VisiCalc is the first spreadsheet program written for the Apple Computer. Unit 12 discusses passing information from an AppleWorks Data Base to the Spreadsheet using DIF files.)

WHAT YOU TYPE	WHY YOU TYPE IT
1 <RETURN>	To select **1. From scratch.**
First	To enter "First" for the file name.
<RETURN>	To complete the name entry.

A blank spreadsheet, like the one shown in Figure 5-1, appears in the display.

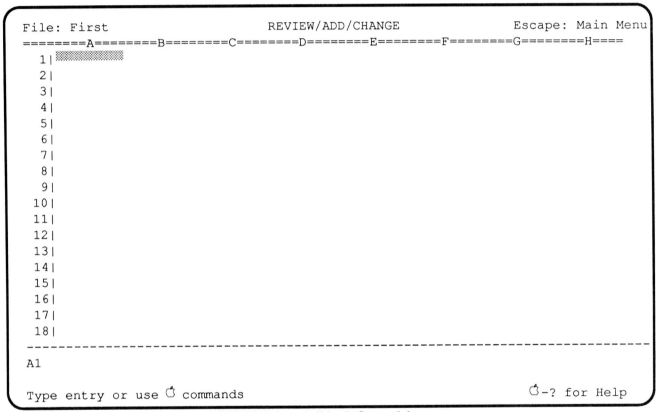

```
File: First                    REVIEW/ADD/CHANGE              Escape: Main Menu
========A========B========C========D========E========F========G========H====
   1|▓▓▓▓▓▓▓▓▓▓
   2|
   3|
   4|
   5|
   6|
   7|
   8|
   9|
  10|
  11|
  12|
  13|
  14|
  15|
  16|
  17|
  18|
------------------------------------------------------------------------------
A1

Type entry or use Ô commands                              Ô-? for Help
```

FIGURE 5-1.   A Blank Spreadsheet.

The top and bottom lines of the screen provide familiar information. They displayed the name of the file (First), the operation that you are performing (REVIEW/ADD/CHANGE), the action taken when you press Escape (display the Main Menu), the actions that you may perform (Type an entry or use the Ô commands), and finally how to obtain help (Ô-?) . The center portion of the screen is not so familiar. Let's look at it.

EXPLORING THE SPREADSHEET

The highlighted block near the top left of the screen is called a **cell**. AppleWorks cells are identified by the letter above the cell and the number at the left edge of the screen. The highlighted cell's location is displayed in the lower left of the screen on the third line from the bottom. The highlighted cell is cell A1. The highlighting block is called a cursor or **cell locator**.

Every cell under the "A" is in **column** A. Likewise, every cell under the "B" is in column B. The letters identify the columns down the spreadsheet. The numbers identify **rows** across the spreadsheet. A1, B1, C1, and D1 are all in the first row across; they are, of course, in different columns. A1, A2, A3, and A4 are in the same column but in four separate rows.

✓ CHECKPOINT

How many rows appear in the display shown in Figure 5-1?

How many columns appear in the display?

How many cells appear in the display?

In order to enter information into a cell in the spreadsheet, you must first move the cell locator to the cell. Cell movement is accomplished with the arrow keys and Open-Apple arrow keys. Let's work on some movement combinations.

GUIDED ACTIVITY: MOVE

WHAT YOU TYPE	WHY YOU TYPE IT
<DOWN-ARROW>	To move the cell locator down one cell.

The highlighted cell is now A2, as indicated by the new position of the cell locator and by the identification line in the lower left corner.

If you try to move off the Spreadsheet by going too far up, left, right, or down, the computer beeps.

WHAT YOU TYPE	WHY YOU TYPE IT
<LEFT-ARROW>	To attempt to move off of the left edge of the spreadsheet. The computer beeps to indicate that you can not do this.

The display shows 8 columns, A to H, and 18 rows, 1 to 18. 144 cells (8X18 is 144) are visible at this time. There are more cells, rows, and columns to the right and at the bottom.

Determine the location of the right edge of the Spreadsheet.

WHAT YOU TYPE	WHY YOU TYPE IT

<RIGHT-ARROW> eight times   To move the cell locator to the right edge of the screen.

When the cell locator reaches the right edge of the screen, the Spreadsheet shifts to the left, the A column disappears off the left edge, and column I appears at the right.

Hold down the <RIGHT-ARROW> key until you hear a beep.

The right edge is at column DW. There are 127 columns (A–Z, AA–AZ, BA–BZ, CA–CZ, and DA–DW for a total of 26+26+26+26+23=127).

Let's move down as far as possible. The Open-Apple and arrow key combination increases the speed of the cursor movement. The combination Open-Apple-down-arrow moves the cursor down one full screen at a time just as it did in the Word Processor and the Data Base. (Isn't integrated software great.)

Hold down ⌂-DOWN-ARROW until you reach the bottom of the Spreadsheet.

The computer beeps when 999 is displayed at the left edge of the screen. The dimensions of the Spreadsheet are thus 127 by 999 or 126,873 cells. Because the Desktop has a limit of 55K of space in a 128K computer, only about 6,000 cells can be used for one file. (There are about 1,000 cells available in a 64K machine.)

There are several other methods of moving from cell to cell in the Spreadsheet. Open-Apple-1 through Open-Apple-9 work the same here as they do in the other applications.

WHAT YOU TYPE	WHY YOU TYPE IT

⌂-1   To move to the first (top) row.

Notice that you are still in column DW. To move back to cell A1 rapidly,

Hold ⌂-LEFT-ARROW until the cell locator moves to cell A1.

Now that you are at the top of the Spreadsheet, Open-Apple-2 through Open-Apple-9 do not move the cell locator down. Remember, they move the cell locator proportionally down through the information that you have entered; since there is no information entered, there is no downward movement.

There is one additional way to move around the worksheet that is not found in either of the other applications. Try the following:

GUIDED ACTIVITY: MOVE   (continued)

WHAT YOU TYPE	WHY YOU TYPE IT
⌘-F	To start the **Find** command.
C	To indicate that you are finding **coordinates** (the row and column identification).
DW999	To enter the coordinates of the cell to which you wish to move.
<RETURN>	To move to cell DW999.
⌘-F	To start the Find command again.
C	To find coordinates.
A1 <RETURN>	To move back to the top left cell.

The highlighted bar in the cell is sometimes referred to as the cell cursor or just the cursor. Remember, this book refers to it as the cell locator to avoid confusion with the entry cursor showing in the lower left corner of the screen.

VALUE TYPE CELLS

There are two types of information that can be entered into the cells, label–type information and value–type information. Label–type information is anything that is not a number or that does not produce a number by a calculation. Value–type information includes numbers, formulas, and calculations. The first character that you type tells the computer which type of information is being entered. Letters indicate label–type information, and numbers indicate value–type information.

GUIDED ACTIVITY: ENTER

Type any letter key.

The letter appears in the highlighted cell and also on the second line up from the bottom after the indicator Label:.

Press <ESCAPE> and the information is removed.
Type any number key.

In the lower left corner, the computer indicates that a value has been entered. (The number does not appear in the cell until you either press Return or move the cell locator with the arrow keys.)

Press <ESCAPE> to remove the number.

TROUBLESHOOTING:

Problem: The Main Menu appears in the display.

Correction: If you press Escape too many times, you return to the Main Menu. Press Escape one more time to return to the spreadsheet, or highlight 2. Work with one of the files on the Desktop and press Return.

ENTERING VALUES

The computer interprets any number key that you press as the first digit of a value. There are four other keys that also indicate that a value is being entered. The keys are: +, -, (, and @. The minus sign (-) allows negative values to be entered. The other symbols are used with formulas. Do the following Guided Activity to practice entering values.

GUIDED ACTIVITY: ENTER

Let's enter the number 9 into cell A1.

If the cell locator is not in cell A1, move the cell locator to cell A1 using the arrows.

WHAT YOU TYPE	WHY YOU TYPE IT
9	To enter a 9. The 9 appears in the lower left corner of the screen.
<RETURN>	To complete the entry. A 9 appears in the cell. The cell locator does not move from the A1 position.

Enter a 10 in cell B1

WHAT YOU TYPE	WHY YOU TYPE IT
<RIGHT-ARROW>	To move to cell B1.
10	To enter 10. The 10 appears in the lower left corner only.
<RIGHT-ARROW>	To complete the entry. The cell locator moves to cell C1. The 10 appears in cell B1.

This time you completed the entry by moving the cursor to cell C1 with the right-arrow key. An entry is completed either by pressing Return or by moving the cell locator with an arrow key. Once the entry has been completed, it can not be removed by pressing return. Remember, you can look in the upper right corner to determine what the Escape key does.

Commas are not used for numbers over 1000. The computer ignores any illegal keystrokes such as a comma, and beeps to indicate that it has done so.

If the cell locator is not in cell C1, move it there.

In cell C1, enter the number 1,234.567
(Remember, do not type the comma, but, do type the decimal point.)
Press the <LEFT-ARROW> key <u>twice</u>.

The left-arrow key completes the entry and moves the cell locator back to cell A1.

MODIFYING

To modify the information in a cell, you would move to the cell and enter the new value or label.

WHAT YOU TYPE	WHY YOU TYPE IT
11 <RIGHT-ARROW>	To enter 11 into cell A1. To move the cell locator to cell B1 and complete the entry in cell A1.

When you press the arrow key, the new value (11) replaces the old value (9) in the cell A1. The value in B1 remains unchanged.

WHAT YOU TYPE	WHY YOU TYPE IT
5	To start to enter 5 in cell B1. Do not press Return or move the cell locator.

If you decide before you press Return or an arrow key that you do not wish to change the information in the cell, press Escape and your new entry is cleared.

WHAT YOU TYPE	WHY YOU TYPE IT
ESCAPE <RIGHT-ARROW>	To leave the value 10 in cell B1. To move to cell C1.

The value in the cell can also be the result of a calculation. The symbols for addition, subtraction, multiplication, and division are respectively: + - * and /.

WHAT YOU TYPE	WHY YOU TYPE IT
1+2 <RETURN>	To enter 1+2 in cell C1. To complete the entry.

The result appears in the cell; and the calculation you entered appears in the lower left corner.

The order of calculation is from left to right. The rules of a calculator rather than the rules of Algebra apply. For example, 1+2*3 is 9 (1+2 is 3 and 3*3 is 9). (In Algebra, the multiplication is done first and the result of 1+2*3 is 1+6 or 7.) The calculation order can be changed with **parentheses.** For example: 1+(2*3) is multiplication first and the result is 7.

There is one additional calculation symbol, the caret (^). The caret is used to indicate exponentiation (power). For example, 10^4 is ten to the fourth power or 10*10*10*10 = 10,000.

If the cell locator is not in cell C1, move it there using the arrow keys.

WHAT YOU TYPE	WHY YOU TYPE IT
10^4	To enter the calculation.
<RETURN>	To display the result, 10000, in cell C1.

✓ **CHECKPOINT**

Write down your answers to the calculations below on a piece of paper. Enter these calculations into cell C1 and determine the result. Compare the result with your answer. If your answer and the results are different, determine why.

1.   15+20/5

2.   15+(20/5)

3.   20/5+15

4.   20/(5+15)

5.   80+90+100/3

6.   100+90+80/3

7.   10^3

FORMATTING

In the last problem, 1000 is displayed in cell C1 without the comma. Even though you can not type the comma in, the format of the display can be changed so that the comma is shown as part of the number. Any changes to the appearance of the spreadsheet are called **layout** changes. Formatting is one type of layout change.

GUIDED ACTIVITY: FORMAT

WHAT YOU TYPE	WHY YOU TYPE IT
⌘-L	To enter the layout command.

You are presented with a series of choices. The first choice asks you to specify what portion of the spreadsheet you wish to change. The possibilities are:

Entry	The single cell at the cell locator's position.
Rows	One or more rows of cells.
Columns	One or more columns of cells.
Block	A block of one or more cells that you specify by moving the cursor.

WHAT YOU TYPE	WHY YOU TYPE IT
\<RETURN\>	To select `Entry`. The change is made to this cell only.

The next choice asks you to specify the type of change you wish to make. For a single cell layout change the choices are: `Value format, Label format, or Protection.` We wish to modify the value format.

WHAT YOU TYPE	WHY YOU TYPE IT
\<RETURN\>	To select `Value format,` the highlighted block.

Finally you're asked to select the type of value format that you wish to use. Here are your choices:

Fixed	Each number entered in this cell is displayed with a specified number of decimal places (0-7). The last place is rounded off. The entire number entered is stored in the computer; only the display changes. Additional zeros are added at the end of the number if needed to provide the required number of decimal places.
Dollars	A dollar sign is inserted before each amount. Commas are inserted for thousands, millions, etc. The number of decimal places is specified (0-7). Negative numbers are displayed in parentheses. The number is moved one space to the left within the cell (a space is inserted to the right of the number).
Commas	This has the same format as the dollars format but without the dollar sign.
Percent	The value in the cell is multiplied by 100 and a percent sign is inserted at the right of the number. The number of decimal places displayed is fixed (0-7).
Appropriate	Numbers are displayed in a way similar to the way you type them. Trailing zeros after a decimal are dropped.

| Standard | The cells selected are displayed in the standard or default format. The standard format is automatically used when no other format is specified. When you first create a spreadsheet, the standard format is Appropriate. You can reset the standard format to any one of the formats above. |

WHAT YOU TYPE	WHY YOU TYPE IT
C	To select **Commas,** the "comma format".
\<RETURN>	To specify zero decimal places.

Note that the number in cell C1 is displayed as 1,000. Let's change the layout again. This time display the number with one decimal place. The cell locator should be in cell C1.

WHAT YOU TYPE	WHY YOU TYPE IT
⌘-L	To change the layout.
\<RETURN>	To select **Entry.**
V	To select **Value format.**
C 1 \<RETURN>	To select **Commas** format and 1 decimal place.

The number is displayed with a decimal point and one digit showing after the decimal. The digit is 0 for this number. Comma type number formats always show the number of digits that you specify. Trailing zeros are added to the number if necessary or if there are more digits than you specify, the number is rounded to the number of digits you request. Care must be taken not to request a number that is too large for the cell. For example, display 1,000.000 in cell C1.

WHAT YOU TYPE	WHY YOU TYPE IT
⌘-L	To change the layout.
\<RETURN>	To select **Entry.**
V	To select **Value format.**
C 3 \<RETURN>	To select **Commas** format and 3 decimal places.

The cell fills with number signs (#). This is a error message which indicates that the number is too large to be printed in the format that you chose. The number in the cell is not lost, however. Note that it is visible on the third line from the bottom in the display (the calculation that you entered, 10^3, appears there).

✓ CHECKPOINT

Does the number 10^3 display in a cell with the format Commas and two decimal places?

What is the indication on the screen that informs you what the layout for a cell is set to? Where does this indication appear?

Change the format for cell C1 to commas with one decimal.

The lower left corner of the screen should now read:

```
C1: (Value, Layout-C1) 10^3
```

USING FORMULAS

You have already entered formulas into your spreadsheet. These formulas have fixed values, 1+2 and 10^3, that are not changed by the contents of other cells. With fixed value formulas, changing the entry in one cell has no effect on any of the entries in the other cells.

The most powerful feature of spreadsheets is that formulas that **reference** (use) values in other cells can be entered. When the value in the referenced cell is changed, the formula is recalculated and the new result replaces the old one.

Let's enter a formula into cell C1 which adds the contents of cells A1 and B1, and displays the results in C1. Remember, the calculation results must change whenever the values in cell A1 or B1 are changed. A fixed value formula such as 1+2 will not do here; the formula must reference A1 and B1. The exact formula is:

> +A1+B1

Note that the formula starts with a plus sign (+). This is absolutely necessary. If you start with a letter, the computer immediately assumes that you are entering a label. You are not; you're entering a formula that reads: in this cell (C1) place the value that is the result of adding the value in A1 to the value in B1. The next Guided Activity explains this and other formulas.

GUIDED ACTIVITY: FORMULAS

Move the cell locator to cell A1.

WHAT YOU TYPE	WHY YOU TYPE IT
1 <RIGHT-ARROW>	To enter 1 into cell A1 and move the cell locator to cell B1.
2 <RIGHT-ARROW>	To enter 2 into cell B1 and move the cell locator to cell C1.
+A1+B1	To enter the formula at the bottom of the screen.
<RETURN>	To complete the formula entry, calculate the result and display the result in cell C1.

Remember, if you make an error, you can press Escape and try again or you can move to an adjacent cell and then return the cursor to cell C1 and try again. When you have successfully entered the formula and pressed Return, the result of the calculation appears in the C1 cell (the result is written 3.0 since the last layout specified for this cell was commas with one decimal). The formula continues to be displayed in the lower left corner of the screen as shown in Figure 5-2.

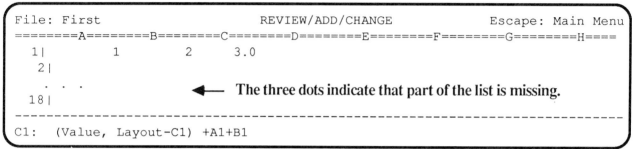

```
File: First                    REVIEW/ADD/CHANGE              Escape: Main Menu
========A========B========C========D========E========F========G========H====
  1|        1        2      3.0
  2|
    .  .  .                   ◄── The three dots indicate that part of the list is missing.
 18|
----------------------------------------------------------------------------
C1:   (Value, Layout-C1) +A1+B1
```

FIGURE 5-2.   Formula in a Spreadsheet.

Move the cell locator to cell A1.

WHAT YOU TYPE	WHY YOU TYPE IT
5 <RETURN>	To change the value in cell A1 to 5. Notice that the value in cell C1 immediately changes to 7 to reflect the new sum, 5 plus 2.
<RIGHT-ARROW>	To move to cell B1.
9 <RIGHT-ARROW>	To change the value in cell B1 to 9 and move the cell locator to cell C1. Again the value in C1 changes, this time to 14, the sum of 9 and 5.

Let's enter a formula in C1 to calculate the average of the two numbers in cells A1 and B1. The formula is:

+A1+B1/2
   or
(A1+B1)/2

Remember, the spreadsheet formulas are calculated left to right unless the order is changed by parentheses. In this example, the calculation order is exactly the same although some people prefer the second expression since it makes the calculation order clearer.

Enter the first formula into cell C1.
Remember to press <RETURN> to complete your entry.

When you signal the computer that the formula is complete by pressing Return or by moving the cell locator to a new cell with an arrow key, the result is calculated and the average, 7, is displayed in cell C1.

A second method of entering formulas is called **pointing**. You indicate the cell or cells that are used in the formula by moving the cell locator to the cell and then entering the next step in the formula. Let's try pointing with the alternate formula for average. Enter the formula in another cell to compare the results.

    Move the cursor to cell C2.

WHAT YOU TYPE	WHY YOU TYPE IT
(	To enter the open parenthesis symbol. In the lower left-hand corner, the computer acknowledges that a value is about to be entered.
<UP-ARROW> once	To move to cell C1. Watch the lower left corner of the screen as you move the locator. The cell label is automatically inserted into the formula as you move from cell to cell.
<LEFT-ARROW> twice	To move to cell A1.
+	To enter the plus sign.

The plus sign is the next step in the formula. When you press the + key, the cell locator jumps back to cell C2. The formula showing in the lower left corner now reads: (A1+

WHAT YOU TYPE	WHY YOU TYPE IT
<UP-ARROW>	To move the cell locator to cell C1.
<LEFT-ARROW>	To move the cell locator to cell B1. The formula in the lower left corner now reads: (A1+B1
)/2	To finish the formula.
<RETURN>	To calculate and display the results.
<UP-ARROW>	To move the cell locator to cell C1.
<LEFT-ARROW> twice	To move the cell locator to cell A1.
25 <RETURN>	To enter 25 into cell A1.

The average of 25 in cell A1 and 9 in cell B1 is calculated, and the result, 17, is displayed in cells C1 and C2. Both C1 and C2 are changed when a change is made in cell A1, since both cells have formulas that reference A1. C1 and C2 also change when a new value is entered in cell B1.

There is yet another way to calculate the average of the values in two or more cells: use the formula for average that is built into the Spreadsheet. Here are some examples of the **average formula:**

1. @AVG(H11...H30)   Average the twenty values in cells H11, H12, H13, and so on up to and including the value in cell H30.
2. @AVG(K5,K10,K15)   Average the three values found in cells K5, K10, and K15.
3. @AVG(M1,R1...R5)   Average the six values found in cells M1, R1, R2, R3, R4, and R5.

As you can see, the formula starts with the characters "@AVG(". The cell locations of the values to be averaged are indicated inside the parentheses. Built-in formulas can be given a **range** of values as in the first example, a set of individual values as in the second example, or a combination of individual values and ranges as in the third example. When a range of values is given, only the first and last cells in the range are listed. **Ellipsis** marks (the three dots) are used to separate the first and last cell location in a range. The cell locations can be entered from the keyboard or by using the pointing method.

Let's recalculate the average one last time using @AVG.

GUIDED ACTIVITY: FORMULAS   (continued)

Move the cell locator to cell C1.

WHAT YOU TYPE	WHY YOU TYPE IT
@AVG(	To begin the formula entry.
<LEFT-ARROW> twice	To move to cell A1. You are using the pointing entry method here.
.	To type the period (decimal point or dot) for the ellipsis. The computer enters two more periods into the formula to indicate the ellipsis. The cell locator remains in cell A1.
<RIGHT-ARROW>	To move the cell locator to cell B1. Both A1 and B1 are highlighted. The highlighting shows all of the cells used in the range.
<RETURN>	To enter B1 into the formula.
)	To complete the formula.
<RETURN>	To calculate and display the average.

Note that cell C1 displays 17.0 and cell C2 displays 17 because the layout format was changed in cell C1 and not in cell C2.

Move to cell A1.

WHAT YOU TYPE	WHY YOU TYPE IT
1.75	To enter the number 1.75 into cell A1.
<RETURN>	To complete the entry and recalculate the averages in cells C1 and C2

The answer that the computer obtains, remembers, and uses is the same for both cell C1 and C2. The display in cell C1 is rounded off (using the rule: 5 rounds to an even digit) to fit the layout format for that cell (commas with one decimal place). Since no layout format has been set for cell C2, the the number displayed there uses the default setting (standard). Figure 5-3 shows the spreadsheet as it now appears.

```
┌──────────────────────────────────────────────────────────────────────────┐
│  File: First                    REVIEW/ADD/CHANGE            Escape: Main Menu│
│  ========A========B========C========D========E========F========G========H====│
│    1|       1.75        9       5.4                                          │
│    2|                          5.375                                         │
│     .  .  .                                                                  │
│   18|                                                                        │
│  --------------------------------------------------------------------------- │
│  C1:   (Value, Layout-C1) @AVG(A1...B1)                                      │
└──────────────────────────────────────────────────────────────────────────┘
```

FIGURE 5-3.   Average Formula in a Spreadsheet.

BLANKING A CELL

Let's clear out the cells that we have been experimenting with and build a more sophisticated spreadsheet model. To blank a cell or a group of cells, use the Open-Apple-B command. You'll try two of the options for this command in the next Guided Activity.

GUIDED ACTIVITY: BLANK

Move the cell locator to cell A1.

WHAT YOU TYPE	WHY YOU TYPE IT
⌂-B	To start the blank command.
<RETURN>	To select Entry.

The contents of the cell A1 are blanked out.

Let's blank a **block** of cells this time. A block is a rectangular or square set of cells that are adjacent to one another. The cell locator must start in a cell that is in one of the corners of the block of cells to be blanked. You need to blank the block that contains cells B1, C1, B2, and C2. Even though some of these cells are already blank, the block is the quickest way to blank the set.

Move the cell locator to cell B1, a corner of the block you need to blank.

WHAT YOU TYPE	WHY YOU TYPE IT
⌘-B	To start the blanking process.
B	To select Block.

The computer displays the following message:

```
Use cursor moves to highlight Block, then press Return.
```

WHAT YOU TYPE	WHY YOU TYPE IT
<RIGHT-ARROW>	To highlight B1 and C1
<DOWN-ARROW>	To add B2 and C2 to the highlight area. The block of cells B1, C1, B2, and C2 are highlighted. Three of these cells contain information and the fourth is blank.
<RETURN>	To blank all four cells.

A WORD OF WISDOM

The computer does not ask you "Are you sure you want to do this?" when you blank cells, so be careful in using this command. Once you blank (or delete) information from cells, the only ways to reenter the information are to retype it, or reload the entire file from the disk.

✓   CHECKPOINT

You are going to blank cells D5, E5, D6,E6, D7, E7, D8, and E8 using the Blank Block commands. There are four correct places that you can move the cell locator to before you enter the Open-Apple-B command. What are they?

LABEL TYPE CELLS

Cells that start with letters are label-type cells as previously mentioned. In addition to letters, quotation marks (") can be used as a first character to signal the computer that the information being entered is label-type. For example, if you wish to enter a date such as 9/10, typing the 9 first would indicate that a value is being entered. If you type 9/10 and press Return, the computer enters the result of the division calculation (0.9) into the cell. To enter a label that starts with a digit or any other nonletter character, first type quotation marks (") and then type the character. The first quotation mark that you type is not displayed. It only serves to signal the computer that a label entry is to follow.

You can mix letters and numbers in labels but you cannot mix numbers and letters in values. Remember, the first character determines the type of entry. Key 1 is an acceptable label even though it includes a number. You would not be able to enter 1st Key, however: the 1 signals that a value is being entered, and since 1st is not a valid computer value, the computer beeps and ignores the "s" and the "t." If you start the entry with a quotation mark, "1st Key is a valid label and AppleWorks has no problem with it.

The example for this section examines what someone earns (income) and what he or she spends (expenses) for ten months. Expenses are subtracted from income to produce an amount for savings. Figure 5-4 shows what the table looks like when it is completed.

```
File:     First                                         Page   1
                                                        7/1/88


        Month Income    minus  Expenses    =     Savings
        ------------------------------------------------------
           1   125.00   minus    65.00     =      60.00
           2   129.00   minus    65.00     =      64.00
           3   133.00   minus    65.00     =      68.00
           4   137.00   minus    65.00     =      72.00
           5   141.00   minus    65.00     =      76.00
           6   145.00   minus    65.00     =      80.00
           7   149.00   minus    65.00     =      84.00
           8   153.00   minus    65.00     =      88.00
           9   157.00   minus    65.00     =      92.00
          10   161.00   minus    65.00     =      96.00
             ---------         ---------        ---------
             1,430.00           650.00          780.00
```

FIGURE 5-4.   Completed Income and Expense Table.

You should make the following observations about this table:

- The word minus is repeated 11 times. The equal sign is repeated 11 times, too.
- The line of dashes (-) is repeated across the top of the columns.
- The number 65.00 is repeated down the fourth column.
- The values in the month column increase by 1 as they move down the column.
- The values in the income column increase by 4 as they move down the column.
- The values in the savings column are the differences of the values in the income and expense columns in the same row.
- There are six columns in the table.

ENTERING

The first task you need to complete in building this spreadsheet is to enter the labels at the top of the six columns. When you first enter them, they do not appear as they do in the figure above. Don't be concerned; your next task will be to modify the layout of the labels.

GUIDED ACTIVITY: INCOME 1

Start to create the income table.

Enter the column headers for the top line of the example by following the steps below.

Move the cell locator to cell A1.

WHAT YOU TYPE	WHY YOU TYPE IT
Month <RIGHT-ARROW>	To enter the label Month into cell A1.
Income <RIGHT-ARROW>	To enter the label Income into cell B1.
minus <RIGHT-ARROW>	To enter the label minus into cell C1.
Expenses <RIGHT-ARROW>	To enter the label Expenses into cell D1.
"= <RIGHT-ARROW>	To enter the label = into cell E1. The quote marks do not appear in the cell.
Savings <RIGHT-ARROW>	To enter the label Savings into cell F1.

It is also possible to type label information in one continuous entry. As you enter the characters, additional cells to the right of the starting cell are highlighted and filled with information. The bottom of the screen, however, shows information entered into the starting cell only. When you press Return or one of the arrow keys, the information is distributed to the cells as it appears on the screen.

Move the cell locator to cell A2.

Type the following as one continuous entry to determine what happens when you fill a cell:

WHAT YOU TYPE	WHY YOU TYPE IT
Now is the time for all good people to compute with a spreadsheet.	
<RETURN>	To complete the entry.
<Right-arrow>	To move across the cells in the row.

The lower left corner of the screen displays what the computer decided to store in each cell. Because you have so little control over the information stored in each column, this entry method is good only when you are entering titles for the entire spreadsheet. Remove the clutter from this row.

Move the cell locator back to cell A2.

WHAT YOU TYPE	WHY YOU TYPE IT
⌘-B	To start the blanking process.
R	To select **Row** as the area to blank.
<RETURN>	To blank the entire highlighted row.

The next label that you are going to enter is the row of dashes under the column headings. Remember that the computer thinks that a value is about to be entered when the dash or minus sign is pressed. You'll need to use the quotation marks to circumvent this.

GUIDED ACTIVITY: INCOME 1   (continued)

WHAT YOU TYPE	WHY YOU TYPE IT
" (quotation mark)	To signal that a label is to be entered.
Press and hold -	To fill the six columns A2 through F2 with dashes.
<RETURN>	To finish the entry.

MODIFYING

The procedure for odifying the contents of a label cell is identical to the procedure for modifying the contents of a value cell. All you have to do is move to the cell and type the new information. Pressing Escape before you press Return or an arrow key cancels the modification. For example, to change the minus signs (-) in row 2 to equal signs (=), you would first move the cursor to cell A2. Then you would type a quotation mark ("); then press and hold the equal key (=) until the six columns are overwritten with equal signs.

Another way to modify the contents of a cell is to edit the cell. Let's edit the contents of cell A1 by adding enough spaces before the word Month to move the word to the right edge of the cell.

GUIDED ACTIVITY: INCOME 1   (continued)

Make sure that you are using the insert cursor, i.e., the underline cursor (_). If necessary, use ⌘-E to change to this cursor.

Move the cell locator to A1, the cell to be changed.

WHAT YOU TYPE	WHY YOU TYPE IT
⌘-U	To enter the cell edit mode. (⌘-E is used to change to the edit cursor. ⌘-U is a different type of edit, a cell edit.) The contents of cell A1 appear in the lower left corner of the screen.
<SPACE BAR>	The word "Month" moves right and a space is inserted before the word.
<SPACE BAR> three times	To insert a total of four spaces. This moves the word to the right edge of the cell.
<RETURN>	To complete the edit process for this cell.

When a word is as far right in a cell as possible, it is said to be **right-justified**.

In the edit mode the arrow keys move the cursor left and right through the information in the cell, allowing you to insert or delete characters in the middle or at the end of the information. After any changes have been made, press Return to signal the computer that you are finished editing.

GUIDED ACTIVITY: INCOME 1   (continued)

Enter the third row of the table.

WHAT YOU TYPE	WHY YOU TYPE IT
Arrows	To move to cell A3.
1 <RIGHT-ARROW>	To enter 1 into cell A3 and move the cell locator to cell B3.
125 <RIGHT-ARROW>	To enter 125 into cell B3 and move the cell locator to C3.
"<SPACE BAR> <SPACE BAR> minus <RIGHT-ARROW>	To enter the label minus into cell C3. That's the word minus preceded by two spaces.
65 <RIGHT-ARROW>	To enter 65 into cell D3 and move the cell locator to E3.
"= <RIGHT-ARROW>	To enter an equal sign into cell E3 and move the cell locator to cell F3.
+B3-D3 <RETURN>	To enter the formula for income minus expense.

Check your entries against those in Figure 5-5. Your entries should line up as they do in the figure. Make sure that the information in each cell of the top three rows is the same. Correct any errors that you have made using the Open-Apple-U command, and then proceed to the next section.

```
File: First                   REVIEW/ADD/CHANGE              Escape: Main Menu
========A========B========C========D========E========F========G========H====
  1|    MonthIncome   minus    Expenses  =         Savings
  2|-------------------------------------------------------------------
  3|      1       125  minus          65=               60
   .  .  .
 18|
-----------------------------------------------------------------------
F3: (Value) +B3-D3
```

FIGURE 5-5.   Beginning of the Income Spreadsheet.

FORMATTING

Let's change the layout format in the label cells to match that of Figure 5-4. Except for the words "Month" and "minus," the labels are as far left in the cell as they can be, that is, they are left-justified. The format of the labels in Figure 5-4 is **centered**.

Move the cursor to cell A1. Note that the lower left corner of the screen reads:

```
A1:  (Label)      Month
```

indicating that the cell contains a standard label " Month".

WHAT YOU TYPE	WHY YOU TYPE IT
⌘-L	To issue the command to modify the layout.
R	To select **Rows.**
<DOWN-ARROW> twice	To highlight the first three rows.
<RETURN>	To signal that you have completed your selection.
L	To select **Label format.**
C	To select **Center.**

The information in the label cells moves to the center to reflect your format change. The information in the value cells remains unchanged. Note that the lower left corner of the screen now reads: A1: (Label, Layout-C) Month. The "C" indicates that this cell now has a centered layout format.

Layout formats for any additional label cells that you type are still standard, i.e., left-justified. If you wanted all of the label cells to have centered as their standard format, you could change the **standard value** of the default format. Similarily, you can set the standard value format for value cells to any format type that you desire.

Let's reset the standard value format for this file to "commas" with two decimal places. This is the format used in Figure 5-4.

WHAT YOU TYPE	WHY YOU TYPE IT
⌘-V	To start the standard values command.
V	To set the standard for Value format.
C	To select comma format.
2 <RETURN>	To specify two decimal places for this format.

Note that the numbers already entered into the spreadsheet all adjust to the new standard value format for numbers. Any new numbers that are entered into any cell in this spreadsheet will be formatted Commas with two decimals. You have made that the default for number entry. If you wish to use a different format for some cells, you change the format for those cells using the layout command as you did before.

✓   __CHECKPOINT__

The Help Screen displays the standard formats at the bottom of the help list. What is listed as the standard format for labels?

What command changes the standard value for the label format?

When most of the values or labels in a spreadsheet use a nonstandard format such as commas, set the standard value to the new format. Individual cells can be changed to other formats as desired. If only a few cells have a non-standard format, change the format of those cells using the layout command.

Standard Value format changes made with the Open-Apple-V command apply to all cells in the spreadsheet. Layout format changes made with the Open-Apple-L command are only for the nonempty cells you specify when you use the command. When you enter information into an empty cell, the standard value setting is the format that is automatically used for the entry.

COPYING

There are many formulas in the spreadsheet that you are working on. There is also a lot of duplicate information. It is not necessary to type all of the information into each cell of a spreadsheet. Duplicate data can be easily copied to several cells with the copy command.

You'll use the copy command in several, progressive stages. First you'll copy a label from one cell to another nonadjacent cell, then from one cell to an adjacent cell, then from one cell to several nonadjacent cells, and finally, you'll copy from one cell to several cells with one cell adjacent to the source cell. That seems like a tall order. We'll go slowly to give you a lot of practice with a very important command.

GUIDED ACTIVITY: INCOME 2

To start, let's copy the contents of cell C3 to cell C6.

> Move the cell locator to cell C3. The cell contains "minus".
> Issue the copy command, ⌂-C.

The computer presents you with three choices: Within (the) worksheet, To (the) clipboard, and From (the) clipboard.

> Select **Within worksheet** by pressing <RETURN>.

Next, the message at the bottom of the display reads: Use cursor to highlight Source, then press Return. Since the single cell, C3, is the source of the copy information and since the cell is already highlighted, you do not need to move the cursor (cell locator); just

Press <RETURN>.

The message `Move cursor to new location, then press "." or Return` appears.

Press the <DOWN-ARROW> key three times to move the cursor to cell C6.
Finally, press <RETURN>.

The contents of cell C3 are now duplicated in cell C6.

The difficulty with moving information into an adjacent cell is that the cell locator's movement is not readily apparent. Move the contents of cell C3 to cell C4 to observe this.

Make sure that the cell locator is in cell C3.

WHAT YOU TYPE	WHY YOU TYPE IT
-C	To start the copy command.
<RETURN>	To select **Within worksheet**.
<RETURN>	To indicate that cell C3 is the source.
<DOWN-ARROW>	Press this key once and observe the screen. Cells C3 and C4 are both highlighted. C3 is the source and C4 is the new location.
<RETURN>	To copy the contents of C3 into cell C4.

Now let's copy information from one cell, C6, to several cells, C8, C9, and C10, that are nonadjacent to the source.

Move the cell locator to cell C6.

WHAT YOU TYPE	WHY YOU TYPE IT
-C	To start the copy process.
<RETURN>	To select **Within worksheet**.
<RETURN>	To select one cell, C6, as the source.
<DOWN-ARROW> twice	To move the cell locator down to cell C8. Notice that both C6 and C8 are highlighted.
.	The period indicates that you are copying the information into a range of cells. Observe that cell C8 is now the only cell highlighted. C8 is the start of the range.
<DOWN-ARROW> twice	To highlight the range . Each time you press the down-arrow key another cell is highlighted. The highlighted cells are C8, C9, and C10.
<RETURN>	To copy the `minus` label into the range of three cells.

Now copy label information from one cell, C3, to several cells, C4 to C12, one of which,C4, is adjacent to the source cell.

WHAT YOU TYPE	WHY YOU TYPE IT
<Arrows>	To move the cell locator to cell C3.
minus <RETURN>	To remove the extra spaces in the front of the word.
⌘-C	To start the copy procedure.
<RETURN>	To select **Within worksheet**.
<RETURN>	To select cell C3 as the source.

The instructions displayed at the bottom of the screen now are:

```
Move to new location, then press "." or Return.
```

WHAT YOU TYPE	WHY YOU TYPE IT
<DOWN-ARROW>	To move down one row to cell C4. Both cell C3 and C4 are highlighted.
.	To indicate the start of a range. Only C4 is highlighted now. The instructions change to: `Use cursor moves to highlight destination, then press Return.`
<DOWN-ARROW> 8 times	To highlight the range of the cells from C4 to C12.
<RETURN>	To complete the copy.

The contents of cell C3 are copied into cells C4 to C12.

UNGUIDED ACTIVITY:

Use the copy command to copy the label in cell E3 into cells E4 to E12.

✓ CHECKPOINT

At one point in the copy command, you are asked to:
```
Move to a new location, then press "." or Return
```
What is the difference between pressing a period or pressing Return at this point?

COPYING VALUE AND FORMULA CELLS

Copying formulas and values is different from copying labels. Consider column D for a moment. You can copy the value 65 into all of the cells from D4 to D12 exactly the same way that you copied the labels. However, if you later wish to change the value of expenses from 65 to say 70, you will need to re-copy the values. A logical question to ask is: Can you set up the cells so that when the value in cell D3 is changed, all of the expense cells, D4 through D12, automatically reflect the change? The answer is: of course; use a formula in cells D4 to D12 that makes them the same as D3. Possible formulas are: 0+D3; 1*D3 or just +D3. Let's use this method to copy the value 65.

GUIDED ACTIVITY: INCOME 2   (continued)

Enter the formula +D3 into cell D4.

WHAT YOU TYPE	WHY YOU TYPE IT
Arrows	To move the cell locator to cell D4 and
+D3	To enter the formula into cell D4.
<RETURN>	To complete the formula and perform the calculation. The value 65 appears in the cell.

Copy the formula in cell D4 to cells D5 through D12. The formula is the same in each cell that it is copied into.

WHAT YOU TYPE	WHY YOU TYPE IT
⌘-C	To start the copy procedure.
<RETURN> twice	To select **Within worksheet** and to select cell D4 as the source.
<DOWN-ARROW>	To move to D5, the start of the range D5 to D12.
.	To indicate that you are coping to a range of cells.
<Down-Arrow>	To highlight cells D5 to D12. (The lower case for this key means that you must determine how many times to press this key.)
<RETURN>.	To complete this part of the copy.

The lower left corner of the screen now displays the following:

```
D4: (Value) +D3
+D3
Reference to D3?  No change   Relative
```

The **D3** in the center line and the words **No change** are highlighted. It is your job to select either "No change" or "Relative" with respect to the cell location referenced in the formula. Let's examine these two options carefully.

First select **No change** by pressing <RETURN>.

Cells D5 to D12 now display a 65. Move the cell locator down through these cells to examine the formula that produced this value. In each cell the formula is the same; it is +D3. The formula was copied without changing the cell reference. This action is exactly what you specified when you selected the "No change" option. The only cell in column D that changes the value of the lower cells when it is changed is cell D3.

WHAT YOU TYPE	WHY YOU TYPE IT
Arrows	To move to cell D9.
75 <RETURN>	To enter 75 into cell D9. This erases the formula in the cell and replaces it with the value. Notice that no other cell is affected. Cell D9 is the only cell with the value 75.
Arrows	To move to cell D3.
60 <RETURN>	To enter 60 into cell D3.

The cells with the exception of D9 change to 60. The only cell change that affects the other cells in the column is a change made in cell D3.

✓ CHECKPOINT

Why didn't the 75 in cell D9 change to a 60? HINT: Compare the contents of cell D9 with other cells in the column.

The second option presented to you near the end of the copy procedure is a bit more complex. It is the **Relative** option.

Look at the formula, +D3, in cell D4. It tells the computer to copy the contents of cell D3 into cell D4. If you think of the cell's relative positions, you are saying: copy into this cell, D4, the contents of the cell above, D3. If you were to continue down the column in terms of relative formulas, the formula in cell D5 would be +D4, in D6 the formula would be +D5, and so on (that is: copy into this cell, D5, the contents of the cell above, D4; copy into this cell, D6, the contents of the cell above, D5; etc). Let's try a Relative formula copy in which the formula in each cell changes to reflect the relation of the cell to its "upstairs" neighbor.

GUIDED ACTIVITY: INCOME 2 (continued)

Blank out cells D5 to D12 with the blank command, Open-Apple-B.

WHAT YOU TYPE	WHY YOU TYPE IT
Arrows	To move the cell locator to either D5 or D12.
⌘-B	To start the blanking process.
B	To select **Block**.
Arrows	To highlight the block from D5 to D12.
<RETURN>	To complete the process and blank the cells.

Re-copy the formula in cell D4 to cells D5 through D12 using the relative formula option.

What You Type	Why You Type It
Arrows	To move to cell D4.
⌘-C	To start the copy procedure.
<RETURN> twice	To select **Within worksheet** and to select cell D4 as the source.
<DOWN-ARROW>	To move down one cell.
.	To indicate the start of the range.
Down-Arrow	To highlight cells D5 to D12.
<RETURN>	To indicate that the selection is complete.
R	To select **Relative** for the formula.

Now, when you examine the contents of cells D5 to D12, you see that the formulas are all different. Each one takes its value from the cell above it.

The values that appear in the cells are still the same. What's different? To find out:

What You Type	Why You Type It
Arrows	To move to cell D9.
75 <RETURN>	To enter 75 into cell D9. This erases the formula in the cell and replaces it with the value. This time all of the cells below D9 are changed to 75.

✓ CHECKPOINT

If the number in cell D3 is changed to 65, what number will you then find in cell D10? Why?

WHAT YOU'VE LEARNED

- The copy command can be used to duplicate labels, values, and formulas.
- Formulas can be copied without change or they can be copied and automatically changed relative to their new position.
- Formulas can be removed with the blanking command or by overtyping them with a new label or value. This may produce unexpected or unwanted results.

Please follow the steps below to restore the spreadsheet.

Move to cell D9.
Type: +D8 <RETURN>   To replace the 75 with the correct formula.

Your display should now match Figure 5-6. If it does not, make the corrections necessary to make your display match the figure.

```
File: First                   REVIEW/ADD/CHANGE              Escape: Main Menu
=======A========B========C========D========E========F========G========H====
  1|    Month Income    minus Expenses     =    Savings
  2|---------------------------------------------------------
  3|    1.00   125.00   minus    65.00     =     60.00
  4|                    minus    65.00
  5|                    minus    65.00
  6|                    minus    65.00
  7|                    minus    65.00
  8|                    minus    65.00
  9|                    minus    65.00
 10|                    minus    65.00
 11|                    minus    65.00
 12|                    minus    65.00
  -----------------------------------------------------------------------
D9: (Value)  +D8
```

FIGURE 5-6. Partially Completed Spreadsheet.

THE FORMULA THAT COUNTS

The months in the first column are nothing more than the counting numbers from one to ten. It would be convenient if a formula could be used to enter these numbers. Consider the formula 1+A3 in cell A4. If all of the cells contained relative formulas, that is, contained a number one higher than the number in the cell above, then the cells would contain the values 2, 3, 4, and so on. (If all of the cells on the A column from row 4 to row 12 contained the same formula (1+A3), each cell would contain a 2 (1+1).)

Let's use relative formula copying to generate the values in column A. Remember, each cell in this column contains a value that is one higher than the value in the cell above it. To obtain the value in cell A4, use the formula 1+A3. To obtain a value in cell A5, the formula is 1+A4; for cell A6, the formula is 1+A5. Continue in this fashion until cell A12, where you use the formula 1+A11.

Finish the Guided Activity, Income 2 by entering all of these formulas.

GUIDED ACTIVITY: INCOME 2 (continued)

WHAT YOU TYPE	WHY YOU TYPE IT
Arrows	To move to cell A4.
1+A3	To enter the first formula.
⌘-C	To start to copy the formula from A4 into cells A5 through A12.

\<RETURN\> twice	To select **Within worksheet** and to select cell A4 as the source.
\<DOWN-ARROW\>	To move down one cell.
.	To indicate the start of a range.
Down-Arrow	To highlight cells A5 to A12.
\<RETURN\>	To indicate that you have completed the range selection.
R	To select **Relative** for the reference to A3.

Examine the contents of cells A5 to A12; the formulas are all different. Each cell has a value one higher than the cell above it.

UNGUIDED ACTIVITY

Each number in the income column is 4 higher than the number above it. Enter the formula 4+B3 into cell B4. Use this formula to generate the formulas in cells B5 to B12. If you do this correctly, the number in cell B12 will be 161.00.

The last task needed to complete this spreadsheet is to enter the formulas for the cells in column F. You have already entered the formula in cell F3. It is +B3-D3. For cell F4 the formula is +B4-D4, for cell F5, +B5-D5. In this case, the formula changes relative to the row its cell is in. Both of the cell references in the formula are relative to the row. Here's how to copy the formula in cell F3 into cells F4 to F12. While you're at it, you'll copy the equal sign too.

WHAT YOU TYPE	WHY YOU TYPE IT
Arrows	To move the cell locator to cell E3.
⌘-C	To start the copy command.
\<RETURN\>	To select **Within worksheet**.
\<RIGHT-ARROW\>	To highlight both E3 and F3.
\<RETURN\>	To complete the selection for the source.
\<DOWN-ARROW\>	To move down one cell.
.	To indicate the start of the range.
\<Down-Arrow\>	To highlight cells E4 to E12 and F4 to F12.
\<RETURN\>	To indicate the selection is complete.

You are now asked to choose "No change" or "Relative" for each cell referenced in the formula.

Type: R <u>twice</u> to select **Relative** for each part of the formula.

The calculations are done and the spreadsheet is now similar to the one in Figure 5-7.

```
File: First                    REVIEW/ADD/CHANGE              Escape: Main  Menu
========A========B========C========D========E========F========G======H====
   1|     Month Income    minus  Expenses    =     Savings
   2|-----------------------------------------------------------
   3|       1   125.00    minus   65.00      =      60.00
   4|       2   129.00    minus   65.00      =      64.00
   5|       3   133.00    minus   65.00      =      68.00
   6|       4   137.00    minus   65.00      =      72.00
   7|       5   141.00    minus   65.00      =      76.00
   8|       6   145.00    minus   65.00      =      80.00
   9|       7   149.00    minus   65.00      =      84.00
  10|       8   153.00    minus   65.00      =      88.00
  11|       9   157.00    minus   65.00      =      92.00
  12|      10   161.00    minus   65.00      =      96.00
   .  .  .
   -----------------------------------------------------------------
F3:  (Value) +B3-D3
```

FIGURE 5-7. Partially Completed Spreadsheet.

You should play with the completed spreadsheet a bit. Change the value in cell D3 to 70. All of the expense values change to 70 and all of the savings values are recalculated. Change the income value in cell B3 to 150. The income values then change from 150 to 186 and the savings values are again recalculated. When you have finished, change the numbers back to their original values.

INSERTING ROWS OR COLUMNS

The only thing our table lacks is a title on the first line. Unfortunately, there is no blank line upon which to place a title. Let's remedy that.

GUIDED ACTIVITY: INCOME 3

WHAT YOU TYPE	WHY YOU TYPE IT
⌘-1	To move to the top of the spreadsheet.
⌘-I	To issue the insert command.
R	To indicate **Rows**.
2 <RETURN>	To insert two rows.

You now have one row for the title and one row to be left blank.

Move the cell locator to cell A1.

WHAT YOU TYPE

Income and Expense for the School Year

```
+----------------------------------------------------------------------+
| File: First                 REVIEW/ADD/CHANGE           Escape: Main Menu|
| ========A========B========C========D========E========F========G========H====|
|   1|Income and Expense for the School Year                            |
|   2|                                                                  |
|   3|    Month Income    minus  Expenses     =     Savings             |
|   4|-----------------------------------------------------------       |
|   5|1          125       minus 65           =     +B5-D5              |
|   6|1+A5       4+B5      minus +D5          =     +B6-D6              |
|   7|1+A6       4+B6      minus +D6          =     +B7-D7              |
|   8|1+A7       4+B7      minus +D7          =     +B8-D8              |
|   9|1+A8       4+B8      minus +D8          =     +B9-D9              |
|  10|1+A9       4+B9      minus +D9          =     +B10-D10            |
|  11|1+A10      4+B10     minus +D10         =     +B11-D11            |
|  12|1+A11      4+B11     minus +D11         =     +B12-D12            |
|  13|1+A12      4+B12     minus +D12         =     +B13-D13            |
|  14|1+A13      4+B13     minus +D13         =     +B14-D14            |
|  15|                                                                  |
|  16|                                                                  |
|  17|                                                                  |
|  18|                                                                  |
| ----------------------------------------------------------------------|
| F5: (Value) +B5-D5                                                    |
|                                                                      |
| Type entry or use ⌘ commands                          ⌘ -? for Help  |
+----------------------------------------------------------------------+
```

FIGURE 5-8.   Income Worksheet Formulas.

The title spreads over several columns automatically. Entering the title last is good practice. (As you'll see in the next spreadsheet unit, changing the column width is easy. However, narrowing a column can eliminate letters in the title display while expanding a column can add unwanted spaces to the title. If you enter the title last, you avoid this problem.)

To see the formulas, give the ⌘-Z command.

Zoom in the spreadsheet means zoom in to see the formulas or zoom out to see the results.

Check out your worksheet by comparing your formulas with those shown in Figure 5-8.

✓ CHECKPOINT

In the next section, you are going to print your file. What should you do before you print?

A WORD OF CAUTION:

If you make an error such as attempting to print a report when there are no printers connected to your computer, AppleWorks may hang (get stuck). The only way to fix this condition is to restart AppleWorks. This means that your file will be lost. To protect yourself, always save your file before you print even if the instruction to save is not part of the listed command sequence. Save your file now to get ready for the next section of this unit.

PRINTING THE SPREADSHEET

It is quite helpful to be able to examine both the results and the formulas used to produce the results. It is even more helpful to have the formulas in printed form. To make a **hard copy** (a paper copy) of the formulas that you may use for future reference:

WHAT YOU TYPE	WHY YOU TYPE IT
⌘-Z	To display the formulas on the screen if they are not already showing. Make sure that the printer is turned on and is selected.
⌘-H	To print a hard copy of the screen.

The Open-Apple-H command produces a hard copy of whatever is showing on the screen. It can be used with the Word Processor, the Data Base, or the Spreadsheet.

To print the results of your calculations, first display them on the screen and then print a hard copy.

WHAT YOU TYPE	WHY YOU TYPE IT
⌘-Z	To display the calculation results.
⌘-H	To print a hard copy of the screen.

The spreadsheet can also be printed with the Open-Apple-P command. The questions and your responses are almost identical to those for the Data Base.

What You Type	Why You Type It
⌘-P	To start the print process.
<RETURN>	To select **all** of the spreadsheet.
A Number <RETURN>	To select your printer.
Today's Date <RETURN>	To enter the date.
<RETURN>	To select one copy.

The spreadsheet prints in a report form. The column letters and row numbers do not appear on the report. The date you entered, the file name, and a page number do appear on the report.

TOTALING COLUMNS

You want to know the total amount that you have put into savings for the ten month period. In addition, you want to find the total income and expense over the same time period. You will use the formula **@SUM** for this. The formula is used in the same way as @AVG which was discussed earlier in this unit. As practice activity for what you have learned in this chapter, you will use three different methods to enter the formulas, 1. straight typing, 2. pointing, and 3. copying from another cell.

GUIDED ACTIVITY: SUM

	What You Type	Why You Type It
1.	<Arrows>	To move to cell B15.
	"---------	To underscore column B.
	<RIGHT-ARROW> twice	To move to cell D15.
	"---------	To underscore column D.
	<RIGHT-ARROW> twice	To move to cell F15.
	"---------	To underscore column F.
	<Arrows>	To move the cell locator to cell B16.
	@SUM(B4.B15)	To enter the formula in cell B15. (The computer adds two additional periods into the middle of the formula when you press an arrow key. You only type one period.)
2.	<Arrows>	To move to cell D16.
	@SUM(	To start the formula entry.
	<UP-ARROW> 12 times	To move to cell D4.
	.	To enter the three dots.
	<DOWN-ARROW> 11 times	To move to cell D15.
	<RETURN>	To signal the end of the range.
	) <RETURN>	To complete the formula and calculation.

3.   The cursor should be in cell D16
        &-C   To start the copy process.
        <RETURN>   To select **Within worksheet**.
        <RETURN>   To specify D16 as the source.
        <RIGHT-ARROW> twice   To move to cell F16.
        <RETURN>   To specify F16 as the new location.
        R twice   To make both the cell references relative.

The formula range, B4...B15, includes the dash line labels at the beginning and end of the values. The dashed lines are not included in the total calculation in any way. The reason for including them in the range will be revealed in the next spreadsheet unit, Mastering the Spreadsheet.

Your finished worksheet should now match the one shown in Figure 5-9.

```
========A========B========C========D========E========F========G========H====
 1|Income and Expense for the School Year
 2|
 3|    Month Income    minus Expenses    =    Savings
 4|-------------------------------------------------------
 5|    1.00    125.00    minus    65.00    =    60.00
 6|    2.00    129.00    minus    65.00    =    64.00
 7|    3.00    133.00    minus    65.00    =    68.00
 8|    4.00    137.00    minus    65.00    =    72.00
 9|    5.00    141.00    minus    65.00    =    76.00
10|    6.00    145.00    minus    65.00    =    80.00
11|    7.00    149.00    minus    65.00    =    84.00
12|    8.00    153.00    minus    65.00    =    88.00
13|    9.00    157.00    minus    65.00    =    92.00
14|   10.00    161.00    minus    65.00    =    96.00
15|           ---------           ---------        ---------
16|         1,430.00           650.00           780.00
-------------------------------------------------------------------
D16:  (Value)  @SUM(D4...D15)
```

FIGURE 5-9. Completed Income and Expense Spreadsheet.

REMOVING A FILE FROM THE DESKTOP

You created the income spreadsheet for practice. Since the file does not contain any information that you would want to store on your disk, let's get rid of it.

    Press <ESCAPE> to return to the Main Menu.
    Select option 4. **Remove files from the Desktop.**

The name of the file that you have just created is displayed and highlighted.

Press <RETURN> to indicate that you wish to remove it from the Desktop.

The computer informs you that you have just created this file and suggests that you save it. Ignore its suggestion and

Select option 3. **Throw out the new file.**
Type: Y to say yes you are sure that you want to do this.

The file is gone. You did not save it on your disk, where it would take up room unnecessarily. You do not have it in electronic form anywhere, and it is not taking room on your desktop and this is just as you wish.

WHAT YOU'VE LEARNED

You created a spreadsheet of over 100 cells. You can easily move the cell locator from one location to another, enter values or labels into a cell, and format the information in a cell in several different ways. In addition, you are now expert in copying information from cell to cell.

REVIEW QUESTIONS

1. What characters indicate a value is to be entered into a cell?

2. What characters indicate that a label is to be entered into a cell?

3. Name two ways to move the cell locator to cell X109.

4. What are the dimensions of the AppleWorks Spreadsheet?

5. Explain the difference between using Open-Apple-V to change the format and using Open-Apple-L.

6. What Open-Apple combination is used to edit the contents of a cell?

7. Explain how you would enter the label   1st Downs.

8. What do #'s in a cell indicate?

9. Cell A1 has the value 1234.654 in it. If ⌘-L is used to change the layout of cell, what will be displayed when the value format below is selected?

    a. Commas, 0 decimal places
    b. Dollars, 2 decimal places
    c. Commas, 2 decimal places
    d. Fixed, 4 decimal places
    e. Fixed, 1 decimal place
    f. Standard

10. What results are displayed if the following calculations are entered into a cell of the AppleWorks Spreadsheet?

    a. 22+10/2
    b. (22+10)/2
    c. 22+(10/2)
    d. 80+90+100/3
    e. 10/5*2
    f. 10/(5*2)
    g. 5+10/5+2*3
    h. 5+(10/5)+(2*3)
    i. (((5+10)/5)+2)*3

11. What results are displayed if the following calculations are entered into a cell of the AppleWorks Spreadsheet?

    a. 11/01/88
    b. "11/01/88

EXERCISES

5.1   Construct a multiplication table. Make the table flexible enough so that changing the value of one cell will change the table. An example of a nine times table is given below.

```
Multiplication Table
**********************************************
      9      X          1      =          9
      9      X          2      =         18
      9      X          3      =         27
      9      X          4      =         36
      9      X          5      =         45
      9      X          6      =         54
      9      X          7      =         63
      9      X          8      =         72
      9      X          9      =         81
      9      X         10      =         90
      9      X         11      =         99
      9      X         12      =        108
```

Change one number in your worksheet so that your table becomes an 8 times table. Change a second number so your table shows the products 8 X 41 to 8 X 52. Print out a hard copy of the formulas that you used. Print a report showing the 8 times table. Hand in both reports to your instructor.

5.2   Construct a spreadsheet to compute the average number of miles per gallon for each of the four cars in the table below. Also, compute the total number of miles and the total number of gallons for the four cars.

Car	Miles	Gallons Used
1	432	26.3
2	512	34.5
3	329	16.1
4	912	30.4

5.3   An old problem suggests that you work for thirty days and be paid as follows. A penny for the first day, two pennies for the second day, four for the third day, and so on (your money doubles for each day that you work until day 30). Determine how much money you would get each day for the thirty days. Determine the total that you would earn under this system. Do this by creating a spreadsheet with two columns, one for days and one for money. HINT: To double the value in cell B1 and store the result in B2, enter the formula 2*B1 in cell B2.

Print out a hard copy of the formulas that you used. Print a report showing the values in the spreadsheet. Hand in both reports to your instructor.

5.4 Keep track of your income and expenses for one week. Construct a worksheet similar to this:

	Mon	Tue	Wed	Thu	Fri	Sat	Sun	Total
EXPENSES								
food								
car								
clothes								
dates								
donations								
movies								
misc.								
TOTAL								
INCOME								
allowance								
salary								
interest								
other								
TOTAL								
SAVINGS								

Print out a hard copy of the formulas that you used. Print a report showing the values in the spreadsheet. Hand in both reports to your instructor.

APPLICATION

B   A CALCULATION COLLECTION

Your instructor will assign one or more of the following problems to you. The first problem is an example that might be used in a home or school wood shop. The second problem might be found in a business office or business class. The third problem might be found in an Earth Science class.

1. THE A-FRAME

You have been asked to build a dog house. The local lumber yard has a pamphlet with plans for the house that you want, an A-frame dog house. Included in the pamphlet is a list of materials you would need to build the dog house. Figure B-1 shows the material list along with the prices that the salesmen gives you.

Quantity	Material	Cost/Unit	Cost
1.0	8' long 4" x 4" pressure treated lumber	$5.59	
5.0	2" x 3" lumber - stud grade	$1.49	
2.5	4' x 8' x 7/16" wafer board panels	$6.99	
18.0	Ty-plates (A-5)	$.27	
12.0	Right Angle Framing Plates	$.33	
1.0	6d nails (pound)	$.59	
3.0	8d nails 1 1/2" long (pound)	$.69	
		Total	

FIGURE B-1.   Material List for A-Frame Dog House.

The amount that you spend for each item on the list is found by multiplying the Cost/Unit by the quantity. The total cost of the dog house is found by finding the sum of the costs for each individual item.

YOUR TASK

Enter the information in Figure B-1 into a spreadsheet. Enter formulas into the last column to calculate the cost of each item. Enter a formula to find the sum of the individual costs. Print out the information in the spreadsheet. Print out a hard copy of the formulas you used. Turn in this information to your teacher.

2. TAKING STOCK

You have made modest investments in the stock market. You decide to build a spreadsheet to total your investments. Your investments are shown in Figure B-2. The figure also shows the dollar value per each share of stock.

```
Stock                         # Shares   $/Share    Value
------------------------------------------------------------
Integrated Apple Works              40   $36.000
Robert's Spreadsheet Service       300     $.875
Mom's Apple Pie Company             75    $5.500
Lyon's Share Oil                    15   $91.750
E. F. Button Keyboards           2,000     $.125
```

FIGURE B-2.   Stock Investments.

The value for all of the shares of a stock is found by multiplying the number of shares by the dollar amount each share is worth ($/Share). The total value of all on the stock is found by taking the sum of the amounts in the value column.

YOUR TASK

Enter the information in Figure B-2 into a spreadsheet. Enter formulas into the last column to calculate the value of each stock. Enter a formula to find the sum of the values. Print out the information in the spreadsheet. Print out a hard copy of the formulas you used. Turn in this information to your teacher.

3. WEIGHTED CALCULATIONS

Because each planet has a different mass and size, how much you weigh depends on what planet you get weighed on. The following table shows what a person who weighs 100 pounds on Earth would weigh on some of the other planets in our solar system.

Earth	100 pounds	
Mercury	39 pounds	(Multiply 100 by 0.39)
Venus	91 pounds	(Multiply 100 by .91)
Mars	38 pounds	(Multiply 100 by ??)
Jupiter	264 pounds	(Multiple 100 by 2.64)
Neptune	141 pounds	(Multiply 100 by ??)

YOUR TASK

Construct a spreadsheet to calculate a person's weight on these five planets , given the number of pounds a person weighs on Earth. Print out the information in the spreadsheet for at least two different Earth weights. Print out a hard copy of the formulas you used. Turn in this information to your teacher.

AN ADDITIONAL (OR ALTERNATIVE) TASK

It is possible to compute a person's Earth weight given his or her weight on another planet. For example, a person who weighs 140 on Earth weighs 140 x 0.39 = 54.6 on Mercury. If a person's weight on Mercury is 54.6 pounds, his Earth weight is 54.6 divided by 0.39 or 140 pounds. You can convert weight on any planet back to weight on Earth by dividing by the number you had originally multiplied by. Once you have Earth weight, you can again calculate weight on the other planets as you did above.

Modify your spreadsheet so that the information given can be weight on any of the six planets and the spreadsheet displays weight on all of the other planets. (Hint - You may want to supply both the weight on a given planet and the multiplication factor to get from weight on Earth to weight on that planet.) Print out and hand in the same information requested above.

2

INTERMEDIATE APPLEWORKS OPERATIONS

UNIT

6 MASTERING THE WORD PROCESSOR

LEARNING OBJECTIVES

1. After completing this unit, you should know ...

   a. how to enhance the printed appearance of a word processor document.

   b. time-saving features that can be used in entering a document.

   c. why you would revise a document's vertical spacing format.

   d. why you would use boldface and underline.

   e. the difference between the copy and the move commands.

2. After completing this unit, you should be able to ...

   a. change the margins in a document.

   b. select single-, double-, or triple-spacing for all or part of a document.

   c. underline parts of a document or make them boldface.

   d. modify the tab settings.

   e. use the find and replace text commands.

   f. use the copy and move text commands.

   g. use indenting to produce outline formats.

ASSIGNMENTS

1. MARGINS: Change the top, bottom, left, and right margins in a document.

2. SPACING: Examine single-, double-, and triple-spacing.

3. EMPHASIZE: Add boldface and underlining to make a document easier to read.

4. FORMAT: Revise a document to produce a newspaper format.

5. OUTLINE: Create an outline using tabs.

6. FORM OUTLINE: Create an outline from a form.

IMPORTANT KEYSTROKES AND COMMANDS

COMMAND KEYS	MEANING
Ć-C	Copy text.
Ć-M	Move text.
Ć-F	Find text.
Ć-R	Replace text.
Ć-T	Set Tab stops.

Print formatting options:

Control-L	Underline begin or end.
Ć-O, UB	Underline begin.
Ć-O, UE	Underline end.
Control-B	Boldface begin or end.
Ć-O, BB	Boldface begin.
Ć-O, BE	Boldface end.
Ć-O, BM	Set bottom margin.
Ć-O, LM	Set left margin.
Ć-O, RM	Set right margin.
Ć-O, TM	Set top margin.
Ć-O, SS	Set single spacing.
Ć-O, DS	Set double spacing.
Ć-O, TS	Set triple spacing.
Ć-O, IN	Set indent.
Ć-O, JU	Start justify.
Ć-O, P1	Set proportional 1 type size (elite).
Ć-O, P2	Set proportional 2 type size (pica).

There are two basic operations in the Word Processor. The first is adding, reviewing, and modifying the text of the file. The Unit, Getting Started with The Word Processor, introduced that process and this unit continues it.

The second operation is **formatting** the text. Formatting lets you plan how the text will look on the printed page. With proper formatting, a good document looks great and a great document looks excellent. With formatting, you can specify the size of the margins , where boldface and underlining start and end, what size characters to use, and so on. You can easily change the format of your text even after you have typed it and printed it several times. Thus you can change the way your text looks almost as easily as you can change a word or a character. In this unit you will learn how to present what you have written in the best possible format.

Modifying Print Options

If you have ever designed the layout of a page on a typewriter, you know how difficult a task that can be. Word processors simplify the formatting job considerably. Short documents can easily be reformatted, evaluated, and printed several times to obtain the most desirable results. Before you start to experiment with margins, double- and triple-spacing, boldface, and underline, you should examine the default settings for these options.

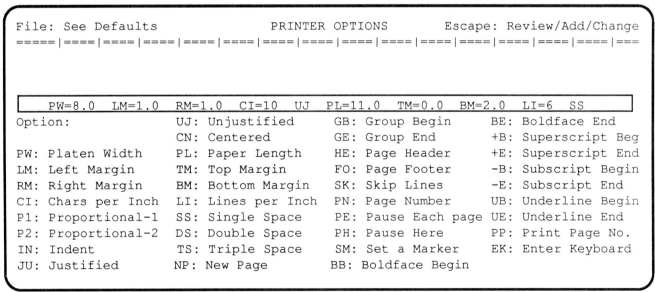

```
File: See Defaults                PRINTER OPTIONS          Escape: Review/Add/Change
=====|====|====|====|====|====|====|====|====|====|====|====|====|====|====|===



    PW=8.0   LM=1.0   RM=1.0   CI=10   UJ   PL=11.0   TM=0.0   BM=2.0   LI=6   SS
Option:                  UJ: Unjustified      GB: Group Begin      BE: Boldface End
                         CN: Centered         GE: Group End        +B: Superscript Beg
PW: Platen Width         PL: Paper Length     HE: Page Header      +E: Superscript End
LM: Left Margin          TM: Top Margin       FO: Page Footer      -B: Subscript Begin
RM: Right Margin         BM: Bottom Margin    SK: Skip Lines       -E: Subscript End
CI: Chars per Inch       LI: Lines per Inch   PN: Page Number      UB: Underline Begin
P1: Proportional-1       SS: Single Space     PE: Pause Each page  UE: Underline End
P2: Proportional-2       DS: Double Space     PH: Pause Here       PP: Print Page No.
IN: Indent               TS: Triple Space     SM: Set a Marker     EK: Enter Keyboard
JU: Justified            NP: New Page         BB: Boldface Begin
```

FIGURE 6-1.   Printer Options List.

Start AppleWorks if it is not already in the computer   or
<ESCAPE> to the Main Menu if AppleWorks is running.
Select **Add files to the Desktop.**
Select **Make a new file for: The Word Processor.**

Select from **Scratch.**
Name the file   See Defaults
Press <RETURN>
Display the printer options with the command ⌂-O.

As you can see, the printer options are given to the computer as two character codes. All 37 options and their corresponding two-character codes are listed on your screen and in Figure 6-1. The highlighted bar near the center of the screen indicates the default settings. Reading from left to right across the bar, the codes, their default settings, and their meanings are as follows:

CODE	MEANING
PW=8.0	The platen width is the standard 8 inch platen; this is the width of most printer carriages. The two most common settings, 8 and 13.2 inches, are used for normal and wide-carriage printers, respectively. Eight-inch printers can not accommodate the larger platen or paper size. Acceptable values for PW range from 1.5 to 13.2 inches.
LM=1.0	The left printing margin is set to 1 inch. That is, printing starts 1 inch from the left edge of the paper. Left margin values are given in tenths of an inch, for example, .3, 1.6, or 2.5 are ok. Acceptable values for LM are 0 to 9 inches.
RM=1.0	The right printing margin is set to 1 inch in from the right edge of the paper. Right margin values are also given in tenths of an inch. The standard width of the printed area is 6 inches (8 inches minus 1 inch each for the left and right margins). In general, the width of the printed line is platen width minus the left margin width, minus the right margin width (PW-LM-RM). This value should be larger than zero. Acceptable values for RM are 0 through 9 inches.
CI=10	The characters-per-inch setting is 10 characters in one horizontal inch, this is sometimes referred to as pica pitch. Acceptable values for CI are 4 through 24 characters. Not all values work with all printers.
UJ	The text is unjustified on the right. The right edge is ragged and the left edge is straight. Other characters that appear in this location on the highlighted bar are CN for centered text and JU for text that is straight on both the left and right margins.
PL=11.0	The paper length is 11 inches including headers, footers, the text printed on the page, and the top and bottom margins. One reason to change paper length is to print mailing labels, which are usually one inch long. Acceptable values for PL are 1 through 25 inches.
TM=0.0	The top margin is 0.0 inches. Printing starts at the top line of the paper. (See the next paragraph.) Acceptable values for TM are 0 through 9 inches.

BM=2.0   The bottom margin is set to 2 inches from the bottom of the paper. Note: If the paper is rolled forward in the printer a few lines, it may appear that the top margin is greater than 0 and the bottom margin is less than 2 inches. This margin setting makes paper adjustment easier on most printers (start the paper forward a few lines). Acceptable values for BM are 0 through 9 inches.

LI=6   Six lines are printed for every vertical inch inside the top and bottom margins. Most printers are capable of either 6 or 8 lines to the inch. The number of lines, including blank lines, printed at 6 lines per inch on 11 inch paper with a 2 inch bottom margin is 54 ((11-2)*6). Acceptable values for LI are 6 or 8 lines.

The default settings can be changed as desired where ever in the document a change is needed.

When the left and right margins are set to 0 inches and the platen width is set to 8 inches, there is still a 1/4 inch margin on the left and right of 8 1/2" paper. (8 1/2 - 8 = 1/2 inch extra space. Half of the 1/2 inch space is on either side of the printed area so there is 1/4 inch on each side.) This means that a 1-inch margin really measures closer to 1 1/4 inches; a 3/4 inch margin measures close to 1 inch, and so on.

Some printer commands such as boldface and underlining begin with the next character printed. Changes in options such as characters per inch or right margin affect the next line, yet others such as top margin affect the next page printed. For example, changing the top margin to 1 inch in the middle of page three does not affect page three; it changes the top margin on page four and on any following pages.

MARGINS

Lounge, the story that you entered in Unit 3 is to be used for the school newspaper. As part of the process of preparing the story for the paper, it is first printed double-spaced for proofreading and for corrections by the paper's editor. After the corrections, if any, are entered, the article is reprinted in a 2 1/2 inch wide column and pasted into the newspaper layout.

Let's simulate this process. First you will print out the story for the editor's corrections, making the following format changes: set the top margin to one inch, set the left and right margins to 1.5 inches (the editor likes lots of margin room to write in), and change the spacing to double-space.

GUIDED ACTIVITY: MARGINS

Bring Lounge back to the display screen with one of the two methods below.

If "Lounge" is not on your Desktop:

Press <ESCAPE> to return to the Main Menu.
Highlight **Add files to the Desktop** and press <RETURN>.
Get the file from your disk.
When the file appears, press <ESCAPE> to return to the Main Menu.

If "Lounge" is on your Desktop:

Press <ESCAPE> to return to the Main Menu.

(If you already have this file on your Desktop, do not add another copy of the file to the Desktop. Having two copies of one file on the Desktop will confuse both the computer and you. If you are ever informed "You are about to have more than one copy of this file on the Desktop." and asked, "Do you really want to do this?", your response should be no. When this happens, you should return to the Main Menu and select "Work with one of the files on the Desktop.")

You now have two different files on the Desktop, Lounge and See Defaults.

Highlight **Work with one of the files on the desktop.** Press <RETURN>.
Highlight the file **Lounge** and press <RETURN>

When the story appears in the display, you are ready to make your changes. The steps are:

WHAT YOU TYPE		WHY YOU TYPE IT
⌂-1		To move to the beginning of the text.
⌂-O		To display printer options.
TM	<RETURN>	To indicate a top margin change to a new value of
1	<RETURN>	one inch.
LM	<RETURN>	To indicate a left margin change to a new value of
1.5	<RETURN>	1.5 inches.
RM	<RETURN>	To indicate a right margin change to a new value of
1.5	<RETURN>	1.5 inches.
DS	<RETURN>	To double-space.

Note that the new values you have entered are indicated in the highlighted line in the center of the screen.

Press <ESCAPE> to exit the options menu and return to the story.

The display line length is reduced to reflect the tighter left and right margins. No change is made in the screen display to indicate the new value for the top margin or double-spacing.

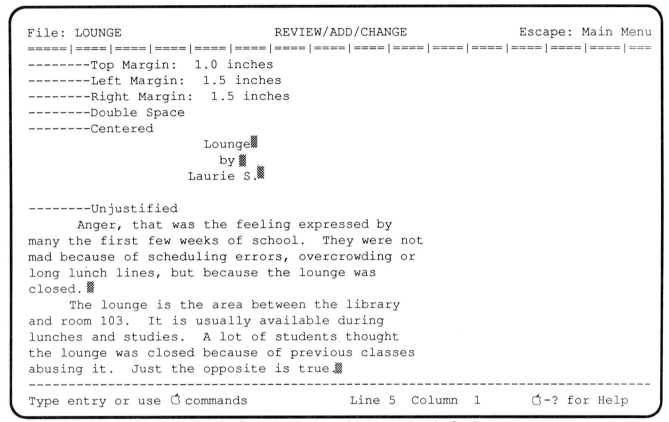

FIGURE 6-2. Screen Display with New Margin Settings.

If the printer commands are not showing, give the ⌃-Z command to zoom in.

The printer commands

```
-------Top Margin: 1.0 inches
-------Double Space
```

appear with other commands at the top of the screen. Figures 6-2 and 6-3 are respectively a screen display showing the changes and a print out showing the effect of these changes.

> Print the modified Lounge Story.
> Write your name and the format settings you used on the back of your printout sheet.

Changing back to the original settings can be accomplished in one of two ways. The first way is to add new settings positioned after the first settings. Let's change the top margin this way.

```
                         Lounge

                           by

                        Laurie S.


    Anger, that was the feeling expressed by

many the first few weeks of school.  They were not

mad because of scheduling errors, overcrowding or

long lunch lines, but because the lounge was

closed.

    The lounge is the area between the library

and room 103.  It is usually available during

lunches and studies.  A lot of students thought

the lounge was closed because of previous classes

abusing it.  Just the opposite is true.

    The lounge was closed for safety reasons.  A

broken air conditioner was spread out over the

benches waiting to be fixed.  It took longer for

this to be taken care of because the town

maintenance crew had to fix it, not High School

custodians.

    The lounge was not closed because of abuse.

Our principal said that students have always kept

the area clean and used it at the proper times.

                    The End
```

FIGURE 6-3. Printout with New Margin Settings.

GUIDED ACTIVITY: MARGINS   (continued)

WHAT YOU TYPE	WHY YOU TYPE IT
(◕-Z)	If they are not visible, zoom in to show the printer settings.
◕-1	To move to the beginning of the text.
<DOWN-ARROW> 4 times	To move below the original **Top Margin** setting.
◕-O	To display the printer options.
TM <RETURN>	To change the top margin.
2 <RETURN>	To enter the "new" value for top margin.
<ESCAPE>	To return to the text.

AppleWorks follows this rule for printer settings: the last valid printer setting is the one used; if no setting is given, the default setting is used. The last top margin setting is 2 inches so that is the setting that is used when the document is printed again.

Print the file to verify that the change worked.
Write your name and the printer settings used for this printout on the back of the printout sheet.
Compare this printout with the first one you made. Remember, the the top and bottom margins are controlled by the settings in the document and by the position of the paper in the printer when you start to print.
Keep both papers together for later use.

If you wish to change a printer setting to a value other than the original default value, move the cursor to the position where you want the change to begin and insert the setting.

The second way to change back to the original settings is to delete the unwanted setting. When a printer command is deleted, the last setting (the default in this case) is used.

The delete key does not delete printer commands. Open-Apple-D must be used. To delete printer commands, follow these steps:

GUIDED ACTIVITY: MARGINS   (continued)

WHAT YOU TYPE	WHY YOU TYPE IT
(◕-Z)	If they are not showing, display the printer commands and Return blots.
◕-1	To move to the beginning of the document.
◕-D	To start the delete process.
<DOWN-ARROW> 4 times	To highlight the first five printer commands.
<RETURN>	To complete the delete process.

The text width changes to reflect the default margin settings.

✓ CHECKPOINT

What does default mean? What are the default margin settings?

SINGLE-, DOUBLE- AND TRIPLE-SPACING

Some of the documents that you print require single-spaced printouts while others require double-spaced printouts. Yet others require a combination of single- and double-spaced printing. When you are working on a document, it is sometimes helpful to print a triple-spaced draft copy. You then have plenty of room for your editing notes.

GUIDED ACTIVITY: SPACING

Make the title and bylines double-spaced, and make the rest of the story triple-spaced. You need two printer commands to do this. At the beginning of the file, insert the command to double-space. At the beginning of the first paragraph, insert the command to triple-space. Here is the command sequence:

WHAT YOU TYPE	WHY YOU TYPE IT
⌘-1	To move the cursor to the top of the file.
⌘-O	To display the printer options.
DS <RETURN>	To insert the double-space option.
<ESCAPE>	To return to the text.
ARROWS	To move down to the beginning of the first paragraph.
⌘-O	To display the printer options.
TS <RETURN>	To set the triple-space option.
<ESCAPE>	To return to the text.

Print the file and examine the changes.

On the Imagewriter printer, "The End" is on a separate page.

⌘-9   To move to the end of the document .

The display shows that two pages were printed. (This happens on the Imagewriter; it may not happen on your printer.) The second page contains only "The   End" and a blank line. The "- - End of Page - -" line does not necessarily mean that the page is full, only that the page ends at this point. Figure 6-4 shows this screen display.

It would save some paper if we could determine where the pages ended before we printed the document. Let's change the bottom margin to 1 inch and determine if the file would then print on one page. Follow these steps:

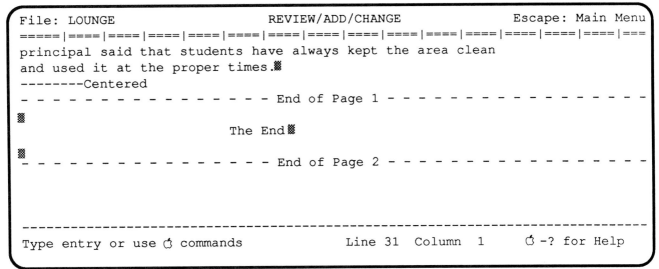

FIGURE 6-4.   Display Showing Page Breaks.

GUIDED ACTIVITY: SPACING   (continued)

WHAT YOU TYPE	WHY YOU TYPE IT
⌘-1	To move to the beginning of the text.
⌘-O	To display printer options.
BM \<RETURN>	To change the Bottom Margin to a new value of
1 \<RETURN>	1 inch.
\<ESCAPE>	To return to the text.
⌘-9	To display the end of the text.
⌘-K	To **calculate page breaks** or page divisions (the calculate pages command uses ⌘-K since ⌘-C is already used for the copy command).
Arrows	To highlight your printer. (Remember, the arrows you use and the number of times you use them are up to you. The lowercase lettering is shown when you need to decide if a key is used and exactly how it is used.)
\<RETURN>	To select the printer.

After the calculation, a message appears in the display at the end of the text to indicate that only one page is needed. Print the text to verify this, if you wish. The printout appears on one page with the bylines double-spaced and the paragraphs triple-spaced.

Let's make one last change to reinforce an earlier concept.

GUIDED ACTIVITY: SPACING (continued)

WHAT YOU TYPE	WHY YOU TYPE IT
⌂-Z	To show the printer commands.
Arrows	To move the cursor to the **Triple Space** command line (the cursor can be anywhere on the line).
⌂-D <RETURN>	To delete the triple-space command.

Think about the following question: If the file is printed now, what spacing is used for the paragraphs? It is not necessary to print the file to answer the question.

Move the cursor to any location in any of the paragraphs.
Issue the ⌂-O command.

The right end of the highlighted line shows "DS" to indicate double-spacing here. When the triple-space command was deleted, the spacing reverted to the last spacing command given. This was the double-space command at the start of the file, not the default command (single-space).

Press <ESCAPE> to return to the text.

The last activity added another concept: to determine the format settings of the file at any point in the file, move to that point, press Open-Apple-O, and examine the highlighted line in the center of the screen.

BOLDFACE AND UNDERLINE

The readability of your document can be improved by the correct use of **boldface** and **underline**. For example, words that are new to the reader can be easily found if they are printed in boldface type as they are in the previous sentence. You would emphasize a particular word or the <u>title of a book</u> by underlining it.

There are two ways to boldface and/or underline text. One way uses more keystrokes than the other. Let's look at the longer way first. When you display the printer options, you find the four boldface and underline options: BB: Boldface Begin, BE: Boldface End, UB: Underline Begin, and UE: Underline End. Let's use these options to underline the title of the story.

GUIDED ACTIVITY: EMPHASIZE

Move the cursor to the letter "L" in the word "Lounge" in the title.

Next, follow this sequence:

WHAT YOU TYPE	WHY YOU TYPE IT
-O	To display the printer options.
UB <RETURN>	To set underline begin.
<ESCAPE>	To return to the text.
Arrows	To move the cursor to the space at the end of the word "Lounge".
-O	To display the printer options again.
UE <RETURN>	To set underline end.
<ESCAPE>	To return to the text.

The caret symbol (^) appears in the text at the beginning and the end of the title. This symbol is a printer setting command and is not printed on the paper copy. As other printer settings do, it tells the printer to perform some special operation. To determine what that special operation is, move the cursor under the caret. The bottom center of the screen displays a message indicating the special printer operation for that caret. Try it. The first caret message is: **Underline Begin**. The second is: **Underline End.**

Let's underline the sentence "Just the opposite is true." the easy way.

WHAT YOU TYPE	WHY YOU TYPE IT
Arrows	To move the cursor to the "J" in "Just".
Hold down <CONTROL>	To start a control command. Control commands are typed the same way that the Open-Apple commands are typed.
L	To give the **Control-L** command. The caret is displayed.
Release <CONTROL>	
LEFT-ARROW	To verify that this caret represents "Underline Begin". Observe the message in the lower center of the display.
Arrows	To move the cursor to the space after the period following "true."
CONTROL-L	To give the command again and display another caret.
LEFT-ARROW	To verify that the second caret represents "Underline End".

To remove an underline, you would delete the carets. Let's make the title and the bylines boldface instead of underline.

WHAT YOU TYPE	WHY YOU TYPE IT
Arrows	To move the cursor to the "L" in "Lounge" in the title.
<DELETE>	To remove the "Underline Begin" caret.
CONTROL-B	To start boldface for the title.

Arrows	To move to the space (or Return blot) after the caret at the end of the title.
<DELETE>	To remove the "Underline End" caret.
CONTROL-B	To end boldface.
Arrows	To move to the "b" in "by".
CONTROL-B	To start boldface.
Arrows	To move to the space after the "y".
CONTROL-B	To end boldface.

On your own, make "Laurie S." boldface.

Move the cursor to each caret and verify that it correctly represents **Boldface   Begin** at the start of the line and **Boldface End** at the end of the line.

Boldface and underlines end automatically at the end of a paragraph when the Return is detected. So there is no danger of boldfacing or underlining all of the text in the file because you missed a boldface or underline end command.

Print the file to see the effect of your changes.
Write your name on the back of the printout.
Write on the back of the printout which printer options you used.

✓ **CHECKPOINT**

What word or words, if any, should be underlined in the sentence below? What word or words, if any, should be boldfaced?

Understanding and Using AppleWorks by Frank Short has helped to make me more productive with the computer.

GUIDED ACTIVITY: FORMAT

The changes the editor suggests are back; you're ready to enter them and print the final copy of the article for the paper. Here are the changes and the requirements for the final printout.

Changes:

1. Change the title to LOUNGE CLOSED.
2. Put by Laurie S. on one line.
3. Delete the blank line between the byline and the first paragraph.
4. Remove the blank line and "The End" from the end of the story.

The following steps will make the required changes:

WHAT YOU TYPE	WHY YOU TYPE IT
1. Arrows	To move to the boldface end caret after the word "Lounge".
<DELETE> five times	To delete "ounge".
"OUNGE CLOSED	To insert the new title.
2. Arrows	To move the cursor to the "L" in "Laurie S."
<DELETE> four times	To remove the two carets and the line return blot. Now "by" and "Laurie S." are on one line.
<SPACE BAR>	A space is inserted between "by" and "Laurie".
3. <DOWN-ARROW>	The cursor moves to the blank line.
⌘-D	The blank line is highlighted.
<RETURN>	The blank line is removed.
4. ⌘-9	Move to the end of the document.
⌘-D	The blank line under "The End is highlighted.
<UP-ARROW> three times	"The End", another blank line, and the centering command are highlighted.
<RETURN>	The lines are removed.

Printout Requirements:

1. Make the width of the print out 2.5 inches. To do this set the left margin to 2.5 and the right margin to 3. (2.5 = 8 - 2.5 - 3)
2. No underlines are allowed.
3. The title is in boldface, 8 characters per inch. (Use 5 or 10 if your printer can not print 8.)
4. Title and bylines are centered.
5. Paragraphs are justified.
6. Proportional pica (P2) characters are used for the paragraphs. (If your printer does not print proportional, use 10 characters per inch.)

To set the printout requirements you need to:

WHAT YOU TYPE		WHY YOU TYPE IT
1. ⌘-1		To move to the top of the document.
⌘-O		To display the printer options.
LM	<RETURN>	
2.5	<RETURN>	To set the left margin to 2.5.
RM	<RETURN>	
3	<RETURN>	To set the right margin to 3.

TM	<RETURN>	
1	<RETURN>	To set the top margin to 1 inch.
<ESCAPE>		To return to the text.

2. Arrows   To move to the "J" in "Just".
    <DELETE>   To remove the Underline Begin caret.
    Arrows   To move to the right of the caret in "true.^".
    <DELETE>   Remove the Underline End caret.

3. Arrows   To move to the "L" in "LOUNGE".
    CONTROL-B   To set bold begin.
    ⌘-O   Display the printer options.
    CI   <RETURN>
    8   <RETURN>   To set 8 characters per inch.
    <ESCAPE>   To return to the text.
    Arrows   To move to the space at the end of "CLOSED".
    CONTROL-B   To set bold end. (This step was not really necessary since boldface ends automatically at the Return Blot.)

LOUNGE CLOSED
by Laurie S.

Anger, that was the feeling expressed by many the first few weeks of school. They were not mad because of scheduling errors, overcrowding or long lunch lines, but because the lounge was closed.

The lounge is the area between the library and room 103. It is usually available during lunches and studies. A lot of students thought the lounge was closed because of previous classes abusing it. Just the opposite is true.

The lounge was closed for safety reasons. A broken air conditioner was spread out over the benches waiting to be fixed. It took longer for this to be taken care of because the town maintenance crew had to fix it, not High School custodians.

The lounge was not closed because of abuse. Our principal said that students have always kept the area clean and used it at the proper times.

FIGURE 6-5. Article Printed in Newspaper Format.

4. The title and bylines should already be centered.

5.	Arrows	To move the cursor to the line containing the printer command:
		------Unjustified
	○-D <RETURN>	To delete the unjustified command.
	○-O	To display the printer options.
	JU <RETURN>	To set the justify option.
	<ESCAPE>	To return to the text.
6.	○-1	To move to the beginning of the text.
	<Down-arrow>	To move down to the byline.
	○-O	To display the printer options.
	P2 <RETURN>	To set the P2 proportional type style.
	<ESCAPE>	To return to the text.

Print the story. It should appear as it does in Figure 6-5.

TABS

Outlines are useful for a great number of things. You have probably been asked more times that you would care to count to produce an outline for a project, paper, or class. For the remainder of this unit you'll look at ways to enter information in an outline form.

There are several ways to enter outlines into the word processor. In this unit, you'll use three distinctly different methods to create an outline that might be a science class assignment.

The first method uses the **TAB** key. Try this:

> Add a new file to the Desktop. (Name it Tab.)
> Press <TAB> a few times and observer the cursor movement.
>
> Press ○-TAB a few times and observe the cursor movement again.

Each time you press Tab, the cursor moves five spaces right to the next tab stop. Each time you press Open-Apple-Tab, the cursor moves five spaces left to the previous tab stop. The tab stops are already set for each new document at positions 6, 11, 16, and so forth. The settings are indicated by the vertical lines in the row of equal signs near the top of the screen. You can change these settings to any position on the line. Here's how:

WHAT YOU TYPE	WHY YOU TYPE IT
○-1	To move the cursor to line 1 column 1.
○-T	To move the cursor to the Tab line.
RIGHT-ARROW 5 TIMES	To move the cursor to a tab marker line.

C	To clear the tab marker line. There is no longer a tab setting at this point.
S	To set a tab at this position. The marker line reappears.
R	To remove all tabs. All of the tab markers disappear.
Arrows	To move the cursor to column 4 (note the column indicator in the lower right corner).
S	Set a tab mark at column 4. This is the only tab mark on the line.
Arrows	To move the cursor to column 8.
S	To set another tab mark at column 8.
Arrows S	Continue to move the cursor and set tabs at columns 12 and 16.
<ESCAPE>	Exit from the tab line and return to Review/Add/Change.

WHAT YOU'VE LEARNED

Tab settings can be removed one at a time or all of them can be removed at once; they can only be inserted one at a time. The default settings for tab positions are always 6, 11, 16, 21, etc.

GUIDED ACTIVITY: OUTLINE

Most outlines have a format that is similar to this one which has indentations of 4, 8, 12, and 16.

```
        I.
            A.
                1.
                    a.
                    b.
                2.
                    a.
                    b.
            B.
                1.
                    a.
                    b.
                2.
                    a.
                    b.
        II.
```

Let's enter an outline with this format.

Make sure that your tab marks are set at 4, 8, 12, and 16 as shown above.

WHAT YOU TYPE

_____

Unit III - Light = Three forms of energy which may or may not be seen by the human eye.
<RETURN>
<RETURN>
<TAB>A.<TAB>Infrared - Invisible light known as heat.
<RETURN>
<TAB> <TAB>1.<TAB>Primary sources - produce heat
<RETURN>
<TAB> <TAB> <TAB>a.<TAB>sun
<RETURN>
<TAB> <TAB> <TAB>b.<TAB>fire
<RETURN>
<TAB> <TAB> <TAB>c.<TAB>human body

Your screen should now show this:

```
Unit III - Light = Three forms of energy which may or
may not be seen by the human eye.

     A.  Infrared - Invisible light known as heat.
       1.  Primary sources - produce heat
          a.  sun
          b.  fire
          c.  human body
```

If your screen does not match the one shown above, adjust your entries by adding or deleting spaces in the incorrect line or lines. Once you have made an entry on a line, you cannot use Tab to adjust the entry. The entry can be moved to the right or left only by adding or deleting spaces.

You will enter the next section of the outline on your own. Remember, the Tab key is pressed once before the capital letter, twice before the number, and three times before the lowercase letters. After you enter a letter or a digit, you press Tab another time before you type the information.

Practice using Tab. Enter this section of the outline:

```
       2.  Secondary sources - reflect or store heat
          a.   water
          b.   metal
          c.   stone

     B.  Visible Light - Can be seen by the human eye.
```

Copying Text

The format or framework of an outline is similar from section to section. Another way of entering an outline is to create the outline framework and then make the entries. You can use the copy command to duplicate the framework as often as needed. You will use this method as you continue the outline.

GUIDED ACTIVITY: FORM OUTLINE

Enter the following frame to continue your outline.

WHAT YOU TYPE

```
<TAB> <TAB>1.   <RETURN>
<TAB> <TAB> <TAB>a.  <RETURN>
<TAB> <TAB> <TAB>b.  <RETURN>
<TAB> <TAB> <TAB>c.  <RETURN>
<TAB> <TAB> <TAB>d.  <RETURN>
UP-ARROW  five times
```

The cursor should now be at the very beginning of the line containing the 1. You're now ready to copy this framework of the outline for part 2 of the Visible Light section.

WHAT YOU TYPE	WHY YOU TYPE IT
⌘-C	To begin the copy command.
<RETURN>	To select **Within document** for the type of copy.
<DOWN-ARROW> 5 times	To highlight the lines you typed and a blank line.
<LEFT-ARROW>	To move back a line. The blank line is no longer highlighted.
<RETURN>	To indicate that you have finished selecting the text to copy.
<DOWN-ARROW>	
⌘-LEFT-ARROW	To move to the new location for the copy, the insertion point.
<RETURN>	To complete the copy.

The outline form appears a second time on the screen. (You need to move down to see all of the entries.)

Now enter the outline information:

Move to the line under the B.

WHAT YOU TYPE	WHY YOU TYPE IT
<TAB>	To move the cursor to the insert location, the space after the 1.
Primary sources - produce visible light (DO NOT PRESS RETURN.)	

	(If you press Return, use the Delete key to erase the Return blot.)
<DOWN-ARROW>	To move down to the next line.
⌘-TAB	To move the cursor to the entry point.
sun	(DO NOT PRESS RETURN.)
<DOWN-ARROW>	To move the cursor down a line.
⌘-TAB	To move to the insertion point.
fire	(DO NOT PRESS RETURN.)
<DOWN-ARROW>	
⌘-TAB	
bulb	(DO NOT PRESS RETURN.)
<DOWN-ARROW>	
⌘-TAB	
firefly	(DO NOT PRESS RETURN.)
DOWN-ARROW	
⌘-TAB	
⌘-TAB.	

Continue to fill in the next section of the outline in the same fashion as above. You'll need to make some small changes as you go along; for example, change the 1 to a 2 for the next section. The section should read:

```
2.   Secondary sources - reflect or store visible light
     a.   glow-in-the-dark frisbee
     b.   moon
     c.   all colors
     d.   not black
```

Don't be concerned about the word light dangling off on the left. You'll go back and fix this shortly.

Notice that the two lines a. sun and b. fire are duplicated in the outline. You can use the Open-Apple-C command to copy these lines. If you have any information in your text that needs to be entered more than once, the copy command makes the job easier.

REPLACING TEXT

A third method of entering the outline involves formatting the information after you have entered it. Enter the text shown below, leaving two spaces after each period. Do not use the tab key. The text should be blocked on the screen exactly as it is shown here. Do not indent when you first enter the text.

WHAT YOU TYPE

C. Ultra Violet Light - Invisible light that causes tanning and kills many germs.
<RETURN>

```
    1. Primary sources
    <RETURN>
    a. sun
    <RETURN>
    b. sunlamp
    <RETURN>
    c. germicidal lamp
    <RETURN>
    2. Secondary sources - reflect or store ultra violet light.
    <RETURN>
    a. water
    <RETURN>
    b. aluminum foil
    <RETURN>
```

To finish formatting the outline, you'll use the replace command to automatically add spaces to the beginning of each line. There are 3 spaces in front of the lines starting with the capital letters, 7 spaces in front of the numbers, and 11 spaces in front of the lines with the lowercase letters.

When you use the replace command, you have the option of replacing **Text** or **Case sensitive text**. With the text option, if you search for X, the computer will find both X and x. With the case sensitive option, if you search for X, you will only find X, not x. Similarily, a case sensitive search for Xx does not find XX, xX, nor xx; the case must match exactly.

WHAT YOU TYPE	WHY YOU TYPE IT
UP-ARROW	To move to the line above the C.
⌂-R	To start the replace command.
C	To select **Case sensitive text** for the type of material to replace.
C. <RETURN>	To indicate that C. (C period) is the information to replace.
<SPACE BAR><SPACE BAR><SPACE BAR>C.<RETURN>	
	To indicate that C. preceded by three spaces is the new information.
<RETURN>	To elect to make the replacements one at a time.
Y	To make the first replacement.
<RETURN>	To indicate that there are no further replacements to make. (The lower case c needs 11 spaces that will be added shortly.)

Now repeat the command for the digits 1 and 2.

WHAT YOU TYPE	WHY YOU TYPE IT
Up-arrow	To move to the line above the C.
⌂-R	To start the replace command.

<RETURN>	To select **Text** for the type of material to replace.
⌘-Y	To erase the previous text.
1. <RETURN>	To identify the text (1 period) to be replaced.
⌘-Y	To erase the previous text.
<SPACE BAR> seven times 1.<RETURN>	
	To indicate the new text (7 spaces followed by 1.).
<RETURN>	To indicate one at a time replacement.
Y	To replace the first occurrence.
Y	To search for the next occurrence.

The computer indicates that no additional occurrences of 1. can be found in the text. All possible replacements have been made.

Press <SPACE BAR> to continue.

The next step is to insert the spaces for the remainder of the numbered entries (in this case only the 2. line needs to be changed). When you do this, you'll use the edit cursor to take advantage of the correct spacing already provided in the last replacement command.

WHAT YOU TYPE	WHY YOU TYPE IT
⌘-R	To start the replace command.
<RETURN>	To select **Text** for the type of material to replace.
⌘-E	To turn on the overstrike cursor.
2 <RETURN>	To replace the 1 with 2.
<RIGHT-ARROW> seven times	
2 <RETURN>	To replace 1 with 2 again.
<RETURN>	To indicate one at a time replacement.
Y <RETURN>	To make the replacement in the outline.

The changes that you are making now would make more sense if you were working with a longer outline; then a number of changes for outline spacing could be accomplished quite rapidly. The process would involve moving to the beginning of the outline and giving the replacement command for each outline level (in this example, since you have already entered the correct spacing at the beginning of the outline, you moved the cursor back to the beginning of the C level). Remember, the replacements are made from wherever the cursor is in the document to the end of the document. Now let's do the lower case levels of the outline.

WHAT YOU TYPE	WHY YOU TYPE IT
UP-ARROW	To move to the line above 1. Primary sources.
⌘-R	To start the replace command.
C	To select **Case sensitive text** for the type of material to replace.

a	To overstrike the 2 with a lowercase a.
Ú-E	To change to the insert cursor.
<RETURN>	To move to the `Replace with what?` question.
<SPACE> four times	To insert four spaces.
Ú-E	To change to the overstrike cursor.
Right arrow	To move to the 2.
a <RETURN>	To overstrike the 2 with a lowercase a.
A	To make all of the changes at once.

You should now be able to change the spacing in the remainder of the outline. Remember, first move the cursor to a section of the outline just above the section to be changed, second, give the replace command, and third, make the replacements one at a time or for all of the remaining text.

✓ CHECKPOINT

The replacement command is given as shown below.

```
Case sensitive text
Replace what?  d.              (Notice the period after the d.)
Replace with what?        d.   (There are 10 spaces before the d.)
Replace?          All
```

Explain what happens to the line in the document that reads:

```
d.   The last word.
```

Why does this happen?

INDENTING

The outline has one final annoying problem. Long lines reach back to the left margin when they wrap around to a second line. All of the lines that do this can be neatly tucked in using the **indent** command.

WHAT YOU TYPE	WHY YOU TYPE IT
Ú-1	To move to the top of the outline.
Ú-O	To start the printer options.
IN <RETURN>	To select "Indent."
11 <RETURN>	To indent 11 characters.
<ESCAPE>	To return to the text mode.

Figure 6.6 shows a finished outline.

```
Unit III - Light = three forms of energy which may or may
           not be seen by the human eye.

    A.   Infra Red - Invisible light know as heat
         1.  Primary sources - produce heat
             a.   sun
             b.   fire
             c.   human body
         2.  Secondary Sources - reflect or store heat
             a.   water
             b.   metal
             c.   stone

    B.   Visible Light - Can be seen by the human eye
         1.  Primary Sources - produce visable light
             a.   sun
             b.   fire
             c.   bulb
             d.   firefly
         2.  Secondary sources - reflect or store visable
             light
             a.   glow-in-the-dark frisbee
             b.   moon
             c.   all colors
             d.   not black

    C.   Ultra Violet Light - Invisible light that causes
         tanning and kills many germs
         1.  Primary sources
             a.   sun
             b.   sunlamp
             c.   germacidal lamp
         2.  Secondary sources - reflect or store ultra violet
             light
             a.   water
            b.   aluminum foil
```

FIGURE 6-6.   Light Outline.

Move down through the text on your display and observe the lines that extended to a second line. All of them are now indented. In fact, any additional lines that you add to the document are indented even if you do not want them to be. Try this:

WHAT YOU TYPE	WHY YOU TYPE IT
Ċ-9	Move to the end of the outline.

Now is the time to test out the range of the indent command as it is
used in this outline.

Notice that the indentation command extends to the end of the document. What you typed is indented
11 characters after the first line. You need to turn off the indentation when it is no longer wanted.

WHAT YOU TYPE	WHY YOU TYPE IT
Arrows	To move the cursor back to the beginning of the sentence you just typed.
Ċ-O	To start the printer options.
IN <RETURN>	To select "indent."
0 <RETURN>	To specify that indent is 0 characters (no indentation).
<ESCAPE>	To return to text mode.
Ċ-Z	To zoom in to display the indentation printer commands.

The last sentence is adjusted and appears in standard paragraph form with no indentation.

FINDING TEXT

You can search through your text rapidly using the **find** command. There are several reasons why you
might want to do this: you wish to determine how often you used a certain word or phrase, you have a
bad habit of spelling a word the same wrong way and you wish to find out if you did it again, or you
want to locate text in a long document so that you can make corrections. Try these examples:

1. Determine how often the word "sun" is in the outline.

WHAT YOU TYPE	WHY YOU TYPE IT
Ċ-1	To move to the top of the outline.
Ċ-F	To start the find option.
<RETURN>	To select **Text**.
Ċ-Y	To remove any previously entered information.
sun <RETURN>	To enter the text to search for.
Y Y Y Y <SPACE>	Each time the computer finds the word it asks if you want to find the next occurence. You respond Y to indicate a yes answer. You found the word four times, the number of Y's you pressed.

2. Remove the paragraph that starts "Now is...".

WHAT YOU TYPE	WHY YOU TYPE IT
⌘-1	To move to the top of the outline.
⌘-F	To start the find option.
<RETURN>	To select **Text.**
⌘-Y	To remove any previously entered information.
Now is <RETURN>	To enter the text to search for.
<RETURN>	To end the search; you are at the start of the deletion point.
⌘-D	To start the deletion process.
<DOWN-ARROW> twice	To highlight the unwanted text.
<RETURN>	To complete the deletion process.

MOVING TEXT

Now that you have finished the outline, your science teacher has added a new twist that you need to accommodate. the order of the outline must be from highwave length light to low wavelength light. This is just the reverse of the way you now have it typed. You need to move the A section of the outline to where the C section is, and move the C section to where the A section is. The **move** command helps you here.

The move command is very much like the copy command. The difference is that there is no copy of the text left in the original text location.

It might be a good idea to save your outline if you have not already done so. If you should suffer a disaster and mess up your outline, you can erase the copy on the Desktop, add a fresh copy from the disk, and start again. Here is an overview of what you are going to do:

    1. Move the entire A section to the end of the outline.
    2. Move the C section above the B section.
    3. Correct the lettering in these sections.

Let's go.

	WHAT YOU TYPE	WHY YOU TYPE IT
1.	⌘-1	To move to the top of the outline.
	<DOWN-ARROW> 4 times	To move to the first line of the A section.
	⌘-M	To start the move command.
	<RETURN>	To select **Within document.**
	DOWN-ARROW 9 times	To highlight the information in the A section and the blank line following it.
	<RETURN>	To complete the selection of the move information.

⌘-9		To move to the end of the file.
<RETURN>		To move the text to this location.

2.

UP-ARROW	12 times	To move the cursor to the first line of the C section.
⌘-M		To start the move command.
<RETURN>		To select **Within document.**
DOWN-ARROW	10 times	To highlight the information in the C section.
<RETURN>		To complete selection of the information.
⌘-1		To move to the top of the document.
DOWN-ARROW	4 times	To move to the beginning of the first line of the B section.
<RETURN>		To complete the insertion.

3.   To complete the move operation, you need to change the capital letters so that they are again in alphabetical order. You are on your own for this change.

REVIEW QUESTIONS

1. The following appears on your screen when you zoom in to examine the printer commands.

```
--------Chars per Inch: 10 chars
Hello
--------Chars per inch: 12 chars
out
--------Chars per inch: 5 chars
there,
Lisa
```

   a. What character size would "Hello" be printed in?
   b. What character size would "out" be printed in?
   c. What character size would "there," be printed in?
   d. What character size would "Lisa" be printed in?

The printer command --------Chars per inch: 12 Chars is deleted.

   e. What character size would "out" be printed in now?
   f. What character size would "Lisa" be printed in now?

2. Explain two methods that can be used to make a word boldface.

3. How do you determine what the caret (^) in your text means?

4. What is the difference between copy and move?

5. The review questions on this page are indented five characters. Explain what this means in terms of how the text appears on the page.

6. Match the abbreviations in Column A and the meanings in Column B. Some of the items in Column B may be used more than once.

Column A	Column B
BB	a. Indent
BE	b. Unjustified
BM	c. Center
CN	d. Top margin
Control-B	e. Bottom margin
Control-L	f. Single space
DS	g. Double space
IN	h. Triple space
SS	i. Bold Begin
TM	j. Bold End
TS	k. Underline begin
UB	l. Underline end
UE	
UJ	

7. Although you did not want it to be, the last half of a paragraph in the middle or your document is underlined. Why did this happen? How can you fix it?

EXERCISES

6.1 Change all of the spacing in the outline that you created in this unit. the capital letters should be indented one space, the numbers indented three spaces, and the lowercase letters indented five spaces. This can be done with one use of the replace command. Think about what you want to do before you do anything. (Hint: replace some number of spaces with a lesser number of spaces.) Print this outline and hand it in.

6.2 Outline this unit. Enter the outline into the AppleWorks Word Processor. Print out the outline and hand it in.

6.3 Look in your local newspaper help wanted section for a job that interests you. Write a one-page letter of application for the job. Use the format for the letter indicated by your teacher or match the format in the sample letter shown in Figure 6-7.

The spacing shown in the figure will not appear on your display until both left margin commands have been inserted in the text. There are no spaces typed at the beginning of the return address lines. They have been modified by the margin commands.

```
File: Letter                REVIEW/ADD/CHANGE           Escape: Main Menu
=====|====|====|====|====|====|====|====|====|====|====|====|====|====|====|===
--------Left Margin:  4.0 inches
                              45 Long Meadow Hill Road §
                              New Haven, Connecticut  06510 §
                              April 5, 1988 §
--------Right Margin:  1.0 inches
--------Left Margin:  1.0 inches
§
§
Mrs. Donna Case, Vice-President §
Apple Bus Scheduling Company §
2 East Avenue §
New Haven, Connecticut   06515 §
§
§
Dear Mrs. Case: §
§
    I am writing in reply to your advertisement in
yesterdays New Haven Register.  I am particularly interested
in the job titled ^General Office Help^.  I have the
following office skills: §
-----------------------------------------------------------------------
Type entry or use Ḉcommands          Line 14  Column  1      Ḉ-? for Help
```

FIGURE 6-7.   Sample Letter of Application.

Print a hard copy of the screen using Open-Apple-H. Print a copy of the letter. Sign the letter turn both papers in for credit.

APPLICATION

THE FUTURE BUSINESS LEADERS' CLUB

The minutes for the first meeting of the Future Business Leaders' Club have been typed into AppleWorks Word processor. They need to be revised as shown in Figure C-1.

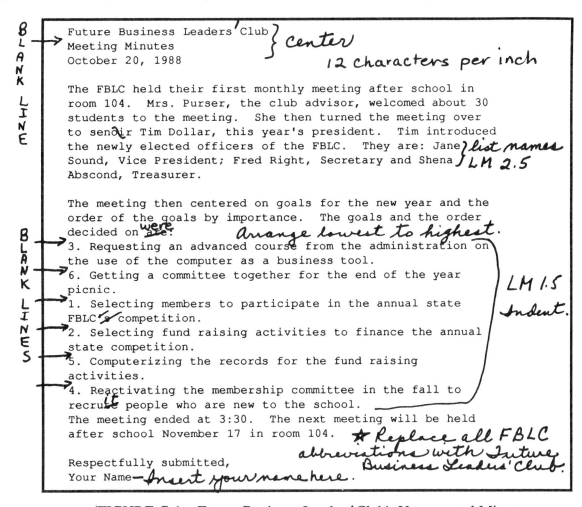

FIGURE C-1. Future Business Leaders' Club's Uncorrected Minutes.

```
                    Future Business Leaders' Club

                          Meeting Minutes
                         October 20, 1988

The Future Business Leaders' Club held their first monthly meeting after
school in room 104.  Mrs. Purser, the club advisor, welcomed about 30
students to the meeting.  She then turned the meeting over to senior Tim
Dollar, this year's president.  Tim introduced the newly elected
officers of the Future Business Leaders' Club.  They are:

               Jane Sound, Vice President
               Fred Right, Secretary
               Shena Abscond, Treasurer.

The meeting then centered on goals for the new year and the order of the
goals by importance.  The goals and the order decided on were:

     1. Selecting members to participate in the annual state
        Future Business Leaders' Club competition.

     2. Selecting fund raising activities to finance the annual
        state competition.

     3. Requesting an advanced course from the administration on
        the use of the computer as a business tool.

     4. Reactivating the membership committee in the fall to
        recruit people who are new to the school.

     5. Computerizing the records for the fund raising
        activities.

     6. Getting a committee together for the end of the year
        picnic.

The meeting ended at 3:30.  The next meeting will be held after school
November 17 in room 104.


Respectfully submitted,
Frank Short
```

FIGURE C-2.   Corrected Future Business Leaders Club Minutes.

YOUR TASK

Load the document FBLC from the Student Data Disk. Save the document on your disk. Make the corrections that are indicated in Figure C-1. When you are sure that your work is complete, save the corrected document on your disk, print it, and turn the printout in to your instructor. Your printout should match the one in Figure C-2. (Make sure that your name appears on the printout and that you remove the pin feed holes from the printout before you turn in your paper.)

UNIT

7 MASTERING THE DATA BASE

LEARNING OBJECTIVES

1. After completing this unit, you should know ...

   a. why you follow an organized pattern to select categories for a data base.

   b. why you organize material for use in a data base.

   c. some efficient methods for data entry.

   d. the consequences of inserting or deleting categories.

2. After completing this unit you should be able to ...

   a. build a data base from scratch.

   b. modify screen layouts to your liking.

   c. change the category names in a data base.

   d. add categories to or delete categories from a data base.

   e. use printer options to modify a report.

   f. group categories on a report.

ASSIGNMENTS

1. CREATE: Develop a data base from scratch.

2. ENTER: Type information into your data base.

3. MULTIPLE RECORD LAYOUT: Modify multiple record screen layouts to your preference.

4. SINGLE RECORD LAYOUT: Modify a single screen layout.

5. DIVIDE AND CONQUER: Add a new category to an existing data base and separate the known from the unknown.

6. SET STANDARD VALUES: Make the data entry into a category automatic.

7. ARRANGE: Put the records in your file into order.

8. CUT AND PASTE: Move selected records from one point in the file to another point.

9. RULES: Set the rules for what appears on the display.

10. PRINT: Print the data base you created in this unit.

11. INTEGRATE: Send information to the Word Processor from a data base file.

IMPORTANT KEYSTROKES AND COMMANDS

COMMAND/KEY	MEANING
Ć-L	Change the layout format displayed on the screen.
Ć-> or <	In the change mode for multiple record layouts, move the position of a category.
Ć-D	In layout change mode for multiple records, delete a category from the display.
Ć-I	In the layout change mode for multiple records, insert a previously deleted category into the display.
Ć-G	In report format mode, group the data on a report.
Ć-M	Move records to (cut) and from (paste) the clipboard.
Ć-V	Set standard values for data entry.
Ć-"	In the multiple record layout, ditto the category information from the record above.

DESIGNING A DATA BASE FILE

Designing a data base file requires several small but rather important steps. If some of these steps seem obvious to you, that's good; it means that you're thinking in the right direction. If any of the steps do not seem necessary, please take a moment to examine why they are important.

1. Decide what information belongs in the file. - For example, in a file of athletes, do you include all of the school athletes in one file, or only basketball varsity and junior varsity? The answer depends on several things. What is the intended use of the file? How much information can the file hold? Are the categories general enough to be used across several different sports? (You would not need home run information in a basketball file. Likewise, records kept in basketball are different from those kept in other sports.)

2. Give the file an appropriate name.- You may not use some of your files for long periods of time. When you return to a file after a few months looking for the address of one of your friends, you do not need to spend time wondering whether your address book is in file X, XX, XXX, or XXXX. File names such as "Address Book," "Videos," "Records," and "Books Read 1988" make life much easier when you need to find something in or to add information to a file that you have not used in a long time.

3. Consider what information the file is to provide to the user. It seems trivial to say that the file cannot provide information that is not categorized in the file. For example, a file of friends' names and addresses that does not contain a category for date of birth can tell you where to send a birthday card but not when you should send the card.

4. Decide what categories are to be recorded in the file and name these categories. For example, an address book file might contain: Name, Address, City, ST, Zip, College Name, College Address, College City, cST, cZip, Phone, College Phone, Birthday, Date Last Contact, and Notes (cST and cZip are the state and zip code for the college address).

    Category names should be general. For example, if you are creating a data base file for the members of a softball team, the category name Player is much better than the name Pitcher or Catcher.

5. Create the data base on your computer system and enter the records.

For some data base files, the list of considerations and decisions is easy. For others, category interrelations and file use make the design of the data base formidable. In the name and address file discussed above, should you include a phone number? It takes up room. Do you really need it if you write to all of your friends? Should you allow for two addresses for friends who have both a school and a home address? Maybe you should have two phone numbers in the file, one for home and one for college.

Category names can have from one to twenty characters. Any character can be used in the name of a category. Category names appear at the top of each category when the file is listed and remind you what information the category holds. It is a waste of room to use a long category name for something that contains only a few characters. For example, if you are going to use the two-character postal abbreviation for the states you enter, "ST" would be a better category name to use than "State of the Union" or even "State." It is a good idea to keep the category name length less than or equal to the length of the data that you will eventually type into the file. Don't go overboard with abbreviations though; category names should be long enough to clearly identify the information in the category.

As you learned in Getting Started with the Data Base, a data base is similar to a file card list. Let's start a data base with a very familiar list, a vocabulary list. The list is to contain all of the vocabulary words for an English class for the year. You would start the list in September and add new words to the list each week. (Typing the list into the computer is one method that can be used to study the words.) Periodically, the list is alphabetized and printed for cumulative review.

After consideration of your goals and objectives for the data base, you decide to name the list "Vocabulary Words 88-89". AppleWorks, however, only allows fifteen characters for the file name and no punctuation other than spaces and the period. "Vocabulary Words 88-89" has too many characters, and the dash is illegal . So "VocabWords88.89" is used to abbreviate your more specific first choice.

You then decide that your list should include the following categories:

> Word,
> Date Given, and
> Definition

Just as a paper 3 by 5 card file has limits on how much information can fit on a card and how many cards can fit in a file box, AppleWorks has limits. Each record must have at least one category and may have no more than 30. The maximum number of records that can be filed in a data base file is 1,350. For the vocabulary words file, this means 1,350 words with their associated dates and definitions can be entered. A quick check with a calculator tells us that 25 words per week for 36 weeks is 900 words (25x36=900), so we appear to have ample space for the file.

The maximum number of characters for one category is 76, including spaces and punctuation. No word or date uses 76 characters. However, this may be a problem in the definition category. If it is, we must use shorter definitions.

The final limit is a subtle one. There is a limit of 55K (55,000) characters on the Desktop. (The Desktop limit is 10K (10,000) characters for Apples equipped with 64K of memory.) If the word, date, and definition use an average of 65 characters per record for the 900 records, that would create a file of 58,500 characters. The Desktop cannot hold this amount of information. In this case, either the file could contain fewer records or each record could be modified to use fewer characters per record on average (for example single word definitions could be used rather than full sentences) AppleWorks gives you a very clear message when your Desktop is full. It also protects your work from loss should this condition occur.

As you become more experienced in using the data base you'll discover several ways to overcome the limits that you might encounter. You may also find, as the majority of AppleWorks users do, that your data base needs fit comfortably within the system limits.

The computer has a great deal of flexibility in terms of file design. As you will see later in the chapter, you can readily add or delete categories from the records in a file. It is, however, advisable to design the file correctly from the start. Since all report formats and layouts must be redone to accommodate category insertions or deletions, category changes may involve considerable time if they are done after report formats have been set up, or layouts have been customized.

It appears that there are a great many things to be concerned about when you set up a data base file. There are, but as you work with the Data Base you'll find that you address most of these concerns with increasing ease. Let's set up the vocabulary words file and then look at some ways that the file can be used for vocabulary study.

GUIDED ACTIVITY: CREATE

>Start at AppleWorks' Main Menu.
>Select **Add files to the Desktop.**
>Select **Make a new file for the Data Base.**

Briefly, here's what the other options (2-4) on the Data Base Menu mean. These options are discussed again in later units.

2. `From a text (ASCII) file:` The AppleWorks Word Processor, like other word processors, can generate a file that contains record information in one long list. This option allows you to place that information into a data base file.

3. `From a Quick File (TM) file:` Quick File is another data base from Apple. Information from a Quick File file can be converted to an AppleWorks' Data Base by selecting this option.

4. `From a DIF (TM) file:` Many spreadsheet programs use the DIF (Data Interchange Format) files for storage. Information for the categories in a data base can be moved to and from a spreadsheet using DIF files.

WHAT YOU TYPE	WHY YOU TYPE IT
<RETURN>	To select 1. **From scratch.**

The computer then asks for a name for your file.

WHAT YOU TYPE	WHY YOU TYPE IT
VocabWords88.89	To enter the name of the new data base.
<RETURN>	To complete the name entry.

The computer displays the "Change Name/Category" screen as shown in Figure 7-1.

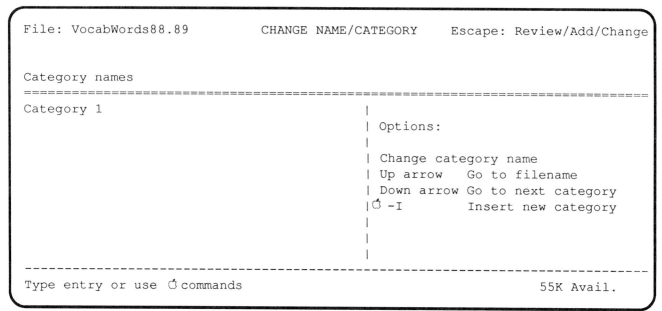

```
File: VocabWords88.89          CHANGE NAME/CATEGORY      Escape: Review/Add/Change


Category names
=====================================================================================
Category 1                                   |
                                             | Options:
                                             |
                                             | Change category name
                                             | Up arrow   Go to filename
                                             | Down arrow Go to next category
                                             |Ú -I          Insert new category
                                             |
                                             |
                                             |
-------------------------------------------------------------------------------------
Type entry or use Ú commands                                          55K Avail.
```

FIGURE 7-1.   Initial Data Base Change Name/Category Screen.

NAMING THE CATEGORIES

The name **Category 1** supplied by the computer insures that there is at least one category in your file. You must have one category, but you do not want "Category 1" as its name. The next part of the Guided Activity removes the unwanted name and adds the correct category names.

GUIDED ACTIVITY: CREATE (continued)

WHAT YOU TYPE	WHY YOU TYPE IT
Ú-Y	To erase Category 1.
Word <RETURN>	To name the first category "Word".
Date Given <RETURN>	To name the second category "Date Given".
Definition <RETURN>	To name the third category "Definition".

That's it! You have set up a data base with three categories: Word, Date Given, and Definition. (Make sure that you have entered the category names correctly. If you did not, move to the line with the incorrect title using the up or down arrows, erase the incorrect category name with Open-Apple-Y, type the correct name, and press Return.)

Press ESCAPE and the following message is displayed:

```
This file does not yet contain
any information.  Therefore, you
will automatically go into the
Insert New Records feature.
```

Press the <SPACE BAR> and a blank record appears ready for you to fill in the first word, date, and definition. The display in the upper left corner indicates that this is record 1 of 1.

ENTERING DATA

Now that your data base has been created, and you are in the Insert New Records mode, let's add some data. Examine the word list below before you enter anything.

```
Word            Date Given    Definition
------------    ------------  --------------------------
altruistic      Sep 21 88     unselfish
brevity         Sep 21 88     shortness
chide           Sep 21 88     berate, scold
console         Sep 21 88     comfort
hamper          Sep 21 88     hold back
mandatory       Sep 21 88     compulsory; necessary
rustic          Sep 21 88     pastoral, of the country
sagacity        Sep 21 88     keenness in judgment
unique          Sep 21 88     one of a kind
wane            Sep 21 88     lose size or power
```

The date is the same for all of the words. An obvious question is, does the date have to be entered for every word? The answer is no, of course not. There are two basic types of similar information for data entry. One type is data that is the same for all or almost all of the records in the file. An example of this would be the state abbreviation in the addresses of all of the students in your school. The second type is information that is the same for a block of records. In the vocabulary list for example, the Date Given is the same for the entire block of words for one week. The following week, the date is again the same for all of the new words, but it is a different date.

Information that is the same for a block of entries can be quickly entered after all of the other entries have been made. Enter the word list from the list below. All of the keystrokes are included in the list. Notice that the date is left blank for all of the entries by pressing Return at the date entry. Enter the list; be careful to see that the words are entered into the Word category and the definitions are entered into the definition category. If you mistakenly enter a word or definition in the date category, move back to the category and use Open-Apple-Y to delete the entry, then enter the information in the correct category.

GUIDED ACTIVITY: ENTER

The blank lines in the list are for clarity. You do not need to type any characters for these lines. Make sure that your cursor is blinking at the beginning of the first Word category entry, then type in entries from the list.

WHAT YOU TYPE

---

altruistic <RETURN>   (The first word.)
<RETURN>   (The date is left blank.)
unselfish <RETURN>   (The first definition.)
                             (You type nothing for this line.)

brevity   <RETURN>
<RETURN>
shortness <RETURN>

chide   RETURN
<RETURN>
berate, scold <RETURN>

console   <RETURN>
<RETURN>
comfort   <RETURN>

hamper   <RETURN>   (Make sure that this is the fifth word.)
<RETURN>
hold back <RETURN>

mandatory <RETURN>
<RETURN>
compulsory; necessary <RETURN>

rustic   <RETURN>
<RETURN>
pastoral, of the country <RETURN>

sagacity   <RETURN>
<RETURN>
keenness in judgment <RETURN>

unique   <RETURN>
<RETURN>
one of a kind <RETURN>

wane   <RETURN>
<RETURN>
lose size or power <RETURN>

<ESCAPE>   To return to the Review/Add/Change mode.

You should now see the multiple record display. (If you do not, press ⌘-Z.) Now finish the data entry by adding the date to each record.

WHAT YOU TYPE	WHY YOU TYPE IT
⌘-1	To move to the top of the list.
<TAB>	To move to the blank date category for the first record.
9/21/88	To enter the date information.
<RETURN>	To complete the date entry.

The cursor drops to the next record; it remains in the same column.

> Give the command   ⌘-"   To ditto the information in the row above. (You do not need to press the shift key to use this command.)

The command duplicates the information from the category above. The date now appears in the first two categories and the cursor has moved down to the third entry.

> Press and hold ⌘-"   To fill the column with the date.

THE SCREEN LAYOUT

The screen layouts can be changed to display the records in your data base in a variety of ways. If you wish the order of the information on either screen to be word - definition - date, instead of word - date - definition, you can arrange it that way. If you wish to display only the definition alone on the multiple record screen, you can arrange that, too.

MULTIPLE RECORD LAYOUTS

When you filled in the date, you probably noticed that several of the definitions were cut off on the multiple record screen display. Each column in the multiple record display was set to a **default width** of fifteen characters; this is not enough to show all of the information in the definition category. The information is not lost; it is just not displayed.

To verify that the information still exists:

> Move to any category in the row containing the word "mandatory".
> Give the ⌘-Z command to display the individual record.
> Verify that "necessary" is completely included in definition category.
> Give the ⌘-Z command to display the multiple records again.

Let's change the layout to expand the definition category by 10 characters and to reduce the width of the Word category by 4 characters.

GUIDED ACTIVITY: MULTIPLE RECORD LAYOUT

Make sure that the multiple record screen shows in the display and follow these steps to modify the screen layout.

WHAT YOU TYPE	WHY YOU TYPE IT
⌘-L	To start a layout change.
⌘-LEFT-ARROW 4 times	To reduce the width of the Word category by 4.
<RIGHT-ARROW> twice	To move to the Definition column.
⌘-RIGHT-ARROW 10 times	To expand the width of the column by ten.
<ESCAPE>	To leave the layout screen.
<RETURN>	To select **down** as the cursor movement when you press Return.

Examine the screen. Notice that the definitions are now fully displayed.

Now you'll change the layout so that the order of the columns is Word - Definition - Date Given.

WHAT YOU TYPE	WHY YOU TYPE IT
⌘-L	To start the layout change.
<RIGHT-ARROW> twice	To move to the Definition column.
⌘-<	To move the Definition column one position left. (Do not shift to get the less than symbol; the Apple key is the shift.)
<ESCAPE>	To leave the layout screen.
<RETURN>	To select **down** as the cursor movement.

Finally, you'll delete the Word category from the multiple record display (this does not delete the words or the Word category from the file; it only removes the them from view).

WHAT YOU TYPE	WHY YOU TYPE IT
⌘-L	To start the layout change.
⌘-D	To delete the word category.
<ESCAPE>	To leave the layout screen.
<RETURN>	To select **down** as the cursor movement.

This multiple record layout which shows only the definitions of your vocabulary words can be used as a study tool. Look at the definition on the multiple record screen and try to recall the vocabulary word that matches the definition. Zoom in to the single record screen to see if you are correct. Alternatively, you can display the vocabulary word on the screen and try to recall the definition.

WHAT YOU TYPE	WHY YOU TYPE IT
Ć-L	To start the layout change.
Ć-D	To delete the definition category.
Ć-I	To insert a previously deleted category.
<RETURN>	To select Word as the category to insert.
<ESCAPE>	To leave the layout screen.
<RETURN>	To select **down** as the cursor movement.

Categories are inserted to the left of the cursor position. If you had wanted the Word category column to follow the Date Given column, you would have moved the cursor to the right with the right-arrow key and then inserted the column.

Categories reinserted into the multiple record display are given their original column width, so the width of the Word column is 15 characters again. If you wish the Word column width to be 11 characters, you need to alter the layout again to reduce the width by four. Please note that the multiple record display now shows only the Word and Date Given categories.

SINGLE RECORD LAYOUT

The single record screen has its own layout command. The command is the same as the multiple record layout command; the difference is that you give the command when a single record is displayed on the Review/Add/Change screen. Changing the multiple record display did not change the single record display in any way.

Give the Ć-Z command to display the single record layout.

(The layout command does not work from the New Record Insert mode. Check the top line of the display; if you are in the New Record Insert mode, press Escape to return to the Review/Add/Change mode.)

GUIDED ACTIVITY: SINGLE RECORD LAYOUT

Observe that the single record layout is unchanged even though the multiple record layout has been changed. Let's change the single record layout.

WHAT YOU TYPE	WHY YOU TYPE IT
Ć-L	To start the layout change.
<DOWN-ARROW> twice	To move the cursor to the "D" in Definition.
Ć-RIGHT-ARROW 25 times	To move Definition 25 places to the right.
Ć-UP-ARROW twice	To move Definition up to the top row.
<ESCAPE>	To exit the layout change mode.
2 <RETURN>	To select **left, right, top to bottom** entry.

There are some important points to note here. (1) you cannot delete a category from the single record layout screen – this screen is used for record entry and all of the categories must be present; (2) you can place a category name almost anywhere you wish on the screen; (3) the order in which categories are entered can be changed by moving the category to a new location on the screen.

You were given a choice of order entry when you pressed Escape to exit the layout change mode. The first choice was to enter the categories in the order that you had defined them. The second choice, the one you selected, was to enter the categories from left to right across the top row, then across the second row, and so on until the bottom of the list is reached. Your placement of the categories means that your entry order is now Word first, Definition second, and Date Given last.

Try this new entry order out by inserting the 10 words in the list below. It is not necessary to move to the bottom of the list as you did when entering a new record in unit 4. An alternate method is to use the insert command.

WHAT YOU TYPE

Ć-I   To start the New Record Insert mode.
adept   <RETURN> (This is the word entry.)
adroit; skilled <RETURN> (This is the definition.)
<RETURN>   (This is the date. It's blank for now.)
                                 (Do not press any keys for the blank lines in the list.)
bona fide   <RETURN> (This is the word entry.)
genuine   <RETURN> (This is the definition.)
<RETURN>   (This is the date blank.)

emulate   <RETURN>
imitate   <RETURN>
<RETURN>

intricate   <RETURN>
complicated   <RETURN>
<RETURN>

laud   <RETURN>
praise   <RETURN>
<RETURN>

lucid   <RETURN>
cloar   <RETURN>
<RETURN>

novice   <RETURN>
amateur   <RETURN>
<RETURN>

ponder	<RETURN>
consider	<RETURN>
<RETURN>	

ruse	<RETURN>
trick, hoax	<RETURN>
<RETURN>	

surmount	<RETURN>
overcome	<RETURN>
<RETURN>	

✓ CHECKPOINT

What command do you use to enter the same date into all of the empty date categories? Which layout, single or multiple, must be displayed when you use this command?

UNGUIDED ACTIVITY

Add the date 9/28/88 to all of the new words you just entered. (Hint: Look at the guided activity "Enter" earlier in this unit.)

ADDING CATEGORIES TO A RECORD

Consider using the data base you created in this unit for study and review over a long period of time. As you add and learn more words, you find that you repeat your practice exercise unnecessarily for the words that you already know well. It would be very helpful if you could separate the words that you know from those that still need practice. Adding a Study category would help: if the category contained "Yes," then you would study the word; if it contained "No," then you could skip it.

Fortunately, AppleWorks makes it easy to add or delete categories in a Data Base file. There is, however, a price to pay for making such a change: the custom layout designs that you entered are lost when you insert or delete a category, and any report formats that you have entered are also lost. (You made a custom single record screen layout when you changed the category entry order.) The reasons for this loss involve problems such as the loss of pointers (place indicators) to existing records in the computer's memory and other technical matters. For example, if you change the entry order of the categories, AppleWorks does not initially know where you would like to place the new category in your custom entry ordering, so it puts all of the layouts back in their original order. Since most changes to the category list occur before extensive layout changes are made or reports are designed, these losses are usually minor.

(One way to avoid the loss caused by adding categories after you have customized layouts and printer reports is to start the file with a few extra categories. Make the names of the extra categories a period or a dash until you need to use them for additional information, then use Open-Apple-N to change the names.)

GUIDED ACTIVITY: DIVIDE AND CONQUER

Add the Study category to the vocabulary data base.

WHAT YOU TYPE	WHY YOU TYPE IT
-N	To display the category names.
<RETURN>	To leave the file name as it is.
<RETURN> 3 times	To move to the blank line under Definition.
Study	To enter the name of the new category.
<RETURN>	To add the name to the category list. Note the message on the right side of the screen.
Y	To answer yes, you really want to do this.

✔ **CHECKPOINT**

a. In your own words, what did the message on the right hand side of the screen say?

b. What categories are now displayed on the multiple record screen? In what order are they displayed? Why are they displayed in this order?

Let's assume that all of the words need to be studied. Enter "Yes" into the study category for each record.

WHAT YOU TYPE	WHY YOU TYPE IT
<ESCAPE>	To return to the multiple record display.
<TAB>	To move the cursor to the Study column.
Yes <RETURN>	To enter "Yes" in the first record.
Hold -"	To enter "Yes" for all records.

Now, as you learn a word, you change its Study category to "No".

STANDARD VALUES

Each new word that you enter would probably have an initial Study category entry of "Yes". You can have AppleWorks automatically supply the Yes for all entries, by changing Standard Values:

WHAT YOU TYPE	WHY YOU TYPE IT
-Z	To display the single record Review/Add/Change screen.
-V	To display the Set Standard Values screen.
<TAB>	To move to the Study category.
Yes <RETURN>	To enter Yes as the standard value for Study (ignore the beep).
<ESCAPE>	To return to Review/Add/Change.

Now the Study category will automatically contain Yes for all new record entries. Try it; enter these five words.

WHAT YOU TYPE	
-I	To start the insert process.
brazen <RETURN>	To enter the first new word.
<RETURN>	To leave the date blank.
bold <RETURN>	To enter the definition.
<RETURN>	To leave the Study entry "Yes".
	Remember, the blank lines are just to make the reading easier.
erroneous <RETURN>	Let's say you already know this word.
<RETURN>	To leave the date blank.
incorrect <RETURN>	
No	To change the Study entry to "No".
CONTROL-Y	To delete Yes .
<RETURN>	To finish the entry and move to the next record.
illustrious <RETURN>	
<RETURN>	
famous <RETURN>	
<RETURN>	
insinuate <RETURN>	
<RETURN>	
hint, suggest <RETURN>	
<RETURN>	
mediocre <RETURN>	
<RETURN>	
average <RETURN>	
<RETURN>	

ARRANGING THE DATA

You get the maximum benefit from your studying if you study the words in different orders. You can use the arrange command to put the word list into several different arrangements. Let's try some.

GUIDED ACTIVITY: ARRANGE

WHAT YOU TYPE	WHY YOU TYPE IT
(⌘-Z)	Display the Multiple Record screen if it does not appear in your display.
<TAB>	To move the cursor to the Word column.
⌘-A	To start the arrangement on this column.
1 <RETURN>	To arrange alphabetically from A to Z.

The multiple record display appears on the screen. The records are in alphabetical order by word. It is possible to arrange the file using any category, even if the category does not appear in the multiple record display. Remove the definition column from the multiple record display.

WHAT YOU TYPE	WHY YOU TYPE IT
(⌘-Z)	Display the Multiple Record screen if it does not appear in your display.
⌘-L	To change the layout.
<RIGHT-ARROW> twice	To move to the Definition column.
⌘-D	To delete the Definition from the display.
<ESCAPE>	To leave the layout screen.
<RETURN>	To select **down** as the cursor movement.

Even though the Definition category does not appear in the multiple record display, the records can be arranged on this category.

WHAT YOU TYPE	WHY YOU TYPE IT
⌘-Z	Display the Single Record screen.
<TAB>	To move the cursor to the Definition category.
⌘-A	To start the arrangement on this category.
2 <RETURN>	To arrange in reverse alphabetical order from Z to A.

When you arrange the file by Definition, the words appear to be scrambled since many of the definitions do not start with the same letter as the word.

✓ **CHECKPOINT**

The words you just entered are no longer together, one after the other in the list. Can you still enter the date for these words using ⌥-"? How?

UNGUIDED ACTIVITY

Enter the date 10/5/88 for all of the blank date categories. Be careful not to change a date that has been previously entered. (Hint: Use Open-Apple-A in the date column.)
Alphabetize the words when you are finished.

THE CLIPBOARD

Information that you cut and paste from one file to another is temporarily stored in an area of the Desktop referred to as the **clipboard.**

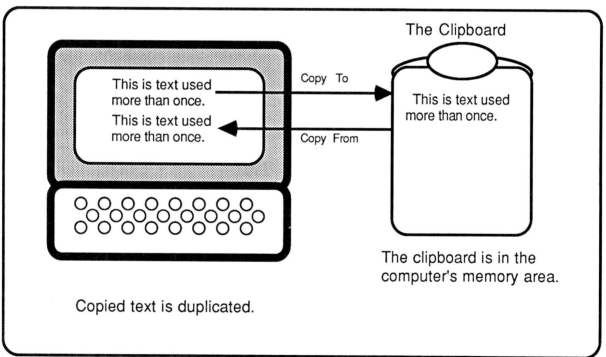

The Clipboard

This is text used more than once.

Copy To

This is text used more than once.

This is text used more than once.

Copy From

The clipboard is in the computer's memory area.

Copied text is duplicated.

FIGURE 7-2. The Clipboard.

Information can be moved or copied to or from the clipboard. Only one piece of information can be on the clipboard at one time. The information can be a small amount such as one letter from a word

202 Understanding and Using AppleWorks

processor file or a very large amount such as one hundred records from a data base file. Information that you store on the clipboard takes up space in the computer's memory.

If you move the information to the clipboard, it will be deleted from the file from which you moved it. If you copy the information to the clipboard, it will be duplicated on the clipboard and will still appear in the file from which you copied it. Similarly, if you move information from the clipboard it will appear pasted into the file moved to and will no longer be on the clipboard. If you copy from the clipboard, the information will appear pasted into the file copied to and a duplicate of the information will remain on the clipboard. You can move information from the clipboard only once. You can copy it from the clipboard as many times as you like.

The copy feature of the clipboard is quite handy for duplicating blocks of information. For example, if a common word or phrase is used several times in a paper you're typing, it can be typed once, copied to the clipboard and then copied back into the text as many times as needed.

Figure 7-2 illustrates the clipboard concept.

CUT-AND-PASTE MOVES

Arrangement orders are limited to alphabetic, numeric, or chronological (by date). Indeed, if you wish to move a single word or a group of words to the top of the list, you may not be able to do it with the arrange command. **Cut**-and-**paste** is much more flexible. You can cut records out of the file from any point, and then paste them back into the file at any other point. Let's move a single word, lucid, to the beginning of the word list.

GUIDED ACTIVITY: CUT AND PASTE

WHAT YOU TYPE	WHY YOU TYPE IT
(Ó-Z)	Display the Multiple Record screen if it is not already showing in your display.
Arrows or Tab	To move to the line containing "lucid".
Ó-M	To start the move command. The "lucid" line is highlighted.
T	To indicate that the information selected is moved **To the clipboard (cut),** that is, cut from the document and stored temporarily in a special section of the computer's memory.
<RETURN>	To indicate that "lucid is the only information selected. The "lucid" line disappears from the display.
Ó-1	To move to the beginning of the records.
Ó-M	To continue the move operation.
F	To indicate that the information is to be moved **From the clipboard (pasted)** into the file at this point. This completes the operation.

Cut- and-paste moves can be made with more than one record at a time as long as the records are next to each other in the file. For example, you can move all of the words that start with "i" to the bottom of the list to test this out.

What You Type	Why You Type It
Arrows or Tab	To move to the Word category.
⌘-A <RETURN>	To arrange the words alphabetically.
Arrows	To move to the first "i" word.
⌘-M	To highlight the first "i" word.
T	To select **To the clipboard (cut).**
<DOWN-ARROW> twice	To highlight all of the "i" words.
<RETURN>	To complete the cut.

It is not necessary to complete the paste operation at this time; however, you will destroy the contents of the clipboard if you move any additional information onto it. There is no warning when you erase the contents of the clipboard, so it is good practice to complete the cut-and-paste operation before you forget that you have left information on the clipboard.

What You Type	Why You Type It
⌘-9	To move to the bottom of the word list.
⌘-M	To continue the move operation.
F	To copy the information **From the clipboard (paste)** into the word list. The information is inserted before the last record. If you wished to have the "i" words be the very last words in the file, you would need to do another move operation to move the word "wane" forward in the list. You cannot paste information after the last record in a file.

RECORD SELECTION RULES

It would be great if the only words that appeared in the display were the ones that you needed to study. The record selection rules do this for you. First, let's check the words that you already know to be sure that you really do know them. Here's how to do this.

GUIDED ACTIVITY: RULES

What You Type	Why You Type It
⌘-R	To set the record selection rules.
4 <RETURN>	To select "Study."

1 <RETURN>	To select "equals."
No <RETURN>	To enter the comparison word as "No".
ESCAPE	To return to the record display.

The only word that appears in the display is "erroneous"; you indicated that you knew the meaning (incorrect) when you entered it. Once you are sure that you know the meaning of all of the words on this list, change the record selection rule to display those words that you need to study.

WHAT YOU TYPE	WHY YOU TYPE IT
Ċ-R	To change the selection rules.
<RETURN>	To indicate not all records are selected.
4 <RETURN>	To select "Study".
1 <RETURN>	To select "equals".
Yes <RETURN>	To enter the comparison word as "Yes".
ESCAPE	To return to the record display.

As you study the words, you will want to mark the ones that you have learned by changing the entry in the Study column to "No". Let's try this.

WHAT YOU TYPE	WHY YOU TYPE IT
(Ċ-Z)	Display the Multiple Record screen (if necessary).
Tab or Arrows	To move to the Study category in the record for the word novice.
No	To enter "No" in this category.
Ċ-Y	To remove Yes.
<RETURN>	To complete the change.

Notice that the category does not immediately disappear from the screen. Move the cursor up the list so that "novice" scrolls off of the bottom. Now scroll back down the list. Novice is no longer there. You must change the display before the word is removed. Try this:

WHAT YOU TYPE	WHY YOU TYPE IT
(Ċ-Z)	If your display does not show multiple records.
Tab or Arrows	To move to the Study category in the "ponder" Record.
No	To enter No in this category.
Ċ-Y	To remove Yes.
<RETURN>	To complete the change.
<UP-ARROW>	To move back up to the "ponder" record.
Ċ-Z	To view the single record display.
Ċ-Z	To return to the multiple record display.

"Ponder" no longer appears in the multiple record display or in the single record display.

✔ <u>**CHECKPOINT**</u>

Ponder this. How do you return all of the records to the display? Now do it (do it correctly on the first try and you should no longer consider yourself an AppleWorks Data Base novice).

PRINTING AND PRINTER OPTIONS

As you saw in the previous data base unit, printing a report is quite simple once the report has been defined. You defined a labels-style report in that unit; and a tables style report had been defined for you. Let's define a tables-style report for the spelling word list and include some special printer options.

GUIDED ACTIVITY: PRINT

A WORD OF CAUTION:

If you make an error such as attempting to print a report when there are no printers connected to your computer, AppleWorks may hang (get stuck). The only way to fix this condition is to restart AppleWorks - this means that your file will be lost. To protect yourself, save your file before you print.

WHAT YOU TYPE	WHY YOU TYPE IT
⌂-S	To save the current version of your file.

Now we'll define and print a tables style report with special printer options. The file VocabWords88.89 should appear in your display.

WHAT YOU TYPE	WHY YOU TYPE IT
⌂-P	To start the print report action.
<RETURN>	To select **Create a new "tables" format** report.
Full File List <RETURN>	To name the report Full File List.
<RIGHT-ARROW>-twice	To move to the definition category.
⌂-RIGHT-ARROW 10 times	To expand the definition category.
<RIGHT-ARROW>	To move to the Study category.
⌂-LEFT-ARROW 7 times	To reduce the Study category width.

Your screen should now look like the one displayed in Figure 7-3. (Your words may not be in the same order or even be the same words as the ones shown in the figure.) Note that the length of the line for the printout is 58 characters.

```
File: VocabWords88.89         REPORT FORMAT         Escape: Report Menu
Report: Full File List
Selection: All records


Group totals on: Date Given
=======================================================================
--> or <--   Move cursor              ⌂-J   Right justify this category
  >  ⌂   <     Switch category positions  ⌂-K   Define a calculated category
--> ⌂  <--   Change column width       ⌂-N   Change report name and/or title
⌂-A   Arrange (sort) on this category ⌂-O   Printer options
⌂-D   Delete this category            ⌂-P   Print the report
⌂-G   Add/remove group totals         ⌂-R   Change record selection rules
⌂-I   Insert a prev. deleted category ⌂-T   Add/remove category totals
-----------------------------------------------------------------------

Word            Date Given   Definition              Study L
-A----------   -B----------  -C--------------------  -D--- e
altruistic     Sep 21 88     unselfish               Yes   n
brevity        Sep 21 88     shortness               Yes   5
chide          Sep 21 88     berate, scold           Yes   8


-----------------------------------------------------------------------
Use options shown above to change report format         52K Avail.
```

FIGURE 7-3.   Full File List - Report Format Screen.

GUIDED ACTIVITY: PRINT (continued)

WHAT YOU TYPE	WHY YOU TYPE IT
<LEFT-ARROW> 3 times	To move to the Word category.
(If the rules are not set to Selection: All records,	
⌂-R Y	To set the rules to display all records.)
⌂-A <RETURN>	To arrange the words alphabetically.
<RIGHT-ARROW>	To move to the Date column.
⌂-A <RETURN>	To arrange the file chronologically (by date).
⌂-O	To modify the printer options.

Examine this screen for a moment. Near the center of the screen in the left column there is a line that reads:

```
Char per line (est)    80
```

This line tells you that the number of characters (letters, digits, spaces, etc.) printed on one line of the report with the current printer settings is estimated to be 80 characters. As you change settings that affect the width of the line, this estimate changes. Watch the setting as you proceed.

WHAT YOU TYPE	WHY YOU TYPE IT
CI <RETURN>	To change the characters per inch setting.
5 <RETURN>	To make the new setting 5.

The estimated number of characters per line is now 40. Remember, the last display indicated that you need at least 58 characters for each line. The 5 character-per-inch setting can not be used for this report since the number of characters per line is insufficient. (If you try to print a report with insufficient line length, you get one of several undesirable results, depending on your printer. Some printers print the extra characters on another line, some print them on the same line, typing over the beginning characters already on the line, and some just ignore the extra characters and do not print them.) Make another change in the characters per inch setting.

WHAT YOU TYPE	WHY YOU TYPE IT
CI <RETURN>	To change the characters-per-inch setting.
10 <RETURN>	To change the setting back to 10.
LM <RETURN> 1 <RETURN>	To change the left margin to 1.
RM <RETURN> 1 <RETURN>	To change the right margin to 1.

Notice that the character per line estimate is now 60. The 1-inch margins reduce the size of the printing width from 8 inches to 6. Ten characters per inch for 6 inches is 60 characters.

✔ CHECKPOINT

If you now change the characters per inch to 12 and make no other changes, how many characters would be printed on a line? Make the change to verify your answer.

The display on your screen should match the display shown in Figure 7-4.

Finally, now that you have defined how the report should look when it prints, print the report.

```
 File: VocabWords88.89          PRINTER OPTIONS          Escape: Report Format
 Report: Full File List
================================================================================


-------Left and right margins--------        ------Top and bottom margins-------
PW: Platen Width            8.0 inches    PL: Paper Length         11.0 inches
LM: Left Margin             1.0 inches    TM: Top Margin            0.0 inches
RM: Right Margin            1.0 inches    BM: Bottom Margin         2.0 inches
CI: Chars per Inch         12             LI: Lines per Inch        6

    Line width              6.0 inches        Printing length       9.0 inches
    Char per line (est)    72                 Lines per page        54

           --------------------Formatting options-------------------
           SC:  Send Special Codes to printer               No
           PD:  Print a Dash when an entry is blank          No
           PH:  Print report Header at top of each page     Yes
                Single, Double or Triple Spacing (SS/DS/TS)  SS




-------------------------------------------------------------------------------
 Type a two letter option code                                52K Avail.
```

FIGURE 7-4. Data Base Printer Options Display.

WHAT YOU TYPE	WHY YOU TYPE IT
ESCAPE	To return to the `Report Format` screen.
♂-P	To print the report.
(A number) <RETURN>	To select your printer, you pick the correct printer number from the list presented on the screen.
Today's Date <RETURN>	To enter the date, type the date and press return.
<RETURN>	To select one copy and start the printer.

You need to make two changes in the report: (1) move the date closer to the center, and (2) print a blank line between each week's list of words. Please save the file again before you proceed. Remember, when you save the file, you're also saving the report that you have just completed formatting.

GROUPING IN A REPORT

Information printed on a Data Base report can be grouped in any category that appears on the report. For our sample file, this means that all of the words for each week can be printed on a separate page or with a separation between each week's words. The file could also be grouped by words to study and those not to study. Only one type of grouping for one category can be indicated on each report.

The computer detects a group change when the information in the category changes. If you want to list the words grouped by the date they were given, you need to do two things. First, arrange the file by the category Date Given. Second, indicate that the records are grouped by this category. If you neglect to arrange the file by the correct category, you'll find that the report prints many small groups since the group changes every time the category entry changes. Let's print two reports to illustrate grouping:

Make these changes to the Full File List report to move the date and page number toward the center and to correctly group the Date Given.

GUIDED ACTIVITY: PRINT   (continued)

The starting point for this list of instructions is the REVIEW/ADD/CHANGE display.

TROUBLESHOOTING

Problem:	This display is not on your screen.
Correction:	You may not have saved your file. Remember, you should always save your file before you print. Save your file with ⌂-S and the Review/Add/Change display appears when the save is complete. If you did save your file, use Escape to return to the Review/Add/Change display.

WHAT YOU TYPE	WHY YOU TYPE IT
⌂-P	To start the print process.
<RETURN>	To select **Get a report format**.
<RETURN>	To select **Full File List**.
⌂-O	To change the printer option.
RM <RETURN>	
2 <RETURN>	To change the right margin to 2 inches.
<ESCAPE>	To return to the Print Format screen.
<RIGHT-ARROW>	To move to the Date Given category.
⌂-A <RETURN>	To arrange the file chronologically.
⌂-G	To group on this category.
<RETURN>	To select No for the question: **Print group totals only?**

<RETURN>	To select No for the question: **Go to a new page after each group total?**
$\circlearrowright$-P	To print the report.
A number <RETURN>	To select your printer.
Today's Date <RETURN>	To enter the date.
<RETURN>	To select 1 copy and start the printer.

The report that you generate should look like the one in Figure 7-5.

```
File:    VocabWords88.89                          Page  1
Report: Full File List                    October, 1988
Word          Date Given    Definition           Study
------------  ------------  ------------------------  -----
altruistic    Sep 21 88     unselfish            Yes
brevity       Sep 21 88     shortness            Yes
chide         Sep 21 88     berate, scold        Yes
console       Sep 21 88     comfort              Yes
hamper        Sep 21 88     hold back            Yes
mandatory     Sep 21 88     compulsory; necessary Ycs
rustic        Sep 21 88     pastoral, of the country Yes
sagacity      Sep 21 88     keenness in judgment  Yes
unique        Sep 21 88     one of a kind        Yes
wane          Sep 21 88     lose size or power   Yes


adept         Sep 28 88     adroit; skilled      Yes
bona fide     Sep 28 88     genuine              Yes
emulate       Sep 28 88     imitate              Yes
intricate     Sep 28 88     complicated          Yes
laud          Sep 28 88     praise               Yes
lucid         Sep 28 88     clear                Yes
novice        Sep 28 88     amateur              No
ponder        Sep 28 88     consider             No
ruse          Sep 28 88     trick, hoax          Yes
surmount      Sep 28 88     overcome             Yes


brazen        Oct  5 88     bold                 Yes
erroneous     Oct  5 88     incorrect            No
illustrious   Oct  5 88     famous               Yes
insinuate     Oct  5 88     hint, suggest        Yes
mediocre      Oct  5 88     average              Yes
```

FIGURE 7-5. A Grouped Report.

✓   CHECKPOINT

When you changed the right margin (RM) to 2.0 inches, what was the new line width setting? What did the character per line estimate change to?

Now print the same report incorrectly sorted to observe what happens to the grouping.

WHAT YOU TYPE	WHY YOU TYPE IT
<LEFT-ARROW>	To move to the Word category.
⌘-A <RETURN>	To arrange the Words alphabetically.
⌘-P	To print the report.
A number <RETURN>	To select your printer (or the screen).
<RETURN>	To accept the previously entered date.
<RETURN>	To select 1 copy and start the printer.

Notice that each group in the report has only one, two, or three words in the group. When the date changes, a new group starts.

To correct this mess, simply rearrange the records chronologically by Date Given and then print the report again.

UNGUIDED ACTIVITY

Arrange the records in the report first alphabetically by Word and then reverse alphabetically by Study. Set group totals on study. Predict to yourself how the report will print out. Print the report on paper or the screen to verify your prediction.

✓   CHECKPOINT

When you print a data base file, there are several printer selections that you can make that do not print the report to a printer. For example, you can elect to print the report on the screen. One of the selections lets you print the report for the Word Processor. According to the selection list, where does this report print?

PRINTING DATA BASE RECORDS TO THE WORD PROCESSOR

AppleWorks is an integrated software package. Not only does this mean that many commands that do one thing in one application also do the same thing in the other applications; but, it also means that information that you enter into one application can be transferred easily to the other applications in the package.

Let's say that a good friend of yours has moved to another town. You write to her regularly and tell her about things that happen in your school. You want to tell her in your next letter how lucky she is that she did not stay, since the vocabulary words are getting brutal. You wish to include the list of words that you entered into the data base in your letter; but, you really do not want to type them all again. You do not have to with an integrated package such as AppleWorks. Here is a Guided Activity to let you work with this feature.

GUIDED ACTIVITY: INTEGRATE

> Start this activity with the VocabWords88.89 file on your Desktop.
> Open a Word Processor file named To Sue 10.20.88.
> Enter the information below into the file:

> 10/21/88

> Dear Sue,

> How are you? So far I'm fine.

> We're doing some great things with the computer this year. We're using it to study our vocabulary words in Mr. Engel's English class. He's ok but the words he gives us are hard. Here are the words that we have had so far:

You are now ready to copy the information from the Data Base to the Word Processor. Follow these steps:

WHAT YOU TYPE	WHY YOU TYPE IT
⌘-Q	To move quickly from one file to another.
<UP-ARROW> <RETURN>	To select the file **VocabWords88.89**.
⌘-P	To start the print process.
2 <RETURN>	To select **Create a new "tables"** format.
To Word <RETURN>	To name the report.
⌘-A <RETURN>	To alphabetize the list.
<RIGHT-ARROW>	To move to the **Date Given** column.
⌘-D 3 times	To delete all of the categories except the Word category.
⌘-P	To start printing.
Arrows <RETURN>	To select **The clipboard (for the Word Processor)**.
<RETURN>	To leave the date blank (or to leave the last date unchanged).

The following message now appears on the screen:

```
The report is now on the clipboard,
and can be moved or copied into Word
Processor documents.
```

To finish transferring the information, proceed with:

WHAT YOU TYPE	WHY YOU TYPE IT
○-Q	To quickly move from one file to another.
<UP-ARROW> <RETURN>	To select the file **To Sue 10.20.88**.
○-M	To start the move command.
F	To select **From clipboard (paste)**.
○-D	To delete the unwanted information from the beginning of the list.
<DOWN-ARROW> 5 times	To highlight the unwanted lines (the report title, date, and column lines).
<LEFT-ARROW>	To remove the highlight from the "a" in the word adept.
<RETURN>	To complete the delete process.
○-9	To move the cursor to the bottom of the file.

Now that the words have been inserted, you can edit them just as you would any other information in a word processor file. Leave the words in a list for now.

Finish this section of the letter by entering the following:

I only sent the word list to you for now because I know how much you like to find the meaning of new words on your own. I'll send you the definitions in my next letter.

UNGUIDED ACTIVITY

Edit the list of vocabulary words in the letter to Sue so that the words are printed across the page, separated by commas. Print the letter and hand it in to your instructor if so requested.

REVIEW QUESTIONS

1. Outline the five steps to consider when you create a data base.

2. Why is the name "Category 1" entered into the category list when you start a new data base?

3. An inventory file has categories for a part number and a part name together with other categories. Almost every part number starts out A2S20064-. What can you do to make data entry easier?

4. Describe two methods you can use to insert new information into an existing file.

5. You have a file with two custom screens (remember, these are the screen layouts that you changed) and five reports. You need to add another category to the file. What happens when you do this? How can you avoid this problem?

6. What is the maximum number of records an AppleWorks data base can hold?

7. What is the maximum number of categories that can be used in an AppleWorks data base file?

8. You are designing a data base file for the basketball historian. The data base file should provide statistical information for the top ten varsity players for each of the last twenty years. The historian is interested in lists of most points scored in a game, number of points per game, total points in a season, high scoring players, and so forth. What categories would you suggest? (You may wish to discuss this with the basketball coach or a basketball player.)

9. You are designing a data base for a book, record, or video tape collection that is to include two or three sentences describing the item in the collection and how well you liked it. Explain exactly how you would include this category.

10. For the data base described in question 9, you want to have a method of arranging the items in the data base from what you consider the best to what you consider the worst. Explain how you might do this.

EXERCISES

7.1 Design and create a name-and-address book data base. Enter at least ten records into the file. Print a hard copy of the file categories list. Print a copy of all of the information in the file.

7.2 Set up a data base that contains information about credit cards, licenses and/or photos that could be lost or stolen from a typical adult wallet. Your data base should include the names of the cards or licenses, their numbers and the phone number or address to contact in the event of such a loss. Enter the data randomly, then sort the file alphabetically based on the name of the item (i.e. American Express card, Driver's License, Mastercard, Photo - Lisa, Photo - Julie, Visa card, etc.). Print a copy of all of the information in the file.

7.3 Write a second letter to Sue. Include an alphabetical list of vocabulary words in the letter that contains both the words and the definitions. The list should appear in the letter in two columns. There should be about 10 spaces between the word and the definition. (Think about how you can use the data base report to add the extra spaces.) Change the left margin in the section of the letter that the vocabulary list appears to 1.5 inches. Feel free to be creative with the other school news that you include in the letter. Print a copy of the letter for your instructor.

7.4   Design a data base for the information in the table below, which gives sprint speeds for several creatures. (A sprint speed is the speed that the creature can run, swim, or fly for a short period of time.) Enter the following information into your data base.

Creature	Speed (MPH)	Type
Bat	15	Mammal
Beaver	8	Mammal
Blue Jay	21	Bird
Blue Shark	33	Fish
Canvasback Duck	72	Bird
Cat	30	Mammal
Cheetah	70	Mammal
Dolphin	23	Mammal
Elephant	22	Mammal
Flying Fish	34	Fish
Golden Eagle	85	Bird
Gorilla	12	Mammal
Green Sea Turtle	21	Reptile
Grizzly Bear	28	Mammal
Horse	43	Mammal
Kangaroo	44	Mammal
Man	20	Mammal
Peregrine Falcon	100	Bird
Rabbit	45	Mammal
Snake	7	Reptile
Swordfish	48	Fish
Tortoise	3	Reptile
Trout	25	Fish
White-tailed Deer	29	Mammal

7.5   Use the data base you created in exercise 7.4 to answer the following questions. Use rule selection, arrangements and the find command to help you. Of the creatures in the list,

a.   which one is the fastest sprinter?
b.   which one is the fastest mammal sprinter?
c.   which one is the slowest sprinter?
d.   which one is the slowest mammal sprinter?
e.   how many sprint faster than man?
f.   how many of the mammals sprint faster than man?
g.   how many sprint slower than the horse?
h.   which fish is the slowest?
i.   There are several birds that sprint faster than the fastest fish sprints. Are there any mammals that can sprint faster than the fastest fish?

D THE MUSIC COLLECTION

You have been asked to organize a very large music collection. Some of the collection is on tapes, some is on long playing records, some is on old 45 rpm records and some is on compact discs (CDs). To add to the complexity of your task, about half of the tapes in the collection are purchased, prerecorded tapes, and the rest are home-recorded. Each record, tape, and CD is numbered, and it appears that there is no duplication of numbers. In other words, if one of the records is number 10, there is no tape or compact disc that is also numbered 10. You have decided to create an AppleWorks data base to help you organize the collection.

```
Record 9 of 18
========================================================================
Number: 204
Title: Revolver
Artist: The Beatles
Type: 60's Rock
Date: 1966
Producer: George Martin
Medium: Record
Favorite of: Mom
::::::::::::::::::::::: -
Song 1: Taxman                          Song 7: Good Day Sunshine
Song 2: Eleanor Rigby                   Song 8: For No One
Song 3: Love You To                     Song 9: I Want To Tell You
Song 4: Here, There and Everywhere      Song 10: Got to Get You Into My Life
Song 5: Yellow Submarine                Song 11: Tomorrow Never Knows
Song 6: She Said She Said               Song 12: -
------------------------------------------------------------------------
```

FIGURE D-1.   An Album Data Base Record.

You have two ideas in mind for the data base. One is to create one data base record for each item; the data base record would include the name of the album, the artist, the type of music, the date the album was produced,who produced it, the medium it is recorded on, the song titles included in the album and who in the family likes this music. One of the records in this data base might look like the one shown in Figure D-1.

The second idea uses one data base record for each song in the collection. The same information would be kept in this data base as in the first one. Figure D-2 is a printout from this second data base file. (Date and Medium are not shown in this report.) This printout includes the album in Figure D-1 as well as a record and a tape that are not in this figure. You should think about how the additional record and tape in Figure D-2 might look when they are arranged as shown in Figure D-1.

Num	Type	Artist	Album	Song	Producer	Favorite of
16	Rock	Springstein	Steve 6/86	Born in the USA	Me	Steve
16	Folk	Crosby,Stills	Steve 6/86	Wooden Ships	Me	Steve
16	Folk	Crosby,Stills	Steve 6/86	Carry On	Me	Virginia
16	Folk	Crosby,Stills	Steve 6/86	Suite: Judy Blue E	Me	Virginia
40	Rock	Springstein	The River	Born to Run		
203	Classical	Fiedler	Grand Canyon Suite	Grand Canyon Suite	RCA	Dad
203	Classical	Fiedler	Grand Canyon Suite	El Salon Mexico	RCA	Dad
204	60's Rock	The Beatles	Revolver	Taxman	Martin	Dad
204	Folk	The Beatles	Revolver	Eleanor Rigby	Martin	Mom
204	60's Rock	The Beatles	Revolver	Love You To	Martin	Mom
204	60's Rock	The Beatles	Revolver	Here, There and Ev	Martin	Mom
204	60's Rock	The Beatles	Revolver	Yellow Submarine	Martin	Bob
204	60's Rock	The Beatles	Revolver	She Said She Said	Martin	Mom
204	Ballad	The Beatles	Revolver	Good Day Sunshine	Martin	Mom
204	60's Rock	The Beatles	Revolver	For No One	Martin	
204	60's Rock	The Beatles	Revolver	I Want To Tell You	Martin	Mom
204	60's Rock	The Beatles	Revolver	Got To Get You Int	Martin	Mom
204	60's Rock	The Beatles	Revolver	Tomorrow Never Kno	Martin	Mom

FIGURE D-2. Alternate File Structure for Album Data Base.

YOUR TASK

Create a data base file to keep track of a music collection. Use one of the two format ideas presented above. Write a short paper (one to two pages double-spaced) explaining why you chose the data base format that you did. Include in your explanation the merits and the faults of each of the two data base organizations and how your choice might change depending on how the data base will be used. If you have another idea for organizing a data base for a music collection, discuss with your teacher the possibility of including your idea in your report. Hand in the report together with a print out of a screen display showing one record of your file.

UNIT

8 MASTERING THE SPREADSHEET

LEARNING OBJECTIVES

1. After completing this unit, you should know ...

   a. how to organize the overall layout of a Spreadsheet.

   b. why you sometimes must deal with oversized spreadsheet files.

   c. how to print oversized spreadsheet files.

   d. additional built-in calculation functions and why you use them.

   e. how to detect forward referencing and why you avoid it.

2. After completing this unit, you should be able to ...

   a. change a Spreadsheet's column width.

   b. format the contents of a spreadsheet document.

   c. implement manual calculation.

   d. arrange the information in a spreadsheet document.

   e. duplicate a large block of a spreadsheet document using the clipboard.

   f. split the screen to display selected rows or columns of information.

   g. print selected columns of information from a spreadsheet document.

ASSIGNMENTS

1. CREATE: Open a spreadsheet file and enter information.

2. LABEL LIST: Enter a list of labels.

3. VALUE LIST: Enter a list of values.

4. STANDARD VALUES: Set the standard values for label and value formats.

5. AVERAGE: Find the simple average for grades entered into a spreadsheet file.

6. WEIGHTED AVERAGE: Calculate student averages where tests count more than quizzes.

7. CLASS AVERAGES: Calculate the averages for the tests and quizzes a class takes.

8. INSERT: Add a new student into the class.

9. DELETE: Remove a student from the class.

10. TITLES: Set and use Spreadsheet titles.

11. WINDOWS: Display selected parts of your spreadsheet file using a combination of titles and windows.

12. BLOCK DUPLICATION: Make a copy of a large section of your spreadsheet file.

13. PRINT: Produce several variations of your spreadsheet file.

IMPORTANT KEYSTROKES AND COMMANDS

COMMAND	MEANING
⌘-A	Arrange or sort rows.
⌘-D	Delete rows or columns.
⌘-I	Insert rows or columns.
⌘-J	Jump from one window to another.
⌘-K	Recalculate formulas.
⌘-O	Display the printer options.
⌘-T	Fix titles in the display.
⌘-W	Change windows in the display.

In this unit you'll examine a more complex spreadsheet file involving a familiar topic, grading. You'll simulate the grades of an AppleWorks class for two grading periods. There are several quiz grades and test grades that must be averaged for each grading period. In addition, the grading periods must be averaged to produce a final average.

There are many grading systems. You'll use one where the average of the tests in each marking period counts three times and the average of the quizzes counts once. Remember that the computer will do all of the arithmetic; all you need to do is supply the formulas and the grades.

The class grades used in this example are number grades such as 71, 74, 79, 87, and 95. Indeed, the Spreadsheet can only be used for keeping number grades. There is no method in the current version of AppleWorks (Version 1.3) to do alphabetic grades.

If you develop a spreadsheet to keep track of your own grades, you can easily examine questions such as, What score do I need on the next test to raise my grade bt one level?" and answer them very precisely, I need 84.27 or higher to have an average in the 80's.

ENTERING LISTS OF LABELS

The first task is to enter the names of the students into the spreadsheet file. The names only need to be entered one time. (The copy command can be used to duplicate the list of names if it is required more than once.)

GUIDED ACTIVITY: CREATE

Start AppleWorks if it is not already running on your computer.
Move to the Main Menu and follow these steps:

WHAT YOU TYPE	WHY YOU TYPE IT
1 <RETURN>	To select **1. Add files to the Desktop**.
5 <RETURN>	To select **Make a new file for the: 5. Spreadsheet**.
1 <RETURN>	To select **1. From scratch**.
Class Grades	To name the file.
<RETURN>	To display the blank spreadsheet file.

Here is the list of names for the example. Examine them for a moment; then we'll discuss their features before entering them.

Arthur, Erica
Bill, Stacy
Canon, Connie
Cutelli, Matt
John, Eric

Kapp, Mary
Keller, Betty
Keller, Sean
Kess, Michael
Luke, George
Shecora, Michelle
Trinski, Bruce

The nine-character standard width of the column doesn't leave enough room for both surname and first name for any of these students. You have the choice of using two columns for the students' names or expanding the width of the first column to accommodate the longest name. Let's expand the width of the first column.

The longest name on the list is 17 characters, counting the comma and the space between last and first names. Add one more character for a space at the end of the name and you need 18 characters in the column. Thus you need to expand the width of all of the cells in the first column by 9 characters. The **layout** command does this.

GUIDED ACTIVITY: LABEL LIST

The first step in entering a list of labels is to set the column width to accommodate the widest label.

WHAT YOU TYPE	WHY YOU TYPE IT
Arrows	If it is not already there, move the cell locator to cell A1.
⌘-L	To change the screen layout.
C	To select **Column** from the choices that appear in the lower left corner of the screen.

The computer indicates that you are to highlight the columns you want to alter by pressing the left or right arrow keys.

WHAT YOU TYPE	WHY YOU TYPE IT
<RETURN>	To select the highlighted column. Since the only column that you wish to change is column one, which is already highlighted, you only needed to press Return.
C	To select **Column width.**
⌘-RIGHT-ARROW nine times	To expand the width of the column by 9. The column width expands in the display as you do this.
<ESCAPE>	To indicate that you are finished expanding the column.
<DOWN-ARROW> three times	To move the cell locator to cell A4, leaving three lines for the title of the spreadsheet file.

You now need to type the twelve names into column one. If you make an error, either move back to the cell and reenter the name correctly, or practice the edit command ($\circlearrowleft$-U) to fix the mistake. The first name is in cell A4, and the last name should occupy cell A15.

WHAT YOU TYPE
_____

```
Arthur, Erica      <DOWN-ARROW>
Bill, Stacy        <DOWN-ARROW>
Canon, Connie      <DOWN-ARROW>
Cutelli, Matt      <DOWN-ARROW>
John, Eric         <DOWN-ARROW>
Kapp, Mary         <DOWN-ARROW>
Keller, Betty      <DOWN-ARROW>      (This name is in cell A10.)
Keller, Sean       <DOWN-ARROW>
Kess, Michael      <DOWN-ARROW>
Luke, George       <DOWN-ARROW>
Shecora, Michelle <DOWN-ARROW>
Trinski, Bruce     <DOWN-ARROW>
```

```
File: Class Grades                REVIEW/ADD/CHANGE              Escape: Main Menu
============A============B========C========D========E========F========G====
  1|
  2|                     Quiz     Test
  3|                     9/21/88  9/27/88
  4|Arthur, Erica           100       95
  5|Bill, Stacy              90       87
  6|Canon, Connie            95       85
  7|Cutelli, Matt                     75
  8|John, Eric              100       90
  9|Kapp, Mary               80       93
 10|Keller, Betty            75      100
 11|Keller, Sean             80       95
 12|Kess, Michael            90      100
 13|Luke, George
 14|Shecora, Michelle       100      100
 15|Trinski, Bruce          100      100
 16|
 17|
 18|
----------------------------------------------------------------------------
A 1

Type entry or use ⌘ commands                              ⌘-? for Help
```

FIGURE 8-1.   First Quiz and Test Grades.

ENTERING LISTS OF VALUES

The grades for the first quiz and the first test are shown in Figure 8-1. The first set of grades is for a quiz given 9/21/88. Cells B2 and B3 contain information about the quiz grades at the top of the column and make it possible to identify the source of the grade at a later date. The second set of grades is for a test given 9/27/88. Again, the cells at the top of the column are used to identify the grades.

GUIDED ACTIVITY: VALUE LIST

Enter all of the grades from the figure column by column. Start at the top of the B column.

WHAT YOU TYPE	WHY YOU TYPE IT
<DOWN-ARROW>	To leave cell B1 blank and move the cell locator to cell B2.
Quiz <DOWN-ARROW>	To enter the title for the column of grades and move the cell locator to cell B3
"9/21/88	To enter the date of the quiz. (Remember, the quotation mark is needed to signal the computer that the date is a label, not a value to be computed.) The cell locator should now be in cell B4.
100 <DOWN-ARROW>	To enter the first grade and move the cell locator down.
The second grade from the quiz list. <DOWN-ARROW>.	
The third grade from the quiz list. <DOWN-ARROW>.	
<DOWN-ARROW>	To leave the cell blank for Cutelli's missing grade.

Type the remaining quiz grades for the column. You're on your own. Don't forget to press Down-Arrow after each entry.

Check your entries. Make sure that your numbers are correct and in the correct rows.

WHAT YOU TYPE	WHY YOU TYPE IT
Arrows	To move to cell C2.

Enter the labels and grades in the C column. You start in cell C2 with the label "Test".

Your display should match Figure 8-1 when you have made all the entries. Please correct any mistakes you might have made by reentering the correct information or by editing the entry.

STANDARD VALUES

The information in a spreadsheet is displayed in a preset, standard fashion. Labels are left justified and values are appropriate unless you change the layout setting. If most of the entries in your spreadsheet file must be displayed in other layout formats, making the changes can be time consuming. For example, if you want most of your labels to be right justified rather than left justified, each time you enter a new label, you need to change its layout. It would be nice in this case if the preset, standard display was right justify and the layout only needed to be changed for the few labels that you wanted to display as left or center justify.

Conveniently, the **standard value** command allows you to select any display format for either values or labels as the standard, automatic, default setting. This change can be made either before or after you enter information into the spreadsheet file.

GUIDED ACTIVITY: STANDARD VALUES

Adjust the information you have already entered by making the default setting for value cells comma spacing with no decimal places.

WHAT YOU TYPE	WHY YOU TYPE IT
⌂-V	To set "Standard Values".
\<RETURN\>	To select **Value** format change.
C	To select **Commas** format.
\<RETURN\>	To select **0** decimal places.

Notice that the comma setting provides one space after the number. The display adjusts to show the new setting.

Make the standard value setting for label cells "Right justify."

WHAT YOU TYPE	WHY YOU TYPE IT
⌂-V	To set "Standard Values" again.
L	To select **Label format** change.
R	To select **Right justify.**

Your new standard value settings are automatically used for any new labels or values that are entered into the spreadsheet file. Unless you specify otherwise, the default setting that you have just selected is used. You specify otherwise by using the layout command as you have previously done. Since the list of names looks better left-justified, we'll specify this format for the first column. The commands to do this are:

WHAT YOU TYPE	WHY YOU TYPE IT
\<LEFT-ARROW\>	To move to column one.
⌂-L	To start a "Layout" change.
C	To select a **Column** change.
\<RETURN\>	To select the highlighted column.
L	To select **Label format** change.
L	To select **Left justify** for the column.

Your display should now be identical to the one shown in Figure 8-2. Notice that the quiz, test, and date labels are all right-justified.

```
File: Class Grades              REVIEW/ADD/CHANGE              Escape: Main Menu
============A============B=======C=======D=======E========F========G====
   1|
   2|                     Quiz      Test
   3|                  9/21/88   9/27/88
   4|Arthur, Erica        100        95
   5|Bill, Stacy           90        87
   6|Canon, Connie         95        85
   7|Cutelli, Matt                   75
   8|John, Eric           100        90
   9|Kapp, Mary            80        93
  10|Keller, Betty         75       100
  11|Keller, Sean          80        95
  12|Kess, Michael         90       100
  13|Luke, George
  14|Shecora, Michelle    100       100
  15|Trinski, Bruce       100       100
  16|
  17|
  18|
-----------------------------------------------------------------------
B4:  (Value)  100

Type entry or use Ô commands                          Ô-? for Help
```

FIGURE 8-2. Formatted Test and Quiz Grades.

To check the value format, move the cell locator to cell B4. The values should all have a space trailing the number. (The trailing space only appears with dollar or comma value formats.) In addition, notice that the format indication C0 does not appear in the lower left corner. The indicator only shows formats that have been changed using the Open-Apple-L command. No indicator means that the standard format (commas with no decimal places since your change) is used.

ARRANGING INFORMATION

The Spreadsheet can arrange rows of information in a manner similar to the way the Data Base arranges information. The Spreadsheet, however, allows you to select the rows containing the information that you wish to sort. You do not need to sort every entry as you do in the Data Base. As you'll see in the next Guided Activity, this is a necessary feature.

Let's look at the quiz grades in rank order; that is, in order from lowest to highest. You must order the information in your spreadsheet file by the quiz grades in the B column. The ordering does not include the labels "Quiz" or "9/21/88" in cells B2 and B3, respectively.

WHAT YOU TYPE	WHY YOU TYPE IT
Arrows	To move the cell locator to cell B4, the first cell in the list of cells to be arranged. This cell contains Erica Arthur's quiz grade of 100.
-A	To start the arrange procedure.
-9	To highlight all of the grades down the column. You are selecting the rows to be arranged.

All the entries in each row (from 4 to 15) are highlighted when you complete these steps indicating that the computer will keep the name, test, and quiz grade in each row together when the quiz grades are rearranged. You requested AppleWorks use column B for the arrangement order by positioning the cell locator in cell B4 at the start or the arrangement procedure. Let's continue.

WHAT YOU TYPE	WHY YOU TYPE IT
<RETURN>	To indicate that you have finished the selection.
Down-Arrow	To highlight option 3. **Values from 0 to 9** (low number to high).
<RETURN>	To complete the arrangement process. The quiz grades are now in rank order.

Note that the names and test grades are also rearranged. The entire row of information is movedwhen a quiz grade is moved so that the students and their grades are not mixed up. Notice, too, that the blank grades are lower than zero and move to the top of the list.

The names within a group of identical grades are still in alphabetical order. For example, the students who have 100 appear in alphabetical order: Erica Arthur, Eric John, Michelle Shecora, and Bruce Trinski. (Recall that rearrangements work the same way in the Data Base.)

Let's arrange the file again, this time in the order of highest test grade to lowest test grade.

WHAT YOU TYPE	WHY YOU TYPE IT
Arrows	To move the cell locator to C4, the first cell in the list of test scores (C4 now contains the 75 for Matt Cutelli).
-A	To start the arrange process.
-9	To highlight the entire list of grades.
<RETURN>	To indicate that the selection is complete.
4 <RETURN>	To select 4. **Values from 9 to 0** (high number to low number) for the sort order.

Now the test grades are in order, but the names and quiz grades are not. Figure 8-3 displays this arrangement.

```
File: Class Grades            REVIEW/ADD/CHANGE            Escape: Main Menu
============A============B========C=======D========E========F========G====
   1|
   2|                      Quiz     Test
   3|                     9/21/88  9/27/88
   4|Keller, Betty          75      100
   5|Kess, Michael          90      100
   6|Shecora, Michelle     100      100
   7|Trinski, Bruce        100      100
   8|Keller, Sean           80       95
   9|Arthur, Erica         100       95
  10|Kapp, Mary             80       93
  11|John, Eric            100       90
  12|Bill, Stacy            90       87
  13|Canon, Connie          95       85
  14|Cutelli, Matt                   75
  15|Luke, George
  16|
  17|
  18|
-----------------------------------------------------------------------
C4:  (Value)  100

Type entry or use ⌕ commands                      ⌕ -? for Help
```

FIGURE 8-3.   Grades Ordered by Test Score.

Note that alphabetical order within groups is no longer preserved. Sean Keller is listed before Erica Arthur in the group of students who scored 95 on the test. The order of the previous quiz arrangement, low quiz to high quiz, is preserved in each test grade group. Sean has a lower quiz grade than Erica, so he is listed first. The quiz arrangement is preserved since it was the last arrangement made before the test arrangement was done.

It appears that you have made a mess of the file. You really want the names in alphabetical order. No problem.

WHAT YOU TYPE	WHY YOU TYPE IT
Arrows	To move the cell locator to A4, the location of the first name on the list, Betty Keller.

☃-A	To start the arrange process.
Arrows	To highlight the list of names.
<RETURN>	To indicate that the selection is complete.
<RETURN>	To select **Labels from A to Z.**

Everything is returned to normal.

In summary, the steps in the arrange command are: move the cell locator to the first cell in the column of cells to be arranged, issue the ☃-A command, highlight the items to be arranged, and select the type of arrangement desired.

✔ __CHECKPOINT__

Why is it necessary to be able to select a range of rows for the arrangement process rather than have to arrange on all of the rows in a column?

AVERAGING THE GRADES

Since there is only one quiz grade and one test grade, let's just take an average of these two grades for the moment. The average could be placed in column D. If you do this, the column for averages would then have to be moved to the right each time that you entered new test or quiz scores. Eventually the average column would move so far to the right that it would no longer be visible on the screen. A simple way to avoid this inconvenience is to place the averages in column B.

Placing the result of a computation to the left of the numbers used in the computation is called **forward referencing**. It causes no problem whatsoever if the cells on the right are numbers and not formulas. (We'll discuss the problems that evolve using formulas and forward referencing later in this chapter.) For now, placing the averages in column B seems like a perfectly logical and convenient way to proceed.

GUIDED ACTIVITY: AVERAGE

Before you can put the average formulas into column B, you need to digress for a moment and insert a blank column at this location.

WHAT YOU TYPE	WHY YOU TYPE IT
Arrows	To move the cell locator to any cell in column B. Column B is the column to be inserted.
☃-I	To start the insert process.
C	To select **Column.**
1 <RETURN>	To indicate one column is to be added and to complete the insert process.

The quiz grades are now in column C and the test grades are in column D. Column B is blank.

WHAT YOU TYPE	WHY YOU TYPE IT
Arrows	To move the cell locator to cell B3.
Average	To enter this label into cell B3.
<DOWN-ARROW>	To complete the label entry and move to cell B4. Note that "Average" is right-justified. (Remember, right justify is the default setting for labels in this file.)
@AVG(C4...D4) <RETURN>	To enter the average formula for cell B4.

Erica's average, 98 , appears in cell B4. The 98 is really 97.5 rounded off. Remember, the default setting for values is commas with no decimal places.

The other students also need formulas for their averages. The formula references are relative to the row that they are in. But before you copy this formula down the column, let's think ahead.

When you enter a new column of grades, the formula will need to be changed to include the new column. If the method of calculating grades is to take the average of all tests, quizzes, and other grades for the marking period, then the formula for the entire marking period can be entered now. For 24 or fewer grades in the marking period, the formula @AVG(C4...Z4) completely defines this grading method. All that needs to be done is add the grades.

GUIDED ACTIVITY: AVERAGE (continued)

Enter the formula   @AVG(C4...Z4)   in cell B4.

You can do this by typing in the formula or by using ⌘-U to edit the cell, changing the "D" to a "Z". After you enter the new formula, Erica's average still appears as a 98 since the average formula only takes the average of non-blank value cells in the range given, so the empty cells from column E to column Z are ignored. As new grades are added into any of these columns, the average is recomputed to include them.

It is important to note that missing numbers are not included in the average. If you wish to average missing grades as zeros or some other number, the zero or number must be entered.

The average displayed is rounded off to the nearest whole number automatically. It can just as easily be displayed rounded to the nearest tenth or hundredth. Remember, the layout command is used to change the format of a value if it is different from the standard (now commas with no decimals). Let's make a change to display the average to one decimal place.

WHAT YOU TYPE	WHY YOU TYPE IT
⌘-L	To start the layout command.
<RETURN>	To change the layout for the **entry**.

<RETURN>	To select **Value format.**
C	To select **Comma** format.
1 <RETURN>	To specify 1 decimal place.

The display changes to show a grade of 97.5.

Copy the formula down the column to compute averages for the other students. Here are the copy instructions; remember, if you make an error, press Escape and try again.

WHAT YOU TYPE	WHY YOU TYPE IT
⌘-C	To start the copy process.
<RETURN>	To select **Within worksheet.**
<RETURN>	To select B4 as the source.
<DOWN-ARROW>	To move to cell B5.
.	To select B5 as the first destination cell in the destination range.
<DOWN-ARROW> ten times	To select B5 to B15.
<RETURN>	To indicate cell selection is complete.
R	To make C4 relative in each new formula.
R	To make Z4 relative in each new formula.

The formula is copied into cells B5 to B15, and the averages for the other students are displayed. The layout format set for cell B4 is also copied. All of the averages are displayed to one decimal place. Figure 8-4 shows your spreadsheet file as it now appears.

ERROR is displayed as the average for George Luke who has no grades at all. The average formula must have at least one grade in order for it to compute an average. If there are no numbers in the range of cells specified, ERROR is displayed. When George makes up his work and the grades are entered, his average will be computed. To verify this,

WHAT YOU TYPE
90 into cell C13 for his quiz grade.
95 into cell D13 for his test.

The error message disappears after you enter the first grade; his average now appears as 92.5.

```
File: Class Grades           REVIEW/ADD/CHANGE             Escape: Main Menu
============A============B========C========D========E========F========G====
   1|
   2|                               Quiz     Test
   3|                     Average  9/21/88  9/27/88
   4|Arthur, Erica         97.5     100       95
   5|Bill, Stacy           88.5      90       87
   6|Canon, Connie         90.0      95       85
   7|Cutelli, Matt         75.0               75
   8|John, Eric            95.0     100       90
   9|Kapp, Mary            86.5      80       93
  10|Keller, Betty         87.5      75      100
  11|Keller, Sean          87.5      80       95
  12|Kess, Michael         95.0      90      100
  13|Luke, George         ERROR
  14|Shecora, Michelle    100.0     100      100
  15|Trinski, Bruce       100.0     100      100
  16|
  17|
  18|
--------------------------------------------------------- ------------------
B4: (Value, Layout-C1) @AVG(C4...Z4)

Type entry or use  commands                          -? for Help
```

FIGURE 8-4.   Spreadsheet with Grade Averages.

CALCULATION MODES

Inserting additional sets of grades into this worksheet is an easy task because we are using a very simple averaging system at the moment. Since your goal for this grade model is to count the test average as three times the quiz average, you need to keep the quiz and test grades physically separated. So, to add a set of test grades, you would move to the last column and add them in the next availabe blank column; to add a set of quiz grades, you would insert a blank column after the last quiz column (and before the first test column), then enter the grades there.

Now let's add a second test into column E.

GUIDED ACTIVITY: AVERAGE   (continued)

WHAT YOU TYPE	WHY YOU TYPE IT
Arrows	To move to cell E2.
Test <DOWN-ARROW>	To enter the label into cell E2 and move the cell locator to cell E3.
"10/05/88 <DOWN-ARROW>	To enter the date of the test into cell E3. (Remember, you must use quotation marks (") to type the date as a label.)
90 <DOWN-ARROW>	To enter Erica's grade.
83 <DOWN-ARROW>	To enter Bill's grade.
80 <DOWN-ARROW>	To enter Connie's grade.
75 <DOWN-ARROW>	To enter Matt's grade.

Did you notice that the computer pauses for a moment after you enter each grade? After each entry is made, the computer recalculates every formula in the spreadsheet file. As the spreadsheet file grows, the recalculation and the pause get longer and longer. The grade entry would certainly be faster if the recalculation could wait until the end of the entry process.

To save entry time and avoid the annoying pause after each grade is entered, let's tell AppleWorks to recalculate only when we want it to. This is called **manual calculation** mode. The sequence of commands to do this is:

WHAT YOU TYPE	WHY YOU TYPE IT
⌘-V	To change standard values.
R	For **Recalculate**.
F	To change the **Frequency** of calculation.
M	To change to **Manual** calculation.

Notice that this command can be used to change the order of calculation as well as the frequency of calculation. The order can be either down the columns from the left to the right or across the rows from top to bottom.

Now enter the rest of the test grades shown below. Notice that there is no recalculation after you enter each grade.

WHAT YOU TYPE	AS A GRADE FOR:
80 <DOWN-ARROW>	John, Eric
95 <DOWN-ARROW>	Kapp, Mary
75 <DOWN-ARROW>	Keller, Betty
75 <DOWN-ARROW>	Keller, Sean
90 <DOWN-ARROW>	Kess, Michael
95 <DOWN-ARROW>	Luke, George

80 <DOWN-ARROW>   Shecora, Michelle
85 <DOWN-ARROW>   Trinski, Bruce

Since there was no recalculation, the averages are no longer correct. The command to manually recalculate the formulas is ⌘-K.

Issue the ⌘-K command.

The averages are recalculated, and your display should now match the one in Figure 8-5.

```
File: Class Grades              REVIEW/ADD/CHANGE           Escape: Main Menu
============A=============B========C========D========E========F========G====
   1|
   2|                             Quiz     Test     Test
   3|                   Average  9/21/88  9/27/88 10/05/88
   4|Arthur, Erica       95.0     100      95       90
   5|Bill, Stacy         86.7      90      87       83
   6|Canon, Connie       86.7      95      85       80
   7|Cutelli, Matt       75.0               75      75
   8|John, Eric          90.0     100      90       80
   9|Kapp, Mary          89.3      80      93       95
  10|Keller, Betty       83.3      75     100       75
  11|Keller, Sean        83.3      80      95       75
  12|Kess, Michael       93.3      90     100       90
  13|Luke, George        93.3      90      95       95
  14|Shecora, Michelle   93.3     100     100       80
  15|Trinski, Bruce      95.0     100     100       85
  16|
  17|
  18|
----------------------------------------------------------------------------
B4: (Value, Layout-C1) @AVG(C4...Z4)

Type entry or use ⌘ commands                          ⌘-? for Help
```

FIGURE 8-5. Grade Worksheet with Second Test.

GROUPING COLUMNS

Columns for test grades and columns for quiz grades must be grouped together so that our goal to average the tests and the quizzes so that the test average counts three times as much as the quiz average, can be accomplished. The problems of grouping information in columns (or rows) together in a spreadsheet file are varied. You'll encounter and examine several of those problems in this section.

To obtain a weighted average, you need to do three things: (1) calculate the test average; (2) calculate the quiz average; and (3) calculate the weighted average of these two averages. Let's take these tasks one at a time.

TEST AVERAGES

Calculating the test average for the two tests already entered is easy at this point. The problem comes when additional tests are added into the average. We would like to make the addition of more test grades to the group of test grades, and recalculation of those grades as easy and as automaticly as possible.

If a new test grade column is inserted before the first test (column D) or after the last test (column F), the test average formulas will not automatically adjust to include the new grades. If you used this method to insert columns of test grades, you would need to change the test average formulas each time you added test grades. This is time consuming, prone to error, and not generally desirable.

Although adding new test grades in the middle of the existing group of test grades does not seem logical, test grades added here are automatically added into the average formulas. Indeed, the formulas are also automatically adjusted to account for changes made by adding a column. For example, the formula @AVG(L22...O22) averages the values in the four cells L22, M22, N22, and O22. If a column is inserted at column O, the formula would adjust to @AVG(L22...P22). (The formula changes because the original O column moves right to column P.) The formula now averages the values in the five cells L22, M22, N22, O22 (the new column), and P22. (P22 contains the value that was in O22 before the insert.) Again, the problem with this method is that the new test grade is inserted into the group of test grades before the last test grades. In other words, the tests are not in chronological order across the columns. The good feature of this method is that the formulas are all adjusted automatically.

There is a way to modify the grouping to take advantage of the good features of the method above while avoiding the bad features. Leave one special column before the first test grade and another after the last test grade. Include the columns in the average formula, but, reserve them to mark the beginning and the end of the test grade section. Remember, cells that are blank or contain labels, will not be included in the average calculation even though they are a part of the formula.

Any test grades inserted between these beginning and ending columns are automatically added into the test average. Using a character like the vertical bar (|) in these columns delineates the test area for the computer and also marks off the test area on the screen for you. (Delineates is a fancy word for marks off.)

Since all of this may be getting a bit complicated, let's review what you are going to do before you do it. You'll insert a new column in column D; type the vertical bar (|) character in cell D1; center the character; copy it down to cell D15, and then repeat the process for column G. The vertical bar labels in the D and G columns mark the beginning and the end of the test score group. The precise steps to take are:

WHAT YOU TYPE	WHY YOU TYPE IT
Arrows	To move to cell D1.
⌂-I	To start the insert process.
C	To insert **columns**.
1 <RETURN>	To specify one column.
"| <RETURN>	Enter the vertical bar in D1.
⌂-L	To start the layout change.
<RETURN>	For the **Entry**.
L	For **Label** change.
C	To select **center**.
⌂-C	To start the copy process.
<RETURN>	To select **Within worksheet**.
<RETURN>	To select cell D1 as the source.
<DOWN-ARROW>	To move to D2. (D2 is the first cell to copy to.)
Down-Arrow	To move down to D15.
<RETURN>	To complete the copy process.

Repeat the process for column G by moving to cell G1 and following the steps above.

Continue with the steps below to compute the average for the tests.

WHAT YOU TYPE	WHY YOU TYPE IT
Arrows	To move the cell locator to cell H2.
Test <DOWN-ARROW>	To enter the label into cell H2. (The names went off the left edge of the display when you moved to the H column.)
Average <DOWN-ARROW>	To enter the label into cell H3 and move the dell locator to cell H4.
@AVG(D4...G4)	To enter the formula for the test averages for the first student.

Note that the calculation is completed for this formula and the result, 92, is displayed.

UNGUIDED ACTIVITY

Copy the formula down the column to cell H15. Select "Relative" for the D4 and G4 cell references in the formula.

(You have used the copy command several times and you should now be able to work through the one cell to many variation on your own. If you need all the steps one last time, here is what to do after you move the cell locator to cell H4: ⌂-C, <RETURN>, <RETURN>, <DOWN-ARROW>, <Period> (.), <DOWN-ARROW> ten times, <RETURN>, R, and R.)

The cells from H5 to H15 have not been recalculated; all contain the value 92.

Issue the ⌘-K command to recalculate and display the correct values in column H.

You would now add new test grades in the following way: add a column after the last test; enter the grades; recalculate the averages. The new test grade is automatically added to the formula and included in the test average.

Figure 8-6 shows the result of your efforts to this point.

```
File: Class Grades              REVIEW/ADD/CHANGE              Escape: Main Menu
========B========C========D========E========F========G========H========I====
   1|                        |                        |
   2|              Quiz       |     Test     Test      |          Test
   3|   Average  9/21/88      |   9/27/88  10/05/88    |        Average
   4|    58.8      100        |     95       90        |           92
   5|    86.2       90        |     87       83        |           85
   6|    85.6       95        |     85       80        |           82
   7|    75.0                 |     75       75        |           75
   8|    88.8      100        |     90       80        |           85
   9|    90.5       80        |     93       95        |           94
  10|    84.4       75        |    100       75        |           88
  11|    83.8       80        |     95       75        |           85
  12|    93.8       90        |    100       90        |           95
  13|    93.8       90        |     95       95        |           95
  14|    92.5      100        |    100       80        |           90
  15|    94.4      100        |    100       85        |           92
  16|
  17|
  18|
-------------------------------------------------------------------------
H4:  (Value)  @AVG(D4...G4)

Type entry or use ⌘ commands                              ⌘-? for Help
```

FIGURE 8-6.   Spreadsheet with Test Averages.

Let's take a detour here to observe a forward referencing problem in this spreadsheet file. Observe that Erica Arthur's average in cell B4 has changed from 95 to 94.4 because the Test Average is incorrectly included in the computation for Average. (Incorrectly including the Test Average is a different error that you'll correct shortly. For the moment, the error of including the Test Average in the overall average can help you to understand the problem of forward referencing.)

Watch what happens when you change one of Erica's test grades and recalculate.

WHAT YOU TYPE	WHY YOU TYPE IT
Arrows	To move the cell locator to cell E4.
0 <RETURN>	To enter a grade of zero for the 9/27/88 test.
⌂-K	To manually recalculate.

Erica's average changes, as expected. However 70.6 is not the correct average for 100, 0, 90, and 45.

Watch cell B4 as you recalculate once more with ⌂-K.

Even though you did not change any grades, her average changes again!

The problem is that the computer must calculate the formulas in a spreadsheet document one at a time in a given order. The default order is column by column. So the average in cell B4 is calculated before the Test Average in cell H4. The first time the computer did the calculations in cell B4, it used the test average from the grades of 95 and 90 rather than the test average from the grades of 0 and 90 since it had not calculated the average of 0 and 90 yet.

To avoid this problem follow the rule: never write a formula that uses the answer from another formula that is in a column to its right or in a row below it. In this example, the formula in B4 incorrectly depended on the answer to a formula to its right in cell H4, causing the forward reference error.

One tell-tale clue when you have a forward reference problem is you get two different answers when you repeat a calculation.

There is no forward referencing problem with values. A formula can reference explicit values (numbers you enter) anywhere in the worksheet.

Before we move on, notice that you cannot see the test averages and the students names on the screen at the same time. Let's fix that by moving the Test Average column to column B (this fixes the forward referencing problem and also fixes the error of including the Test Average in the overall Average.)

WHAT YOU TYPE	WHY YOU TYPE IT
Arrows	To move the cell locator to cell H1.
⌂-M	To start the move command.
<RETURN>	To select **Within worksheet**.
C	To select **columns**.
<RETURN>	To indicate that you are finished highlighting columns (only one column is highlighted).
<LEFT-ARROW> six times	To move to column B, the new location for the highlighted column.
<RETURN>	To complete the move command and to move the column.

✓ CHECKPOINT

A formula in a spreadsheet file in cell D9 uses the results of another formula in cell C5. Could this be an example of forward referencing?

QUIZ AVERAGES

Calculating quiz averages is the second part of an involved problem to compute weighted averages. Many times, when you set a difficult goal, you must solve and understand several side problems on the route to your goal. If you think about it, this is how you usually learn many new things. However, even though you have gone off on several good learning tangents, you cannot lose sight of your overall goal. Keep in mind that you are working on calculating a weighted average for the test and quiz grades.

The first step to take for finding the quiz average is to mark off the quiz average area the way you did the test average area. You'll need to move to column D and insert another column of vertical bars to provide the start column for the quiz grades. The vertical bar column that marks the end of the quiz area can be the same vertical bar column that is used to mark the start of the test area. Here is the procedure to follow to insert the one additional column:

GUIDED ACTIVITY: WEIGHTED AVERAGES   (continued)

WHAT YOU TYPE	WHY YOU TYPE IT
Arrows	To move the cell locator to D1.
⌘-I	To start the insert process.
C	To insert `columns`.
1 <RETURN>	To indicate one column is to be inserted.

Complete the procedure by copying all the vertical bars from column F to column D. The source is 15 cells in the F column from row 1 to row 15; the destination is the D column from row 1 to 15.

Move the cell locator to cell F1 to start.

WHAT YOU TYPE	WHY YOU TYPE IT
⌘-C	To start the copy process.
<RETURN>	To select `Within worksheet`.
Down-Arrow	To highlight cells down to F15.
<RETURN>	To complete the source selection.
Arrows	To move the cell locator to cell D1.
<RETURN>	To complete the move process.

Now insert a new column B for the quiz averages and enter the formula for the averages.

Move to cell B2 to start the process.

WHAT YOU TYPE	WHY YOU TYPE IT
Ś-I	To start the insert process.
C 1 <RETURN>	To insert one column.
Quiz <DOWN-ARROW>	
Average <DOWN-ARROW>	To label the column.
@AVG(E4...G4) <RETURN>	To enter the formula for the quiz averages.

The average, 100, is displayed for Erica Arthur.

```
File: Class Grades           REVIEW/ADD/CHANGE              Escape: Main Menu
============A===========B========C========D========E========F========G====
  1|                                             |                  |
  2|                  Quiz     Test               |         Quiz     |
  3|                  Averages Average  Average   |         9/21/88  |
  4|Arthur, Erica       100      45      63.3     |          100     |
  5|Bill, Stacy          90      85      86.7     |           90     |
  6|Canon, Connie        95      82      86.7     |           95     |
  7|Cutelli, Matt      ERROR     75      75.0     |                  |
  8|John, Eric          100      85      90.0     |          100     |
  9|Kapp, Mary           80      94      89.3     |           80     |
 10|Keller, Betty        75      88      83.3     |           75     |
 11|Keller, Sean         80      85      83.3     |           80     |
 12|Kess, Michael        90      95      93.3     |           90     |
 13|Luke, George         90      95      93.3     |           90     |
 14|Shecora, Michelle   100      90      93.3     |          100     |
 15|Trinski, Bruce      100      92      95.0     |          100     |
 16|
 17|
 18|
-------------------------------------------------------------------
B7: (Value)  @AVG(E7...G7)

Type entry or use Ś commands                        Ś-? for Help
```

FIGURE 8-7. Grade Spreadsheet with Test and Quiz Averages.

UNGUIDED ACTIVITY

Copy the formula from cell B4 into the cells from B5 to B15 making the E4 and G4 references relative.

✓ **CHECKPOINT**

When you finish the copy work in the Unguided Activity, all of the cells show a Quiz Average of 100. Why? How can you correct this?

Recalculate the worksheet with ⌂-K.

The current display of your work should match Figure 8-7.

The ERROR shown for Matt Cutelli in cell B7 appears because Matt has no quiz grades. The error message will disappear as soon as Matt has at least one quiz grade added to his record.

WEIGHTED AVERAGES

The goal is near. After you have looked over some of the possible formulas for obtaining a weighted average, you'll calculate it. There are several formulas that can be used to obtain the desired weighted marking period average - counting the test average as three times the quiz average. Three of these formulas are:

1. $\underline{\text{Quiz Average + Test Average + Test Average + Test Average}}$
                                        4

2. $\underline{\text{Quiz Average + 3 times Test Average}}$
                        4

3.   0.25 times Quiz Average + 0.75 times Test Average

In each case, the quiz average is counted once and the test average is counted three times. Remember that formulas in a spreadsheet file are calculated from left to right and parentheses are sometimes needed to insure that the calculation is done correctly.

Once you have entered a formula, you should test it with a set of grades with a known average. For example, a student with all grades of 100 should have an average of 100; entering the second formula below without the parentheses would give this student an average of 2,575.

With the Quiz Average in B4 and the Test Average in C4, the correct formulas for cell D4 for the formulas given above are:

1. (B4+C4+C4+C4)/4 or +B4+C4+C4+C4/4

2. (B4+(3*C4))/4   or +B4+(3*C4)/4

3. (.25*B4)+(.75*C4)

GUIDED ACTIVITY: WEIGHTED AVERAGE (CONTINUED)

Here are the last steps that you need to take in order to compute the final weighted average.

> Move the cell locator to cell D2.
> Type: Mk PER to indicate that the column now contains the weighted grades.
> Type one of the formulas above into cell D4 to calculate Erica's weighted average.
> (Erica's Quiz average is 100, her test average is 45, and her weighted average is 58.8.)
> Copy the formula into cells B5 to B15, making each cell reference "Relative".
> Recalculate the spreadsheet file for the remaining students using ⌘-K.

Notice that the lack of a quiz grade for Matt Cutelli produced errors in his Quiz Average and in his Marking Period Average. Both of these errors will be corrected when Matt obtains a quiz grade. If the ERROR message annoys you, give him a zero for now and then recalculate .

> Check the formula you entered by changing the two test grades for Erica Arthur to 100; recalculate the spreadsheet file. If all is correct, her Quiz, Test, and Weighted Marking Period Averages should all be 100.

✓ CHECKPOINT

> You have done a lot of work on this file. What should you do now to insure that you do not lose the work that you have done?

CLASS AVERAGES

Students like to know if they are above or below the class average. It is, therefore, helpful to calculate the average that the class obtained on a test or quiz. Let's decide that the class average formulas should be as flexible as the formulas that compute the test and quiz averages. In other words, if you add a new student to your class list, the formulas should automatically correct for the new entry. Make the formula extend from one row above the grades to one row below the grades to avoid any problems with formula readjustment if students are inserted or deleted. This also avoids problems that occur when the list is rearranged. If a formula uses a cell that changes rows in a new arrangement, the formula is changed to use the new location of the cell. By writing a formula using cells that remain above and below any cells that may be moved, you stop the formula from changing.

GUIDED ACTIVITY: CLASS AVERAGES

Let's use a row of dashes as the fixed cells in the formula for the class average.

> Insert one row at row 4 using the Open-Apple-I command.
> Fill the row with dashes starting in cell A4 and ending in cell J4.

(There are several ways to enter the dashes; one is to fill cell A4 with dashes and then copy the dashes into cells B4 to J4. Remember that you must start the entry with a quote mark or the computer expects that you are going to type a negative value.)

> Fill row 17 from column A to J with dashes.
> Move the cell locator to cell B18.
> Type: @Avg(B4...B17) <RETURN>.

If there is no quiz grade for Cutelli, the ERROR message is displayed; if you have not already done so, give him a zero for his missing quiz grade.

```
 File: Class Grades            REVIEW/ADD/CHANGE              Escape: Main Menu
 ============A============B========C========D========E========F========G====
  1|                                            |                |
  2|                  Quiz    Test   Mk Per     |        Quiz    |
  3|                Averages Average Average     |       9/21/88  |
  4|-------------------------------------------------------------------------
  5|Arthur, Erica     100      45     58.8      |        100     |
  6|Bill, Stacy        90      85     86.2      |         90     |
  7|Canon, Connie      95      82     85.6      |         95     |
  8|Cutelli, Matt       0      75     56.2      |          0     |
  9|John, Eric        100      85     88.8      |        100     |
 10|Kapp, Mary         80      94     90.5      |         80     |
 11|Keller, Betty      75      88     84.4      |         75     |
 12|Keller, Sean       80      85     83.8      |         80     |
 13|Kess, Michael      90      95     93.8      |         90     |
 14|Luke, George       90      95     93.8      |         90     |
 15|Shecora, Michelle 100      90     92.5      |        100     |
 16|Trinski, Bruce    100      92     94.4      |        100     |
 17|-------------------------------------------------------------------------
 18|                   83      84      84                83
 -------------------------------------------------------------------------
 B18:  (Value)  @AVG(B4...B17)

 Type entry or use ⌘ commands                           ⌘-? for Help
```

FIGURE 8-8.   Spreadsheet with Class Averages.

To obtain averages for all of the other columns, copy the formula across the spreadsheet.

> Copy the formula from B18 into cells C18 to I18 making both cell references relative.
> Recalculate with ⌘-K.
> Blank cells E18 and G18.
> (Remember, to blank a cell, move the cell locator to the cell and give the ⌘-B command followed by <RETURN>.)

You now see before you the spreadsheet file shown in Figure 8-8.

You should feel free to adjust the formatting to suit your own tases. For example, some values have one decimal place and others have no decimal places. To make all of the values display one decimal place, you would change the standard values (⌘-V) to commas with one decimal place. Alternatively, to make the Marking Period Averages display values in the same form as the rest of the worksheet, you would change the layout of the column to "standard." (Remember you have already set the standard value to commas format with no decimal places.)

✓ CHECKPOINT

> Would you use Open-Apple-L or Open-Apple-V to change the format of the averages in row 18 to commas with one decimal place? Explain your choice.

UNGUIDED ACTIVITY

> Change the layout for the values displayed in row 18 to commas with 1 decimal place.

INSERTING

Inserting rows or columns in a spreadsheet is quite easy. Practice the insert command by inserting a new student. You'll insert a new row, type in the student's name, and copy the formulas into the row.

GUIDED ACTIVITY: INSERT

Insert student Sally Wills into the class.

> Move the cell locator to row 17 and insert a row using Open-Apple-I.
> Copy the formulas, vertical bars, and grades from cells B16 to J16 into row 17.
> Type: Wills, Sally   into cell A17 and press <RETURN>.
> Change the layout format to **Left justify** the name.
> Blank out the grades from cells F17, H17, and I17.
> Recalculate.

The recalculation displays ERROR for all of Sally's averages, since she has no grades yet. As her grades are entered, the error messages will disappear. It is not likely that the first three test and quiz grades will be made up by this student. If no entry is made for the missing grades, they are ignored in calculating the average.

DELETING

The delete command in the Spreadsheet can be dangerous. You delete entire rows or columns including the parts of the rows and columns that do not appear on the display. It is wise to be sure that you are not deleting information you really wish to keep by moving up and down the column or across the row before you delete it.

Matt has decided to drop the course. Practice the delete command; remove him from the file.

GUIDED ACTIVITY: DELETE

Move the cell locator to any cell in Matt's row.

WHAT YOU TYPE	WHY YOU TYPE IT
○-D	To start the delete process.
<RETURN>	To delete the row.
○-K	To recalculate the spreadsheet file and update the test and quiz average calculations.

That's it. The student is removed from the file, and his grades are removed from all averaging calculations.

SPLITTING THE SCREEN

The worksheet is too large to see at one time. When a new test is added, the list of names disappears off the screen to the left, making it difficult to know who is getting what grade. It would be helpful to be able to look at the left side and the right side of the spreadsheet file simultaneously. At other times it may be helpful to examine an upper portion of the worksheet in relation to a lower portion. Splitting the screen allows you to arrange the display in these two ways.

There are two ways to split the screen: by **titles** or by **windows**. Titles allow one or more columns to remain on display on the left side of the screen while you examine cells to the right. Alternately, one or more rows can remain at the top of the display while you examine rows farther down the worksheet.

WHAT YOU TYPE	WHY YOU TYPE IT
Arrows	Move to cell B5. The location of the cell locator is important. Titles are set to the left of this location, or above it, or both to the left and above it.

| ○-T | To start the procedure to set the titles. |
| B | To select the option to set the titles on both the top and the left side. |

Watch the screen as you type the next command.

| ○-RIGHT-ARROW twice | To move the cell locator off of the right side of the screen. |

The names still appear on the screen. Look at the column heading at the top of the screen and check to see that column A is now displayed next to column H.

WHAT YOU TYPE	WHY YOU TYPE IT
<RIGHT-ARROW> twice	To move move column J right next to column A.

Adding additional grades into column J is easier now that you can visually match the names with the corresponding cell.

WHAT YOU TYPE	WHY YOU TYPE IT
Arrows	To move to column J.
○-I C 1 <RETURN>	To insert a new column.
Arrows	To move the cell locator to cell J2.

Two row 2's are displayed, one in the title section and the other in the worksheet section. Enter these labels and test grades: (Press the Down-Arrow key after each entry. Do not enter the names.) Keep your eye on the titles at the top of the screen as you enter the grades

WHAT YOU TYPE

Test	
"10/12/88	
"---------	
90	(Erica)
88	(Stacy)
89	(Connie)
90	(Eric)
90	(Mary)
80	(Betty)
85	(Sean)
85	(Michael)
90	(George)
85	(Michelle)
83	(Bruce)

95   (Sally)
"---------
⌂-K   To recalculate and to include the new grades in the average.

Sometimes the titles to the right appear twice in the display, once as part of the title section and once as part of the worksheet. This is confusing but no problem.

⌂-LEFT-ARROW twice   To observe the double list of names.

There are two ways to remove the double list.

Move right until the extra list of names disappears,
     or
Issue the ⌂-T command again and select "None" to remove the titles.

Now let's work with the other method of splitting the screen, the **windows**. Windows let you split the screen so that you can look at any two pieces of the spreadsheet simultaneously. You can look at the information in each window independently of the other window or you can lock the two windows together so movement in one window is reflected in the other window.

Even though you can examine the spreadsheet through two windows, you still have only one spreadsheet. Any change you make in either window changes the file. Let's explore.

GUIDED ACTIVITY: WINDOWS

Move the cell locator to column C.

WHAT YOU TYPE	WHY YOU TYPE IT
(⌂-T Return)	If titles are still showing, turn them off with this command.
⌂-W	To start the "window" command.
<RETURN>	To select **Side by side** windows.

The cell locator is in the right window.

Move the cell locator to cell C21 with the Down-Arrow key.

Notice that there is no corresponding movement in the right window. In fact, the names are no longer beside the correct grades. Movement in one window is independent of movement in the other window.

Move the cell locator to cell A21.

The same columns can be displayed in both windows. Again, observe that movement in one window is independent of movement in the other window.

Move the cell locator to cell D5.
Jump to the left window with Ⓒ-J and move to cell A21.
Move to cell G25.

It would be hard to realign the two windows at this point so that the name in one window is next to the corresponding grade in the other window. Fortunately, the computer can do this for us.

Issue the Ⓒ-W command and select **Synchronized**.
Move to cell A1 and note that the left window now lines up with the right.

Give the Ⓒ-W command one more time and select **One** to turn off the windows.

Here is a detailed example that uses windows and titles to allow selected columns to be displayed. You want to enter the quiz grades listed below. As you do, you want to compare them to both the 10/12/88 test grades and the Marking Period Average. So, follow the steps given below to display all of the following columns: A, the names; D, the Marking Period Averages; G, the entry column for the new quiz grades; and K, the column for the 10/12 test.

Move the cell locator to cell B1.

WHAT YOU TYPE	WHY YOU TYPE IT
Ⓒ-T L	To set titles on the left side.
Ⓒ-RIGHT-ARROW twice	To move right.
<RIGHT-ARROW> 3 times	To move column K next to A.
Arrows	To move the cell locator to cell L1.
Ⓒ-W S	To select windows that are **side-by-side**.
Ⓒ-T <RETURN>	To remove titles from the right side window.
Arrows	To move the cell locator to cell D1 to display the D column.
Arrows	To move the cell locator to cell G2.
Ⓒ-I C 1	To insert one column.

Enter the list of column labels and grades below. (Do not enter the names.) Remember to press the Down-Arrow key after each entry.

```
Quiz
"10/19/88
"---------
95          Arthur, Erica
93          Bill, Stacy
94          Canon, Connie
95          John, Eric
```

```
100                 Kapp, Mary
 88                 Keller, Betty
 85                 Keller, Sean
 90                 Kess, Michael
 95                 Luke, George
100                 Shecora, Michelle
 83                 Trinski, Bruce
 95                 Wills, Sally
"---------
```

This window arrangement is shown in Figure 8-9.

```
 File: Class Grades           REVIEW/ADD/CHANGE             Escape: Main Menu
 ============A============K============D========E========F========G====
   1|                        1|          |
   2|                Test    2|  Mk Per   |          Quiz     Quiz
   3|             10/12/88   3|  Average  |        9/21/88 10/19/88
   4|------------------------ 4|----------------------------------------
   5|Arthur, Erica     90    5|   96.9    |          100       95
   6|Bill, Stacy       88    6|   87.4    |           90       93
   7|Canon, Connie     89    7|   87.1    |           95       94
   8|John, Eric        90    8|   89.4    |          100       95
   9|Kapp, Mary        90    9|   92.0    |           80      100
  10|Keller, Betty     80   10|   84.1    |           75       88
  11|Keller, Sean      85   11|   84.4    |           80       85
  12|Kess, Michael     85   12|   91.2    |           90       90
  13|Luke, George      90   13|   93.1    |           90       95
  14|Shecora, Michelle 85   14|   91.2    |          100      100
  15|Trinski, Bruce    83   15|   89.9    |          100       83
  16|Wills, Sally      95   16|   95.0    |                    95
  17|------------------------ 17|----------------------------------------
  18|                        18|   90.1    |         90.9

 --------------------------------------------------------------------------
 G16: (Value) 95

 Type entry or use ⌂ commands                              ⌂-? for Help
```

FIGURE 8-9. Example of a Window Arrangement.

⌂-W <RETURN>   To set the display back to one window.

Since the cell locator was in the right window where no titles were set, there are no titles in the single window now displayed.

DUPLICATING A LARGE BLOCK

Duplicating a large block of information is quite a common task in building a spreadsheet file. When different information is calculated the same way, but, with different numbers, it is much easier to duplicate a section of the worksheet that has already been entered and tested and then enter the new numbers, than to re-enter all of the formulas and numbers. For example, in a business spreadsheet, cost comparisons for purchasing the same materials are made in sections of a spreadsheet that are identical except for the numbers. In the example you have been developing, the second marking period is quite similar to the first marking period, so why not just duplicate the first marking period and blank out all of the grades? While doing this, you also need to add some label information to clearly identify the first and second grading periods.

GUIDED ACTIVITY: BLOCK DUPLICATION

MOVE to cell A1.

WHAT YOU TYPE	WHY YOU TYPE IT
AppleWorks Course	To enter a title for the worksheet.
<DOWN-ARROW>	To move to cell A2.
Marking Period 1 <RETURN>	To identify the information that has already been entered as part of the first grading period.
<UP-ARROW>	To move back to cell A1.
⌃-C	To start to copy information for the next marking period.
T	To select **To clipboard**.
Arrows	To highlight all of the rows down to row 18.
<RETURN>	To complete the first part of the block duplication.
Arrows	To move the cell locator to cell A21.
⌃-C F	To copy the block of information **From** (the) **clipboard**.

The spreadsheet for the first marking period has now been duplicated in the rows below its original location. Look at the formula in cell B25. Notice that all of the formula references have been copied **relative** to their new locations. With a few more changes you will be ready for the next marking period.

> Move the cell locator to cell A22.
> Edit the information with the ⌃-U command to read "Marking Period 2".

In a real grade file, you would blank all of the grades with Open-Apple-B at this point, but to save time, you will not do that for this sample grade file. (NEVER DELETE COLUMNS. If you delete columns, you'll delete grades from the first marking period that are unseen but are still at the top of the column.) In a real grade file, you would use the blank command to blank out blocks of quiz grades, then to blank out blocks of test grades. You would then fill in new grades as the marking period progressed.

If you need additional space as the second marking period progresses, you can add columns as you did for the first marking period. If you do this, you will have extra blank columns in the first marking period section but they will not affect the averages in any way. Once the grading system is set, adding additional marking periods is not too difficult.

Leave the grades from the first marking period entered into the second marking period so that we can finish the example. Make the following changes so that the two marking periods are not exact duplicates. Be careful not to change any of the formulas in the average columns.

> Change all of the quiz grades in cells G25 to G36 to 75.
> Change all of the test grades in cells J25 to J36 to 100.
> Recalculate with ⌘-K.

RELATIVE FORMULAS WITH DISTANT LOCATIONS

So far, you have worked with relative formulas for calculations that are close together in the worksheet. There is no confinement for "relative" other than the 127 columns by 999 rows size limit of your worksheet. In other words, relative can mean the cell directly above or a cell twenty-five rows above. To illustrate this, you'll compute the final averages for the AppleWorks Course .

First make sure that the same students are listed for each quarter and that they're listed in exactly the same order. If necessary, arrange, delete, or insert so that all of the marking periods' student lists match exactly.

> Copy the first marking period records, rows 1 to 18, "To clipboard" just as you did in the last section.
> Move to cell D41 and copy the information "From clipboard".
> Blank the block of cells from B41 to L59. (Use ⌘-B.)

All that is left at the bottom of the spreadsheet file is the list of names and titles in the A column from row 41 to 57.

> Enter a Final Exam grade of 83 into cell B45 for the first student.
> Move to cell D45.
> Type: +B45+D5+D5+D25+D25/5 To enter the formula for the final average.

This formula computes the course average for the first student. It counts the two marking periods equally and counts the exam as one-fifth of the grade. An alternate and equally correct formula is:

> (B45)+(2*D5)+(2*D25)/5

The choice of column D for the final average computation was not arbitrary. The formula you entered for the final average uses answers from other formulas in column D. Placing the final average formula in column C would have caused a forward reference error since the values from column D needed in the formula are computed after column C is computed. That is, if the new formula had been placed in column C, it might find averages using numbers that were not correct.

All of the entries are now complete for the first student.

> Copy the formula in D45 for the other students making each cell reference "Relative".
> Type the label Final Grades in cell A42.
> Enter the other headings in rows 42 and 43 in Figure 8-10.
> Enter the final exam grades as shown in Figure 8-10.
> Recalculate and you're finished.

```
File: Class Grades          REVIEW/ADD/CHANGE          Escape: Main Menu
===========A============B========C========D========E========F========G====
 41| AppleWorks Course
 42|      Final Grades                    Course
 43|                       Exam          Average
 44|----------------------------------------------
 45|Arthur, Erica          83.0           93.1
 46|Bill, Stacy            85.0           87.7
 47|Canon, Connie          89.0           88.5
 48|John, Eric             76.0           87.7
 49|Kapp, Mary             90.0           90.8
 50|Keller, Betty          67.0           82.5
 51|Keller, Sean           80.0           85.5
 52|Kess, Michael          90.0           91.2
 53|Luke, George           97.0           93.4
 54|Shecora, Michelle      81.0           90.0
 55|Trinski, Bruce         93.0           91.6
 56|Wills, Sally           98.0           94.3
 57|----------------------------------------------
 58|
-------------------------------------------------------------------
D45: (Value, Layout-C1) +B45+D5+D5+D25+D25/5

Type entry or use Ĝ commands                      Ĝ-? for Help
```

FIGURE 8-10.   Final Grades.

✓ CHECKPOINT

Examine the formulas in cells D46 and D47. What did relative mean for each cell reference when you copied the formula from D45?

PRINTER OPTIONS

There are several options available for printing out spreadsheet files like the one that you just developed. Some options concern what you print and others concern how you print. The organizational work that you did in building the worksheet has increased your printing options. For example, if you wish to print just the students' names and averages, the averages should be placed physically next to the students' names. You have already done this; so all you need to do is select the information to print and print it.

The printing examples in this unit illustrate the problems you may encounter printing any spreadsheet document; many of them concern fitting a large document on a narrow page.

Let's print out the entire worksheet.

> If you are just starting up after a break, add the Class Grade file to the Desktop from the disk. If the file is already on the Desktop, select option 2 from the Main Menu to work with the Class Grade file.

GUIDED ACTIVITY: PRINT

The information in the worksheet is too wide to fit on 8.5 inch paper. To verify this:

> Issue the ⌘-P command.
> Select **All** to determine exactly how wide the information is.

The top of the screen displays:

```
The information that you identified
is 112 characters wide.

The Printer Options values allow
80 characters per line.
```

The message indicates that the width of the lines that you selected to print (112 characters) is greater than the actual print line, 80 characters. The document can be printed, but it will not be satisfactory, to read since information from each line will appear on two lines, or (with some printers) run off the paper, and with others it will not be printed at all. Increasing the number of characters printed on a line will solve this problem. Here's what to do:

WHAT YOU TYPE	WHY YOU TYPE IT
<ESCAPE>	To return the spreadsheet file to the display.
⌘-O	To select print options.
CI <RETURN>	
15 <RETURN>	To change **Characters per inch** to 15.

```
File:    Class Grades                                                                              Page  1

AppleWorks Course                                        |                         |
   Marking Period 1    Quiz     Test     Mk Per          |    Quiz      Quiz       |     Test     Test     Test      |
                       Average  Average  average         |   9/21/88  10/19/88     |    9/27/88  10/27/88 10/20/88   |
---------------------------------------------------------|-------------------------|----------------------------------
Arthur, Erica            98       97      96.9           |    100       95         |     100      100       90       |
Bill, Stacy              92       86      87.4           |     90       93         |      87       83       88       |
Canon, Connie            94       85      87.1           |     95       94         |      85       80       89       |
John, Eric               98       87      89.4           |    100       95         |      90       80       90       |
Kapp, Mary               90       93      92.0           |     80      100         |      93       95       90       |
Keller, Betty            82       85      84.1           |     75       88         |     100       75       80       |
Keller, Sean             82       85      84.4           |     80       85         |      95       75       85       |
Kess, Michael            90       92      91.2           |     90       90         |     100       90       85       |
Luke, George             92       93      93.1           |     90       95         |      95       95       90       |
Shecora, Michelle       100       88      91.2           |    100      100         |     100       80       85       |
Trinski, Bruce           92       89      89.9           |    100       83         |     100       85       83       |
Wills, Sally             95       95      95.0           |              95         |                        95       |
---------------------------------------------------------|-------------------------|----------------------------------
                        92.0     89.5     90.1           |    90.9      92.8       |     95.0     85.3     87.5


AppleWorks Course                                        |                         |
   Marking Period 2    Quiz     Test     Mk Per          |    Quiz      Quiz       |     Test     Test     Test      |
                       Average  Average  average         |   9/21/88  10/19/88     |    9/27/88     0     10/20/88   |
---------------------------------------------------------|-------------------------|----------------------------------
Arthur, Erica            88       97      94.4           |    100       75         |     100      100       90       |
Bill, Stacy              82       92      89.4           |     90       75         |      87      100       88       |
Canon, Connie            85       91      89.8           |     95       75         |      85      100       89       |
John, Eric               88       93      91.9           |    100       75         |      90      100       90       |
Kapp, Mary               78       94      90.1           |     80       75         |      93      100       90       |
Keller, Betty            75       93      88.8           |     75       75         |     100      100       80       |
Keller, Sean             78       93      89.4           |     80       75         |      95      100       85       |
Kess, Michael            82       95      91.9           |     90       75         |     100      100       85       |
Luke, George             82       95      91.9           |     90       75         |      95      100       90       |
Shecora, Michelle        88       95      93.1           |    100       75         |     100      100       85       |
Trinski, Bruce           88       94      92.6           |    100       75         |     100      100       83       |
Wills, Sally             75       98      91.9           |              75         |              100       95       |
---------------------------------------------------------|-------------------------|----------------------------------
                        82.3     94.2     91.2           |    90.9      90.9       |     95.0     100.0    100.0


AppleWorks Course
   Final Grades

------------------------------------------------
Arthur, Erica            83.0              93.1
Bill, Stacy              85.0              87.7
Canon, Connie            89.0              88.5
John, Eric               76.0              87.7
Kapp, Mary               90.0              90.8
Keller, Betty            67.0              82.5
Keller, Sean             80.0              85.5
Kess, Michael            90.0              91.2
Luke, George             97.0              93.4
Shecora, Michelle        81.0              90.0
Trinski, Bruce           93.0              91.6
Wills, Sally             98.0              94.3
------------------------------------------------
```

FIGURE 8-11.   Printout of Class Grades.

Note that an estimate of the number of characters printed per line (Char per line (est)) is displayed on the center left on the screen. As you change the number of characters per inch, the estimated number of characters per line changes. The estimate reads 120 characters. The line of 112 characters now fits.

Press <ESCAPE> to return the spreadsheet file to the display.

(Both the AppleWorks reference manual and your printer manual indicate what characters per inch are available for your printer. Remember, too, that AppleWorks may need to be informed of the exact codes for your printer if you are using a custom printer. If you have not set up your printer yet, see Appendix C.)

Print a copy of your file.

WHAT YOU TYPE	WHY YOU TYPE IT
⌘-S	Always save your file before you print.

Make sure that your printer is on, properly connected, and the select light is lit.

WHAT YOU TYPE	WHY YOU TYPE IT
⌘-P	To start the printing process. Read the screen messages to verify that the printer option settings allow sufficient characters per line.
<RETURN>	To select **all**.
Arrows	To highlight your printer's name.
<RETURN>	To select the printer.
Today's date <RETURN>	To enter the date
<RETURN>	To accept 1 for the number of copies

If your printer is on, loaded, and connected properly, the file will print out as shown in Figure 8-11.

As a variation, print only the averages for each marking period including the final grade averages. Print this report in 10 characters per inch.

WHAT YOU TYPE	WHY YOU TYPE IT
⌘-O	To enter printer options.
CI <RETURN>	
10 <RETURN>	To change characters per inch to 10.
<ESCAPE>	To return to the spreadsheet file display.
Arrows	To move the cell locator to cell A1.
⌘-P	To start the print process.
B	To select **Block**.
Right-Arrow	To the cells in columns A to E.
⌘-9	To select all of the rows in columns A through E.
<RETURN>	To indicate the selection is complete. You have selected the block from A1 to E1 down to A57 to E57.

Select your printer, press <RETURN> and finish answering the printer prompts.

The printout is shown in Figure 8-12.

For another printing example, let's print the quiz grades from the first marking period beside the names. To do this, the Names column needs to be temporarily moved adjacent to the quiz grades.

Move the cell locator to cell A1.

```
File:    Class Grades                              Page  1
                                                   12/23/88

AppleWorks Course                          |
  Marking Period 1    Quiz    Test   Mk Per |
                    Averages Average Average |
-------------------------------------------------------
Arthur, Erica          98      97    96.9   |
Bill, Stacy            92      86    87.4   |
Canon, Connie          94      85    87.1   |
John, Eric             98      87    89.4   |
Kapp, Mary             90      93    92.0   |
Keller, Betty          82      85    84.1   |
Keller, Sean           82      85    84.4   |
Kess, Michael          90      92    91.2   |
Luke, George           92      93    93.1   |
Shecora, Michelle     100      88    91.2   |
Trinski, Bruce         92      89    89.9   |
Wills, Sally           95      95    95.0   |
-------------------------------------------------------
                      92.0    89.5   90.1

AppleWorks Course                          |
  Marking Period 2    Quiz    Test   Mk Per |
                    Averages Average Average |
-------------------------------------------------------
Arthur, Erica          88      97    94.4   |
Bill, Stacy            82      92    89.4   |
Canon, Connie          85      91    89.8   |
John, Eric             88      93    91.9   |
Kapp, Mary             78      94    90.1   |
Keller, Betty          75      93    88.8   |
Keller, Sean           78      93    89.4   |
Kess, Michael          82      95    91.9   |
Luke, George           82      95    91.9   |
Shecora, Michelle      88      95    93.1   |
Trinski, Bruce         88      94    92.6   |
Wills, Sally           75      98    91.9   |
-------------------------------------------------------
                      82.3    94.2   91.2

AppleWorks Course
  Final Grades                          Course
                      Exam             Average
-------------------------------------------------------
Arthur, Erica         83.0              93.1
Bill, Stacy           85.0              87.7
Canon, Connie         89.0              88.5
John, Eric            76.0              87.7
Kapp, Mary            90.0              90.8
Keller, Betty         67.0              82.5
Keller, Sean          80.0              85.5
Kess, Michael         90.0              91.2
Luke, George          97.0              93.4
Shecora, Michelle     81.0              90.0
Trinski, Bruce        93.0              91.6
Wills, Sally          98.0              94.3
```

FIGURE 8-12.   Printout of Marking Period Averages.

WHAT YOU TYPE	WHY YOU TYPE IT
⌖-M	To start the move sequence.
W C	To select **Within worksheet** and **Columns**.
<RETURN>	To select only the one column, column A.
Arrows	To move the cell locator to column E.
<RETURN>	To move the column.

```
File:   Class Grades                                  Page  1
                                                      12/23/88


  AppleWorks Course    |                      |
   Marking Period 1    |       Quiz    Quiz   |
                       |    9/21/88 10/19/88  |
---------------------------------------------------------
Arthur, Erica          |       100      95    |
Bill, Stacy            |        90      93    |
Canon, Connie          |        95      94    |
John, Eric             |       100      95    |
Kapp, Mary             |        80     100    |
Keller, Betty          |        75      88    |
Keller, Sean           |        80      85    |
Kess, Michael          |        90      90    |
Luke, George           |        90      95    |
Shecora, Michelle      |       100     100    |
Trinski, Bruce         |       100      83    |
Wills, Sally           |                95    |
---------------------------------------------------------
                              90.9    92.8


  AppleWorks Course    |                      |
   Marking Period 2    |       Quiz    Quiz   |
                       |    9/21/88 10/19/88  |
---------------------------------------------------------
Arthur, Erica          |       100      75    |
Bill, Stacy            |        90      75    |
Canon, Connie          |        95      75    |
John, Eric             |       100      75    |
Kapp, Mary             |        80      75    |
Keller, Betty          |        75      75    |
Keller, Sean           |        80      75    |
Kess, Michael          |        90      75    |
Luke, George           |        90      75    |
Shecora, Michelle      |       100      75    |
Trinski, Bruce         |       100      75    |
Wills, Sally           |                75    |
---------------------------------------------------------
                              90.9    75.0
```

FIGURE 8-13.   Printout of Names and Quiz Grades.

The names are now adjacent to the quiz grades and can be included in a block of information for printing. Figure 8-13 shows the printout. Try to make this print out on your own. You should be able to get an duplicate of Figure 8-13 from your computer.

Before you continue, return the names to column A. Here are the steps:

WHAT YOU TYPE	WHY YOU TYPE IT
Arrows	To move to cell D1.
⌘-M	To move a column.
<RETURN>	To select **Within worksheet**.
C	To move **Columns**.
<RETURN>	To move one column, column D.
<LEFT-ARROW> 3 times	To get to A1.
<RETURN><RETURN>	To complete the move and return the names to column A.

PAPER SIZE LIMITS

When you try to print a file, you often find that the width of a spreadsheet document is greater than the width of the 8.5 inch paper used in the standard Imagewriter and most other printers.

There are several possible solutions to this problem. One is to keep the spreadsheet files that you develop narrow enough to print on the widest paper available to you. This solution doesn't mean that you must limit the amount of information that you enter into a spreadsheet document. It means that you should look for ways to have the spreadsheet grow longer rather than wider. For example,in the Class Grades spreadsheet all of the test grades could be entered below the quiz grades and the weighted averages below the tests. The spreadsheet width would then be determined by the larger of the number of test columns or the number of quiz columns, not by the total number of test and quiz columns.

A second solution is to print the spreadsheet file in the smallest type size possible, thus permitting more characters to be printed on the same width paper. The imagewriter can print as many as 17 characters per inch (136 characters across 8.5 inch paper, or about 15 standard size Spreadsheet columns wide). The Apple Daisy Wheel printer has a wide carriage (13.2 inches) and can print as many as 24 characters per inch (316 characters on 14 inch paper or about 35 standard size columns). (AppleWorks' limit is 255 characters per line, so even with the Apple Daisy Wheel printer the maximum is 255 characters per line.)

A third solution is to print a wide spreadsheet in pieces. First, you need to select the portion of the spreadsheet file that you wish to print for each piece using block print. For example, the first piece could be columns A through G, the second could be columns H through M, and so on. Then, once the pieces are printed, you need to physically cut and paste them together. The advantage of this method is that the limit of the width of your spreadsheet is the column limit of AppleWorks (127 columns or 255 characters). Another advantage is that the spreadsheet file can be printed in any character size that you wish; larger type sizes just require more pieces.

A fourth solution is to reduce the size of each column to include more columns on the printout. This solution can, of course, be combined with any of the other solutions suggested above.

A WORD OF WISDOM

Since neither the computer nor you, its operator, are infallible, opportunities for error exist. The computer can detect an incorrectly entered formula (for example, one with a missing parenthesis) and beep at you, but it has no way of detecting an incorrect value entry (the wrong number) or an error in the logic you use in building your worksheet.

Your most important worksheet task is developing a method of checking your work. The method can be as simple as entering information that has a known answer and checking the answer that the spreadsheet gives, or as elaborate as devising a second method of computing your results a second time in the same or in another spreadsheet file. The answers found by the two different methods should agree.

Check your formulas as you enter them. Check them again when you arrange, move, insert, or delete rows or columns. Make sure that they still include all the correct cell references.

Remember, the order of arithmetic operations is left to right, so 1+2*3 is 9 while 2*3+1 is 7. If you are in doubt about the order in which a formula is calculated, you might try this: move the cell locator to the cell containing the formula and write the formula down or make a printed copy with Open-Apple-H. (Open-Apple-H prints the information showing on the screen on your printer.) Now you have your formula written down for later reference. Using numbers instead of cell references, try your formula again in an adjacent, blank cell. You may, for example, find that you have left out necessary parentheses. You'll find that you pick up a lot of these omissions just by reentering the formula with number values rather than cell references and checking the result against what you expect.

Check for forward referencing of formulas. If you suspect that you have a forward referencing problem, make a change in a value in the suspected area of the worksheet and recalculate twice. Formula results change from the first calculation to the next if you have a forward referencing problem.

REVIEW QUESTIONS

1. Indicate the Open-Apple command used to:

    a. change the width of one or more columns.

    b. change the format of the value displayed in one cell.

    c. copy a block of information to the clipboard.

    d.   arrange a list of values from highest to lowest.

    e.   create windows.

    f.   clear out the information from the cursor location to the end of a cell.

    g.   fix titles at the top of the display.

    h.   recalculate values.

    i.   change from manual to automatic recalculation.

    j.   edit the contents of a cell.

2. Create a blank spreadsheet file. Enter the following four values and formula in column A.

```
=======A===
1 |        10
2 |        40
3 |        30
4 |        20
5 | @AVG(A1...A4)        (This  is the formula in cell A5.)
```

The value displayed in cell A5 is 25. Arrange the values in cells A1 to A4 from lowest to highest. The average changes to 15. Why? How did the worksheet you developed in this unit avoid this problem?

3. What is the advantage of setting the standard value for recalculation to manual?

4. In cell G40 you have entered a formula that is to calculate the total of the values in cells G31 to G35 and then add 10% to that total. The formula you use is:

```
@SUM(G31...G35) + @SUM(G31...G35)*0.10
```

Explain how you would test the formula. If the formula is incorrect, determine the correct formula.

5. Which of the following formulas calculate the same results for the same values in cells A1, A2, A3, and A4?

    a. +A1*A2+A3*A4   b. (A1*A2)+(A3*A4)
    c. ((A1*A2)+A3)*A4   d. +A1*A2+(A3*A4)

EXERCISES

8.1 Create a new worksheet called Circle. Enter the formula 1+A1 into cell A1. Calculate the worksheet several times with Open-Apple-K. The worksheet you have created is an example of circular referencing, a cell that references itself.

Circular references can be within one cell or they can be spread out over several cells. Try this; enter these formulas into cells A1 through A4.

In A1,   1+A4
In A2,   1+A1
In A3,   1+A2
In A4,   1+A3

Calculate several times with Open-Apple-K. Notice that the calculation results are different even though you did not enter any new numbers. Circular references can easily invalidate the results of any spreadsheet file. How can you determine if your spreadsheet contains a circular reference?

8.2 You have a part time job making deliveries for a local Pizza Shop. In addition to your hourly pay, you are paid 21 cents per mile for each mile that you drive. You are expected to keep a record of the miles and determine how much you should be paid. The record must show the date, customer name, the starting and ending odometer reading for each delivery, the miles for each delivery, and the amount of money earned for each delivery. Set up a spreadsheet file to keep these records. Your file might look something like the printout shown on the next page.

Print the spreadsheet twice, showing the values on one printout and the formulas on the other.

8.3 The $4.20 result shown in the sample spreadsheet for the last problem can be found by adding the dollar amounts for the day or by multiplying the 20 miles by $.021. It is unlikely that either of these calculations would produce an incorrect result. An error in entering the odometer readings can, however, produce incorrect results (for example, if the end odometer reading is entered as 19,350 for the first delivery and the beginning reading for the next delivery is 19,340, an extra 10 miles is added). Add a second calculation to check the total milage results displayed in the spreadsheet. Assume that once you start working, the car is only used for pizza delivery.

```
File:    Pizza                                              Page   1
                                                            6/3/88

             CUSTOMER     BEGIN       END                    DOLLAR
    DATE     NAME         ODOMETER    ODOMETER    MILEAGE    AMOUNT
    -----------------------------------------------------------------
    Tue 6/1  Anderson     19,230      19,241      11         $2.31
             Owens        19,241      19,249       8         $1.68
             Smith        19,249      19,266      17         $3.57
             Sauer        19,266      19,268       2          $.42
             Pepper       19,268      19,275       7         $1.47
             Malcolm      19,275      19,279       4          $.84
             Perrone      19,279      19,281       2          $.42
             Jones        19,281      19,292      11         $2.31
             Park         19,292      19,301       9         $1.89
    Total                                         71        $14.91

    Wed 6/2  Chesmadia    19,352      19,355       3          $.63
             Gladu        19,355      19,361       6         $1.26
             Pearson      19,361      19,366       5         $1.05
             Paradis      19,366      19,371       5         $1.05
             Landia       19,371      19,372       1          $.21
    Total                                         20         $4.20
```

E COMPOUND INTEREST

There are many ways to save money, ranging from no savings at all, to occasional saving, to saving on a very regular basis. The spreadsheet model that you develop in this section examines a regular method of saving. At the beginning of every month a fixed number of dollars is added to your savings account. In addition to the money that you add, the savings institution adds interest to your account at the end of each month.

```
========A========B========C========D==========E======
  1|Monthly Interest Rate in decimal:          .0058333===
  2|
  3|          Month #  Deposit  Interest End of Month
  4|             0 Balance Forward:            $0.00<===
  5|    ===>      1   $65.00      $.38        $65.38
  6|              2   $65.00      $.76       $131.14
  7|              3   $65.00     $1.14       $197.28
  8|              4   $65.00     $1.53       $263.81
  9|              5   $65.00     $1.92       $330.73
 10|              6   $65.00     $2.31       $398.04
 11|              7   $65.00     $2.70       $465.74
 12|              8   $65.00     $3.10       $533.84
 13|              9   $65.00     $3.49       $602.33
 14|             10   $65.00     $3.89       $671.22
 15|             11   $65.00     $4.29       $740.52
 16|             12   $65.00     $4.70       $810.22
 17|                     ==================
 18|Totals              780.00   $30.22
-----------------------------------------------------
E1: (Value) 7/100/12
```

FIGURE E-1. Compound Interest Table.

The interest is compounded monthly, that is, you are paid 1/12th of the yearly interest each month. Interest is paid on your balance at the beginning of the month. This beginning balance is the sum of the money you had at the end of the last month and the money you added at the beginning of the month. Let's look at the example in Figure E-1.

As you can see from the lower left corner of the figure, the monthly interest is entered in meaningful numbers and the computer calculates the decimal it needs for each month. The monthly interest rate (0.0058333) is calculated from 7/100, the fractional form of 7% per year, divided by 12. (If the .0058333 bothers you, try the monthly interest value 0.01 (1%). This is calculated from 12/100/12, the fraction for 12%, 12/100, divided by 12. 12% interest per year compounded monthly is 1% interest per month.)

Cells E1, B4, E4, and C5 are the only cells that do not contain formulas to produce the value in the cell. The value in B4 remains the same while the values in the other three cells change for each different problem that you might wish to do. The cells that need to have information entered into them are indicated by arrows made up of the less than (<) or greater than (>) symbol and three equal signs. The formula cells remain the same for each problem. Here's an outline of how the formulas should work.

Interest Dollars = The total of the end-of-month balance from the line above
                         plus
                    the deposit made at the beginning of the month
                         times
                    the monthly interest rate in decimal form.

End of Month = The total of the end-of-month balance from the line above
                         plus
                    the deposit made at the beginning of the month
                         plus
                    the interest dollars paid that month.

Totals   The totals at the bottom of the first two columns sum all of the deposits and all of the interest payments.

YOUR TASK

Recreate this spreadsheet on your computer. Test your work with the data given in Figure E-1 and test it again with the data given in Figure E-2. (The .006875 is the monthly interest for 8.25%; this is the fraction 8.25/100 divided by 12. Hand in a printout of both of your tests along with a hard copy of the formulas that you used to your instructor.

```
========A========B========C========D==========E======
 1|Monthly Interest Rate in decimal:        .00687S===
 2|
 3|           Month #  Deposit   Interest End of Month
 4|               0 Balance Forward:         $780.00<===
 5|    ===>        1   $85.00    $5.95      $870.95
 6|                2   $85.00    $6.57      $962.52
 7|                3   $85.00    $7.20    $1,054.72
 8|                4   $85.00    $7.84    $1,147.56
 9|                5   $85.00    $8.47    $1,241.03
10|                6   $85.00    $9.12    $1,335.15
11|                7   $85.00    $9.76    $1,429.91
12|                8   $85.00   $10.42    $1,525.33
13|                9   $85.00   $11.07    $1,621.40
14|               10   $85.00   $11.73    $1,718.13
15|               11   $85.00   $12.40    $1,815.52
16|               12   $85.00   $13.07    $1,913.59
17|                       ==================
18|Totals              1,020.00   $113.59
-----------------------------------------------------
E1: (Value) 8.25/100/12
```

FIGURE E-2.   Compound Interest Table Variation.

3

ADVANCED APPLEWORKS OPERATIONS

UNIT

9

ADVANCED WORD PROCESSOR APPLICATIONS

LEARNING OBJECTIVES

After completing this unit, you should be able to ...

a. type a form letter and address it to at least two different people.

b. use markers to move about quickly in a large document.

c. use the clipboard to copy or move up to 250 lines of text from one location in a file to another.

d. use the clipboard to copy information from one file to another.

e. control the page breaks in a long document.

f. insert headers and footers in a document.

IMPORTANT KEYSTROKES AND COMMANDS

COMMAND/KEY	MEANING
⌘-K	Calculate the page breaks.

All of the commands that follow are printer options. They are used with ⌘-O.

EK	Enter information from the keyboard as a document is printed.
SM	Set markers in the text.
HE	Indicate that the next line is header information.
FO	Indicate that the next line is footer information.
PP	Print the page number in the text.
GB	Group Begin.
GE	Group End.
NP	Set a new page.

ENTERING INFORMATION FROM THE KEYBOARD

You have, no doubt, seen a form letter addressed to you or to your family. For example, many contest letters are addressed to an individual or family. They usually start - "**Dear Mr. and Mrs. Short,** The **Short** family of **Brookfield** may have already won one-million dollars." The bold information in the previous line is automatically inserted into the letter by a computer. Examples of similar letters, sent to several different people, and personalized with individual names and addresses include personal notices of an upcoming important event, a friendly note to several friends, or business letters to advertise a product or service.

```
File: Congratulations          REVIEW/ADD/CHANGE          Escape: Main Menu
=====|====|====|====|====|====|====|====|====|====|====|====|====|====|===
Mr. and Mrs. ^ ,
^

^



Dear Mr. and Mrs. ^,

We are very happy to announce that your daughter, ^, has
been elected as tri-captain of this year's tennis team.
I am very pleased with the choice of tri-captains for this
year.   Your daughter's expertise is certain to be an
inspiration to the other members of the team.


I have enclosed a copy of this year's schedule for your
convenience.  I look forward to seeing you at the meets.


Congratulations and good luck for the new season.



Sincerely,
---------------------------------------------------------------------------
Type entry or use Ć commands          Line 25  Column  1       Ć-? for Help
```

FIGURE 9-1.   Form Letter Showing Entry Blanks.

AppleWorks does not automatically insert information into a form letter, however, you can use AppleWorks to manually insert information into form letters. You enter this information from the keyboard as the letter is printing. To do this, you embed a special command in your text at the point where you want the information inserted. When you print the document, the computer stops at this point and requests that you enter up to 50 characters. These characters are then inserted into the printed document. Since the number of characters entered may be different for each printing, AppleWorks automatically adjusts the text as it is printed to compensate for what you type. The special command that you insert in your document is called the **Enter Keyboard** command.

Suppose you have been hired by the tennis coach to do some paper work for him. Each year, when the captain is selected for the tennis team, he sends a note of congratulations to the captain's parents. This year's team has elected three captains. You need to send out three letters that all say the same thing. The only difference is that the letters are addressed to three different people and the names in the body of the letter are different.

Figure 9-1 shows the screen for part of the tennis form letter (The signature line is missing from the bottom of the letter). Each of the carets (^) that appears in the display is an enter keyboard command caret. The computer stops at each of these points and asks for information.

> Type the letter into your computer. Use Figure 9-1 as a guide. Notice that the information that is the same for all letters is typed into the form. This information includes the "Mr. and Mrs." part of the salutation, the comma in the salutation, and the commas surrounding the girl's name. The town and zip code are not included; they are different for all three players.

> For each caret shown in the figure, use the enter keyboard command. Here are two methods you can use to include the command in the document:

Method 1:

WHAT YOU TYPE	WHY YOU TYPE IT
Arrows	To move to the insertion point. (If you enter the commands as you type, this is not necessary.).
⌘-O	To display the printer options.
EK <RETURN>	To insert the Enter Keyboard caret into the text.
<ESCAPE>	To exit the printer options.

Method 2:

> Enter the first Enter Keyboard caret into the text using method 1.

WHAT YOU TYPE	WHY YOU TYPE IT
Arrows	To move the cursor to the caret. The cursor should blink under the caret.
⌘-C T <RETURN>	To copy the caret to the clipboard.

> At each point that you wish to insert the caret into the text:

> ⌘-C F <RIGHT-ARROW> To insert the enter keyboard command into the text.

The enter keyboard command allows information to be entered for only one line at a time; so the address line at the top of the screen has two separate enter keyboard carets: one for the street address line and one for the city, state, and zip code.

When you print the letter displayed in Figure 9-1, the computer prints the document on the printer up to the first caret. This part of the document is then reprinted on the display. The caret is highlighted so that you know what information is needed and where it will be inserted into the document. The bottom of the screen displays a question:

Information? _

You type in the information, George Smith, and press Return. The printer then prints the document up to the next enter keyboard caret, the printed part of the document is displayed, and you enter the next piece of information. This process continues until the document is complete.

```
              45 Long Meadow Hill Road
              Brookfield, Connecticut 06804
              March 29, 1988


              Mr. and Mrs. George Smith,
              512 Charlotte Street
              Brookfield Center, CT 06805


              Dear Mr. and Mrs. Smith,

              We are very happy to announce that your daughter, Jennifer,
              has been elected as tri-captain of this year's tennis team.
              I am very pleased with the choice of tri-captains for this
              year.  Your daughter's expertise is certain to be an
              inspiration to the other members of the team.

              I have enclosed a copy of this year's schedule for your
              convenience.  I look forward to seeing you at the meets.

              Congratulations and good luck for the new season.


              Sincerely,


              John Lee, Tennis Coach
```

FIGURE 9-2. Sample Form Letter.

Figure 9-2 shows one of the printed letters. The information that was entered from the keyboard is underlined in the figure to make it easy for you to see. The copy that you produce is not underlined unless you include the underlining. (The underlining was easily accomplished: just include underline begin and end commands in your text before and after the enter keyboard caret. Boldface can be done in a similar manner.)

Save the form letter for use in Exercise 9.1.

MARKERS

As you enter a long text, you may find that you have a question about something in the text that needs to be checked. You have the option of halting your work and consulting your reference material at that moment or **marking** the text for to go bcak and check it at a later time.

The marking that you insert into the text is similar to a printer control character. It appears on the screen only when you have zoomed in to display the Return blots and the printer commands, and it is not printed on paper when the text is printed.

There are several reasons why you might want to mark locations in the file. Generally you mark locations so that you can return to a point of interest in a long document without spending a lot of time searching. Suppose you want to check the spelling of a word. You would move the cursor to a point in the text near the word in question. Then you would type: (Notice that the what you type and why you type it headings are missing. This is because you are not expected to do this now. This information is provided for your future use.)

⌘-O	Issue the printer options command.
SM <RETURN>	Start the Set Marker command.
1 <RETURN>	Set the marker to marker number one.
<ESCAPE>	Return to the text.

Markers can have any number from 1 to 254. The same number can be repeated as often as you wish or you can use a different number for each marker. The meaning, if any, of the numbers is left to you. For example, 1 could mean check spelling, 2 could mean verify a fact, and so forth.

Once markers have been entered into a file, there are two ways to find them. One method allows you to find all markers with the same number in the order that they appear in the file. The other method allows you to find all of the markers in the order that they appear in the file, that is it finds markers without regard for the marker number. Both methods require you to move to the start of the file before you begin.

⌘-1	Move the the beginning of the file.
⌘-F	Start the Find command.
M 1 <RETURN>	Find marker number 1.

The computer moves the cursor to the first occurrence of marker 1. It then gives you the option to find additional occurrences of marker 1. Press Return or "N" to select no; press "Y" to select yes. If you select yes, either the cursor moves to the next occurrence of marker 1 or you are informed that there are no more marker 1's found in the file.

The following commands are used with the second method of finding markers, the method that finds all of the markers in the text no matter what their number.

⌂-1		Move to the beginning of the file.
⌂-F		Start the Find command.
O		Find Options for the printer.
SM	\<RETURN\>	Specifically the Set Marker option.

The computer moves the cursor to the first marker it finds in the file. The marker number is ignored. If you press "Y" to find the next occurrence, the cursor moves to the next marker, if any, in the file. The next marker may have the same number or a different one.

THE CLIPBOARD

In the last word processing unit, you worked with the move and copy commands. You copied or moved one block of text from one location to another. If you needed to duplicate a section of the text more than once, you had to select the text for each copy you wished to make and then select the location for the new text. This could be a tedious process if you needed to make several copies of even a few lines of your work. Fortunately, the clipboard can be used to save some of the repetitive steps in this process. Here is a general outline of the steps you need to take to copy a section of your document with the aid of the clipboard:

1. Move the cursor to the beginning of the text that is to be copied.
2. Give the copy command, Open-Apple-C.
3. Select "To clipboard (cut)."
4. Highlight the information that is to be copied and press Return.

The information that you have selected is then copied onto the clipboard. This information remains on the clipboard until you do one of the following: copy other information onto the clipboard, move other information onto the clipboard, or move information from the clipboard.

Once the information is copied onto the clipboard, you can copy it back into your document as often as you desire. Here's a general description of how to do that:

1. Move the cursor to the location for the insertion. This location must be exact, since the copy insertion can start anywhere, even in the middle of a word.
2. Give the copy command Open Apple C.
3. Select "From clipboard (paste)."

The information on the clipboard, including spaces, blank lines, printer instructions and carriage returns is copied into the text. A duplicate of this information remains on the clipboard so you can repeat the paste process as often as necessary.

Here is a specific example of this cut-and-paste process. Get the Student Data Disk from your instructor before you proceed.

WHAT YOU TYPE	WHY YOU TYPE IT
<ESCAPE>	To return to the Main Menu.
<RETURN>	To select **Add a file to the Desktop.**
<RETURN>	To select **The current disk.** (Make sure that you are using the Student Data Disk.)
Arrows	To highlight the file **Overview.** (If you have a 64K computer, the file is provided in two parts. You should highlight Overview Part 2.)
<RETURN>	To move a copy of the file onto the Desktop.

Remove the Student Data Disk from the disk drive and return it to your instructor. Insert your data disk into the drive.

WHAT YOU TYPE	WHY YOU TYPE IT
⌘-S	To save the file on your own data disk.
⌘-9	To move to the end of the file.
⌘-UP-ARROW twice	To see question 7 in the display.
<DOWN-ARROW>	To move to the beginning of the line containing the A answer to the question.
⌘-C	To start the copy (cut) command.
T	To select **To clipboard (cut).**
<DOWN-ARROW> 3 times	To highlight the three answers and the blank line beneath the answers.
<RETURN>	To copy the highlighted information onto the clipboard.

The answers can now be copied back into the text as often as you like. Here are the precise steps:

WHAT YOU TYPE	WHY YOU TYPE IT
DOWN-ARROW six times	To move to the space before the 9.
⌘-C	To start the copy (paste) command.
F	To select **From clipboard (paste).**

The answers appear under question 8.

WHAT YOU TYPE	WHY YOU TYPE IT
DOWN-ARROW 6 times	To move to the 1 in the number 10.
⌘-C	To start the copy (paste) command.
F	To select **From clipboard (paste).**

The answers again appear. This time they are under question 9.

✓   CHECKPOINT

Where do you place the cursor so that the answers can be inserted under question 10? Where should you place it to insert the answers for question 11? For 12?

Verify that the answers to the Checkpoint are correct by inserting the answer set for questions 10, 11, and 12 into the version of Overview on your computer.

HEADERS AND FOOTERS

Headers are single lines of information that are printed at the top of each page. **Footers** are single lines of information that are printed at the bottom of each page. Headers and footers are used to identify the document or pages within the document.

Header information is inserted in the file at or before the beginning of the first page on which it appears. A header inserted in the middle of page one, for example, would appear at the top of each page starting with page two. Footer information is inserted at or before the end of the first page it appears on. A footer inserted anywhere on page one appears at the bottom of each page starting on page one. Footers and headers in AppleWorks are printed within the top and bottom margins and are limited to one line of text. When they are printed, two blank lines are printed after each header and before each footer. The header or footer or both can also print the page number.

Figure 9-3 shows the header and footer inserted into the Overview unit. They have both been inserted after the title of the unit so the header will appear on page 2, 3, 4, etc.; the footer will appear on page 1, 2, 3, etc.

The page header and page footer commands are not in the copy of the Overview file that you just copied from the Student Data Disk. Enter them as follows:

WHAT YOU TYPE	WHY YOU TYPE IT
⌘-Z	To display the printer commands (if they are not already displayed).
⌘-1	To move to the top of the file. (People with 64K computers need to remove Part 2 from their Desktop and load Overview Part 1.)
<Down-Arrow>	To move down to the line. ------- Unjustified.
⌘-O	To display the printer commands.
CN <RETURN>	To center the header.
HE <RETURN>	To indicate that a page header follows on the next line.
<ESCAPE>	To return to the text.
<RETURN> <UP-ARROW>	To open a blank line for the header.

An Overview of AppleWorks	To enter the header text.
<RETURN>	To complete the header line and open a line for the footer.
Ć-O	To enter the printer options again.
FO <RETURN>	To indicate that a page footer follows on the next line.
<ESCAPE>	To return to the text.
Page-	To enter part of the footer text.
Ć-O	To enter the printer options for one last time.
PP <RETURN>	To print the page number after the text "Page-".
<ESCAPE>	To return to the text.

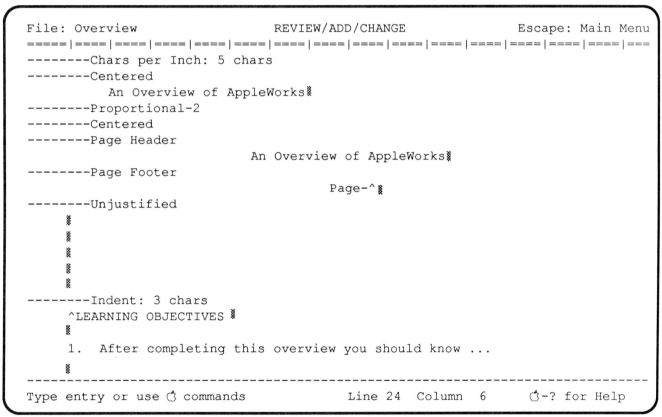

```
File: Overview              REVIEW/ADD/CHANGE            Escape: Main Menu
=====|====|====|====|====|====|====|====|====|====|====|====|====|====|===
--------Chars per Inch: 5 chars
--------Centered
          An Overview of AppleWorks▓
--------Proportional-2
--------Centered
--------Page Header
                        An Overview of AppleWorks▓
--------Page Footer
                              Page-^▓
--------Unjustified
     ▓
     ▓
     ▓
     ▓
     ▓
     ▓
--------Indent: 3 chars
     ^LEARNING OBJECTIVES ▓
     ▓
     1.  After completing this overview you should know ...
     ▓
-----------------------------------------------------------------------
Type entry or use Ć commands          Line 24   Column   6     Ć-? for Help
```

FIGURE 9-3.   Header and Footer Inserts.

Check your display with Figure 9-3. The display and the figure should match at this point.

| Ć-Z | To zoom out and hide the printer options. |

The page header and page footer printer commands still appear in the display to remind you that the lines that follow these commands are special. The commands do not appear in the printed copy of the file. Like other commands in AppleWorks, the header and footer commands remain the same from the point where they are inserted in the file to the end of the file. If you enter a new header or footer command, the new command is used from that page on to the end of the file.

✓ **CHECKPOINT**

What type style will the headers and footers you entered into the Overview file be printed in? (Hint: Notice that the footer and the header are both centered even though you only entered one center command?)

PAGE CONTROLS

AppleWorks automatically determines where one page ends and another starts by counting the number of lines between the top and bottom margins. AppleWorks is programmed to avoid word processing **widows** and **orphans**. A word processing widow is the first line of a new paragraph left at the bottom of a page; AppleWorks moves such a line to the top of the next page. A word processing orphan is the last line of a paragraph alone at the top of a new page; in this case AppleWorks moves another line of the paragraph to the new page.

The treatment of widows and orphans, however, is not applied to lists of information or any information that is only one line long. There are several lists in the Overview unit ; including the individual questions and answers at the end of the unit. AppleWorks treats each answer line as a separate paragraph; so it would have no problem putting question 10 and answers A and B on page 7 and putting answer C all alone at the top of page 8, but readers would find this arrangement confusing.

There are two ways to control this page break problem: the first is to group blocks of text together, the second is to manually mark the page breaks. Either option is an acceptable solution. Page breaks are easier to insert but may need to be changed if the document is revised. Grouping is time-consuming initially but usually does not need revision if the document is changed. In most cases, the best way to control the page breaks in a document is to use some combination of the two methods.

The computer seldom breaks the page in the middle of a group. If a group does not fit on one page, the entire group of text is moved to the next page. Logical groups for the Overview unit are lists of information, entire figures, and the questions and answers at the end of the unit.

Look at the automatically calculated page breaks before you make any changes to the file. Although it is unlikely that all of the page breaks automatically fall where you want them, it is very likely that many of the page breaks automatically fall in acceptable places. To have the computer calculate the page breaks, give the command:

WHAT YOU TYPE	WHY YOU TYPE IT
Ć-K	To calculate page breaks.

Highlight your printer and press <RETURN>.

After a few moments the text reappears in the display. Move down through the document until you see the message - - - End of Page 1 - - -. The first page break presents the first problem for discussion; it is shown in Figure 9-4.

```
    application and how the parts interact or ^integrate^.▧
    ▧

    ▧

    ^The Word Processor
    ▧
- - - - - - - - - - - - - - - - End of Page 1 - - - - - - - - - - - - - - - - - -
    A word processor can be thought of as a tool that produces the same
    results as a typewriter.  With a word processor, however, words are first
```

FIGURE 9-4.   A portion of the screen showing a page break.

The problem is that the title of a section appears at the bottom of page 1 while the section text starts on page 2. Let's choose to correct this problem by manually inserting a page break so that page 1 ends after "The Word Processor."

WHAT YOU TYPE	WHY YOU TYPE IT
Arrows	To move to the blank line below the line that reads: The Word Processor.
Ć-O	To display the printer options.
NP <RETURN>	Insert a new page command into the text.
<ESCAPE>	To return to the text.

When any change is made to the text, the page calculations disappear. (AppleWorks does not know what effect the changes have on the page breaks that it calculated before the change, so it demands that the page calculation be repeated.)

Calculate page breaks again using Ć-K, <RETURN>. (Your printer is still highlighted.)

Now check the page 2 break. It falls in the middle of Figure 1. Let's use the grouping method to correct this problem.

WHAT YOU TYPE	WHY YOU TYPE IT
Arrows	To move the cursor to the start of the group. In this case, it is the **Left Margin** **0** indicator above Figure 1.
Ó-O	To display the printer options.
GB <RETURN>	To indicate **Group Begin.**
ESCAPE	To return to the text.
ARROWS	To move the cursor to the end of the group. It is the **Left Margin** **.5** setting at the bottom of Figure 1.
Ó-O	To again display the printer options.
GE <RETURN>	To indicate **Group End.**
ESCAPE	To return to the text.
Ó-K <RETURN>	To calculate the page breaks again.

Other groups can be formed by repeating the steps above. As an alternative, you can copy the "————Group Begin" printer instruction to the clipboard and copy it back into the text at the start of each group. Repeat the coping procedure for the "————Group End" instruction.

The new page break calculation ends page 2 before the figure is printed. This creates a problem that may not be apparent until the document is printed: page 2 is now quite short. There are two possible ways to correct this: (1) move some text from before the figure to after the figure, or (2) move some text from after the figure to before the figure. In the first case, the figure would be moved to page 2; in the second, the additional text fills out page 2.

Setting the page breaks for a file, especially a file that includes figures, requires a lot of work. The steps given above are repeated for each page of the document. In general, you should group information that must be kept together on one page first. Let the computer calculate the page breaks and then, if you need to, override its calculation by manually inserting a new page command previous to the computer's page break in the text. (If you put your page break after the computer's, you will get a page with only a few lines on it.)

The page calculation and insertion must be done one page at a time, since changing the location of the end of one page changes the location of the end of all of the pages that follow. The only shortcut to this process is to accept as many automatic page break indicators as possible.

A NEAT TRICK

Some times the document that you have created does not all fit into memory at one time. The Overview file, for example, does not fit into a computer with 64K of memory. If you create a document that is too large for the computer, you can still print it so that it looks like one file to your reader. All you need to do is make sure that the first part of the file ends at the bottom of a page. (If you are using page numbers you also need to set the page number in the second part of the file to the correct starting page number.) You do not need to retype any part of the file to accomplish this feat. You can use the clipboard.

This is what you would do:

1. Calculate and set the page breaks in the first part of the file. If the last page happens to be a full page, you're finished; if not, continue down this list.
2. Make sure that you have a backup of both parts of your file in case you make a serious error in one of the next steps.
3. Calculate the page breaks for the first part of the document.
4. Move the last page of the first part of the document onto the clipboard.
5. Return to the Main Menu and remove Part 1 from your Desktop. Since you made a change in the file, you will be prompted to save your Part 1 file. Make sure that you do this.
6. Add Part 2 of the file onto the Desktop.
7. Move the information from the clipboard into the beginning of the Part 2 file. (Neither removing a file from nor adding a file to the Desktop changes the contents of the clipboard.)

The use of the clipboard to pass information from one Word Processor file to another is an example of the integration feature of the AppleWorks software. Now that you know how easy it is to do this, you'll probably find many other reasons to make transfers from one file to another. If both the from and to transfer files fit on your Desktop, the process is even easier. You would clip from the first file; use Open-Apple-Q to move quickly to the second file; and finally clip into the second file. If you have the room on your Desktop, you do not need to remove the first file from the Desktop before you paste information into the second.

WHAT YOU'VE LEARNED

The way a document appears on paper is entirely up to you. You have a great deal of control over all of the functions of AppleWorks, even the ones that appear automatic. Your control can even extend over a multiple file document. Exercising the control takes time, practice, and patience.

REVIEW QUESTIONS

1. Give two reasons for using a marker.

2. Explain how you would change the header and footer so that they print in 15 characters per inch. (If your printer does not have this type size, use another that is available.)

3. Do the headers and footers have to be the same for every page in the document? If not, how do you change them?

4. You have a five-page term paper that includes a title page and a bibliography.
   a. How can you get the title page to print separately from the text of the paper?
   b. How can you get the bibliography to start on its own page at the end of the text?

5. Why is it sometimes necessary for you to modify the location of page breaks?

EXERCISES

9.1 Some suggestions for typing a research paper are given in the following essay. These suggestions are also in a file called Suggestions on the Student Data Disk. Add this file to your Desktop. Insert the necessary bold, underline, center, and indent commands so that the file is printed as it appears below.

Mechanics of typing

Type on 8 and 1/2" by 11" paper. Use only one side of the paper and double space. The left-hand margin should be 1 and 1/2 inches; the right hand margin, 1 inch. On all pages but the first leave a one inch margin at the top of the page and a one inch margin at the bottom of the page. The first page should have a top margin of three inches. Number each page after the first, one inch from the top right hand corner and three lines from the top. Use just the Arabic number (2,3,4, etc.), no dashes or parentheses.

The footnotes and bibliography should be on separate pages, single spaced with a double space between each entry.

Sources used to compile this information are listed below.

Selected Bibliography

Dangle, Lorraine F. and Alice M. Haussman. <u>Preparing the Research Paper</u>. Fairfield, N. J.: Cebco Standard Publishing, 1984.

Schwartz, Steven, ed. <u>The Research Paper Made Easy: From Assignment to Completion</u>, Teacher's Guide to the sound-slide program. White Plains, N.Y.: The Center for the Humanities, 1977.

Wintcrowd, W. Ross and Patricia Y. Murray. <u>English Writing and Language Skills</u>. New York: Harcourt Brace Jovanovich, Publishers, 1983.

9.2 Write one of your term papers or research papers using AppleWorks. Use as many of the AppleWorks Word Processor features as you need. Follow the specific suggestions given above in exercise 9.1.

9.3 Use the Congratulations file you entered in the beginning of this unit to print two additional letters. Send one letter to your parents; send the other letter to the parents of a friend.

9.4 Write three notes to three different friends or relatives announcing your upcoming completion of the AppleWorks course. The body of the note should be written only once. Use the enter keyboard command to enter the name of the person to whom the note is sent and to enter information special to the person (i.e. you should take an AppleWorks course, too, or thanks for telling me about the course). Print a screen image of your file using Open-Apple-H. Hand in all four pages to your instructor.

9.5 Add the file Overview to your Desktop. Set markers in the file at the beginning of each figure. The marker number should be the same as the figure number. Use two methods to move to the markers in the order that you inserted them. Demonstrate your ability to use markers to your instructor.

9.6 Finish setting page breaks in the Overview file. Keep pages balanced throughout the file; that is, keep about the same amount of material on each page. Print the file. (You will not get pages that match this book exactly since there have been many revisions made to the final copy printed in the text. You may find it interesting to compare the electronic first draft you print to Unit 1 as it appears in this text.) (Note to instructors: the file is about eight pages long and will take some time to print. If you have limited printing time you may wish to check the students results by examining the file on the screen.)

10 ADVANCED DATA BASE APPLICATIONS

LEARNING OBJECTIVES

After completing this unit, you should be able to ...

a. use the Find command to locate desired records.

b. set compound Rules for record display.

c. use Find and Rules to selectively delete or copy records.

d. subtotal and total value categories.

e. create calculated categories.

f. change the printer options to accommodate non standard paper sizes.

IMPORTANT KEYSTROKES AND COMMANDS

COMMAND/KEY	MEANING
⌘-F	Find information in the file.
⌘-R	Change the rules used to select records.
⌘-G	Add or remove report group totals.
⌘-T	Add or remove report category totals.

287

```
PLAYER                 TEAM                  CARD #  YEAR COMPANY LOC.  VALUE
-------------------    -------------------   ------  ---- ------- ----  -----
4 PLAYERS              '78 ROOK. PITCHERS    703     1978 TOPPS   7C     3.00
4 PLAYERS              '78 ROOKIE SS's       707     1978 TOPPS   2I     7.00
AARON HANK             BRAVES                100     1973 TOPPS   1B     6.50
AARON HANK             BRAVES                100     1969 TOPPS   4G    10.00
BOGGS WADE             RED SOX               498     1983 TOPPS   7D     3.25
BOGGS WADE             RED SOX               498     1983 TOPPS   7E     3.25
BOGGS WADE             RED SOX               498     1983 TOPPS   7F     3.25
BOGGS WADE             RED SOX               498     1983 TOPPS   7G     3.25
BOGGS WADE             RED SOX               498     1983 TOPPS   7H     3.25
BOGGS WADE             RED SOX               498     1983 TOPPS   7I     3.25
BROCK LOU              CARDINALS             170     1978 TOPPS   2B     1.00
BROCK LOU              CARDINALS             665     1979 TOPPS   6F     1.00
BROCK LOU              CARDINALS             320     1973 TOPPS   1I     2.25
CARLTON STEVE          PHILLIES              25      1979 TOPPS   1D     1.50
CARLTON STEVE          PHILLIES              300     1973 TOPPS   4I     5.50
CARTER GARY            EXPOS                 120     1978 TOPPS   3G     1.35
CEPEDA ORLANDO         ATHLETICS             545     1973 TOPPS   2C     1.45
CLEMENTE ROBERTO       PIRATES               173     1962 POST    2D    10.00
DAWSON ANDRE           EXPOS                 72      1978 TOPPS   3H     1.65
DEROUCHER LEO          ASTROS                624     1973 TOPPS   2G     1.15
FINGERS ROLLIE         ATHLETICS             84      1973 TOPPS   3F     1.15
GOODEN DWIGHT          METS                  190     1985 DONRUSS 6A     2.00
GOODEN DWIGHT          METS                  82      1985 FLEER   6B     2.00
GOODEN DWIGHT          METS                  82      1985 FLEER   6C     2.00
GOODEN DWIGHT          METS                  620     1985 TOPPS   6D     3.00
GOODEN DWIGHT          METS                  620     1985 TOPPS   6E     3.00
HENDERSON RICK         ATHLETICS             482     1980 TOPPS   1E     6.50
HENDERSON RICK         ATHLETICS             482     1980 TOPPS   1F     6.50
HERZOG WHITEY          RANGERS               549     1973 TOPPS   2F     1.15
HOWARD FRANK           TIGERS                560     1973 TOPPS   1A     1.45
LYNN FRED              A.L. COMM. SET        7/22    1984 TOPPS   30B    0.35
LYNN FRED              ANGELS                19/33   1984 DRAKE'S 27C    0.25
LYNN FRED              SUPER STAR            626     1984 FLEER   103D   0.12
MATHEWS ED             BRAVES                155     1955 TOPPS   5B    11.00
McCOVEY WILLIE         GIANTS                410     1973 TOPPS   2A     2.00
MORGAN JOE             REDS                  100     1977 TOPPS   6I     1.00
MORGAN JOE             REDS                  230     1973 TOPPS   1C     1.45
MORRIS JACK            TIGERS                251     1979 TOPPS   6G     1.00
MURPHY DALE            BRAVES                274     1980 TOPPS   4H     2.00
MURRAY EDDIE           ORIOLES               160     1980 TOPPS   2H     2.00
MURRAY EDDIE           ORIOLES               36      1978 TOPPS   3E    16.00
PERRY GAYLORD          RANGERS               686     1978 TOPPS   7B     1.00
RICE JIM               RED SOX               200     1980 TOPPS   7A     1.25
ROBINSON FRANK         ANGELS                175     1973 TOPPS   4C     2.50
RUTH BABE              ALL-TIME RBI LDR      474     1973 TOPPS   4D     2.25
SANDBERG RYNE          CUBS                  83      1983 TOPPS   6H     3.75
SCHMIDT MIKE           PHILLIES              360     1978 TOPPS   4B     2.75
SMITH OZZIE            PADRES                116     1979 TOPPS   4A     1.75
SOTO MARIO             REDS                  427     1978 TOPPS   2E     2.50
SPAHN WARREN           BRAVES                31      1955 TOPPS   5A     9.00
STRAWBERRY DARRYL      METS                  102     1984 TOPPS   4E     2.50
UPSHAW WILLIE          BLUE JAYS             341     1979 TOPPS   3A     2.00
UPSHAW WILLIE          BLUE JAYS             341     1979 TOPPS   3B     2.00
UPSHAW WILLIE          BLUE JAYS             341     1979 TOPPS   3C     2.00
WILSON WILLIE          ROYALS                409     1979 TOPPS   1G     2.00
WILSON WILLIE          ROYALS                409     1979 TOPPS   1H     2.00
WINFIELD DAVE          PADRES                390     1977 TOPPS   3I     2.50
YASTRZEMSKI CARL       RED SOX               230     1976 TOPPS   4F     4.00
YOUNT ROBIN            BREWERS               173     1978 TOPPS   3D     2.00
```

FIGURE 10-1.   Best Cards Data Base File

Load the data base file `Best Cards` from the Student Data Disk. Save a copy of the file on your data disk. You will use this file extensively in this unit. For reference, the complete file is listed in Figure 10-1. (The sixth category name, LOC., is an abbreviation for location in the card file.)

THE FIND OPTION

The **find option** is a data base feature that allows you to single out records that contain a desired phrase, name, or any specified set of characters. The find option is easy to use; however, it sometimes gives you unexpected information, especially if you are like most people and try to enter the shortest comparison information possible. Work through the examples below to see how this can happen.

First, use the find option to list all of the cards in the collection for the Cincinnati Reds team. The team is listed as REDS in the file.

WHAT YOU TYPE	WHY YOU TYPE IT
⌂-F	To start the Find option.
Reds <RETURN>	To enter "Reds" as the comparison information.

Notice that you did not need to use capital letters even though the file listing is all in capitals. The display now shows the information in Figure 10-2.

```
PLAYER                    TEAM                  CARD #  YEAR  COMPANY  LOC.  VALUE
--------------------      --------------------  ------  ----  -------  ----  -----
MORGAN, JOE               REDS                   100    1977  TOPPS    6I    1.00
MORGAN, JOE               REDS                   230    1973  TOPPS    1C    1.45
SOTO, MARIO               REDS                   427    1978  TOPPS    2E    2.50
```

FIGURE 10-2.   Results of Finding "REDS".

This is exactly what was expected.

Second, display the records for the Boston Red Sox. This team is listed in the file as RED SOX. It would seem that the word "Red" alone would produce the display that we want. Let's try it.

WHAT YOU TYPE	WHY YOU TYPE IT
⌂-F	To start the find option.
<RIGHT-ARROW> 3 times	The previous entry "REDS" appears in the comparison information line. The right arrow moves the cursor to the "S".
⌂-Y	To delete the "S".
<RETURN>	To enter "RED" as the comparison information.

The display now shows the information in Figure 10-3.

```
PLAYER                 TEAM                 CARD # YEAR COMPANY LOC. VALUE
-------------------    -------------------  ------ ---- ------- ---- -----
BOGGS,  WADE           RED SOX              498    1983 TOPPS   7D   3.25
BOGGS,  WADE           RED SOX              498    1983 TOPPS   7E   3.25
BOGGS,  WADE           RED SOX              498    1983 TOPPS   7F   3.25
BOGGS,  WADE           RED SOX              498    1983 TOPPS   7G   3.25
BOGGS,  WADE           RED SOX              498    1983 TOPPS   7H   3.25
BOGGS,  WADE           RED SOX              498    1983 TOPPS   7I   3.25
LYNN,  FRED            A.L. COMM. SET       7/22   1984 TOPPS   30B  0.35
LYNN,  FRED            ANGELS               19/33  1984 DRAKE'S 27C  0.25
LYNN,  FRED            SUPER STAR           626    1984 FLEER   103D 0.12
MORGAN,  JOE           REDS                 100    1977 TOPPS   6I   1.00
MORGAN,  JOE           REDS                 230    1973 TOPPS   1C   1.45
RICE,  JIM             RED SOX              200    1980 TOPPS   7A   1.25
SOTO,  MARIO           REDS                 427    1978 TOPPS   2E   2.50
YASTRZEMSKI,  CARL     RED SOX              230    1976 TOPPS   4F   4.00
```

FIGURE 10-3.   Results of Finding Records that contain "RED".

You seem to have gotten a lot more than you asked for. The find command found RED in **RED** SOX, in **RED**S, and in the name LYNN, **FRED**. The display contains all of the occurrences of the three letter sequence RED, even if the sequence is in the middle of a word. You need to change the comparison information to "RED " (that is, RED with a trailing space) to get what you want, only the RED SOX records. Try it.

WHAT YOU TYPE	WHY YOU TYPE IT
⌂-F	To start the find option.
<RIGHT-ARROW> 3 times	The previous entry "RED" appears in the comparison information line. The right arrow moves the cursor past the "D".
<SPACE BAR> <RETURN>	To enter "RED " (that's RED followed by a space) as the comparison information.

Now you have what you want, and you typed the shortest comparison information to get it. You might wonder why LYNN, FRED didn't appear in the display this time. The answer is that there is no space after FRED. The data base removes all extra spaces from the right end of a category and places a special character called an **end of category mark** after the last nonspace character in the category. Since "RED " does not match "RED-end-of-category-mark", LYNN, FRED is not found. Similarly, " RED" (space RED) will not find any information. REDS and RED SOX do not start with a space; and neither does the sequence RED in the word FRED.

✓ CHECKPOINT

You want to display the records for 4 PLAYERS. What is the shortest find comparison information that will find only these records?

When you have completed your work with the find command, press

<ESCAPE>   To select all records and remove any restrictions on what is displayed.

RECORD SELECTION RULES

In unit 7 you used the record selection rules to select only one option for one category. The record selection rules can be expanded to three options using from one to three categories. The conjunctions **"and,"** **"or,"** and in some cases **"through"** are used to form more specific rules. In forming these rules, keep in mind that "and" is more restrictive than "or." For example, there are only seven records where the team is RED SOX and the value of the card is over $3.00; there are 19 records where where the team is RED SOX or the value of the card is over $3.00.

Try these examples:

Display only Red Sox cards.

WHAT YOU TYPE	WHY YOU TYPE IT
⌘-R	To start the rules option.
2 <RETURN>	To select **Team.**
1 <RETURN>	To select **equals.**
RED SOX <RETURN>	To enter "Red Sox" as the comparison information.
<ESCAPE>	To complete the rule.

Eight records are displayed; all of them are for Red Sox cards.

Display only cards with a value over $3.00.

WHAT YOU TYPE	WHY YOU TYPE IT
⌘-R	To start the rules option.
<RETURN>	To select "No" for the question **Display all records?**

What You Type	Why You Type It
7 <RETURN>	To select **Value**.
2 <RETURN>	To select **is greater than**.
3 <RETURN>	To enter 3 ($3.00) as the comparison information.
<ESCAPE>	To complete the rule.

Eighteen records are displayed; all of them have a value over $3.00.

Display Red Sox cards that have a value over $3.00. In other words, the card must be for a Red Sox player and it must also have a value over $3.00.

What You Type	Why You Type It
⌘-R	To start the rules option.
<RETURN>	To select "No" for the question **Display all records?**
2 <RETURN>	To select **Team**.
1 <RETURN>	To select **equals**.
RED SOX <RETURN>	To enter Red Sox as the comparison information.
1 <RETURN>	To select **and** as the conjunction.
7 <RETURN>	To select **Value**.
2 <RETURN>	To select **is greater than**.
3 <RETURN>	To enter 3 ($3.00) as the comparison information.
<ESCAPE>	To complete the rule.

Seven of the eight Red Sox records are now displayed. Notice that for all seven records the card has a value of more than $3.00.

If you now set the rules to display those cards that are either Red Sox cards or that have a value over $3.00, you might expect to see the eight Red Sox cards and the eighteen cards whose values are more than $3.00. That is, you might expect to see 26 cards listed. Let's try it and see.

What You Type	Why You Type It
⌘-R	To select the rules option.
<RETURN>	To select "No" for the question **Display all records?**
2 <RETURN>	To select **Team**.
1 <RETURN>	To select **equals**.
RED SOX <RETURN>	To enter "Red Sox" as the comparison information.
2 <RETURN>	To select **or** as the conjunction.
7 <RETURN>	To select **Value**.
2 <RETURN>	To select **is greater than**.
3 <RETURN>	To enter 3 ($3.00) as the comparison information.
<ESCAPE>	To complete the rule.

There are only 19 cards listed. Why? Seven of the 8 Red Sox cards also have values over $3.00; 7 of the 18 cards on the over $3.00 list are also Red Sox players. Our arithmetic (18+8=26) counted these seven cards twice. The correct arithmetic is: number of Red Sox cards + number of cards with values over $3.00 – number of Red Sox cards that also have a value over $3.00. (You subtract the cards that you counted twice so they are only counted once.) This calculation gives us the correct number of records displayed (8+18-7=19).

WHAT YOU'VE LEARNED

Cards that meet both "or" conditions are only listed and counted once. Another way to state an "or" rule in words is: include in the list all records that meet only the first condition, all records that meet only the second condition, and all records that meet both conditions. Some uses of the word "or" do not include the possibility that both conditions are allowed; this use is referred to as the **exclusive or**. You have also learned that AppleWorks' "or" does include the possibility that both conditions are met; its "or" is referred to as the **inclusive or**.

Here is one last example using a rule with three parts. Let's list those records for cards from the 1970's whose value is greater than or equal to $2.00 but only for the Reds, Red Sox, Royals or Rangers teams. Whoops! That does not sound as if it can be done using a rule with only three parts. Two parts might be needed to select cards from the 1970s:

> Selection: YEAR is greater than 1969
>   through YEAR is less than 1980

Setting the rules for greater than or equal to $2.00 also looks as if it should take two parts:

> Selection: VALUE equals 2
>   or   VALUE is greater than 2

The rule for the team sounds is if it could take as many as four parts. However, another observation about the four teams will simplify the rule.

This problem requires using a little creative thought: If the year is in the 1970s, it must have the digits 97 in the year (or it must begin with 197). Another way to say greater than or equal to $2.00 is to say greater than $1.99. The four team names start with the letter "R";and no other teams start with this letter.

Figure 10-4 shows the listing you obtain when you set the rule.

✓   **CHECKPOINT**

> How many records in the Best Cards file meet the following conditions:
> The card is from the 1980s, for any of the following teams - the Angels, Athletics, Blue Jays, Braves, Brewers, Cardinals, Cubs, Expos, Giants, Mets, Padres, Rangers, Reds, Royals, or Tigers, and it is not from the Topps Card Company?

```
Selection:  YEAR contains 97
   and          VALUE is greater than 1.99
   and          TEAM begins with R
PLAYER                  TEAM                    CARD #  YEAR COMPANY LOC.  VALUE
--------------------    --------------------    ------  ---- ------- ----  -----

SOTO, MARIO             REDS                    427     1978 TOPPS   2E    2.50
WILSON, WILLIE          ROYALS                  409     1979 TOPPS   1G    2.00
WILSON, WILLIE          ROYALS                  409     1979 TOPPS   1H    2.00
YASTRZEMSKI, CARL       RED SOX                 230     1976 TOPPS   4F    4.00
```

FIGURE 10-4.　Results of a Compound Rule Selection.

DELETING RECORDS

You have already used the Open-Apple-D command to delete records in the Spreadsheet. Using the command to delete one or more records in the Data Base is no different. In general, you can remove all of the records you want from the multiple record display by moving to the first record, pressing Open-Apple-D, highlighting the records to be removed, and pressing Return.

It is also possible to use the delete command in conjunction with the record selection commands. This makes it possible to delete several records that are related in some way. For example, you might want to eliminate all records for cards that have a value less than one dollar. You follow this procedure:

WHAT YOU TYPE	WHY YOU TYPE IT
⌘-R	To set a rule.
(<RETURN>)	To select "No" (if you are asked the display all records question).
7 <RETURN>	To select **Value.**
3 <RETURN>	To select **is less than.**
1 <RETURN>	To enter 1 as the comparison information.
<ESCAPE>	To complete the rule. Three records appear on the screen.
Tab/Arrows	To move the cursor to the first row.
⌘-D	To start the delete process.
<DOWN-ARROW>-twice	To highlight all three records for deletion.
<RETURN>	To delete the records.

The three records are deleted and the display reappears with all records selected.

Delete can also be used with the find option to select a specific set of records for removal from a data base. You would find to display the records you wish to remove and then you use Open-Apple-D to delete them.

COPYING RECORDS

The find and rule selection commands can also be used together with copy and move. Here is an example using the copy command. You have just purchased a large collection of cards. Most of them are Braves cards. You find that you now have two new duplicates of all the Braves cards in your Best Cards file. (You now have three of each card.) Here's how you might enter the ten new cards into your collection:

WHAT YOU TYPE	WHY YOU TYPE IT
⌘-R	To start the rule selection process.
2 <RETURN>	To select **Team.**
<RETURN>	To select **equals.**
BRAVES <RETURN>	To enter BRAVES as the comparison information.
<ESCAPE>	To end the selection process. The five Braves cards appear in the display.
Tab/Arrows	To move the cursor to the first row.
⌘-C	To start the copy process.
T	To select **To the clipboard.**
⌘-9	To highlight all five records.
<RETURN>	To copy the five records onto the clipboard.
⌘-C	To start the copy command again.
F	To copy the five records from the clipboard.
⌘-C	To start the copy process yet again.
F	To copy the five records a second time.
⌘-R Y	To select all records again.

The ten entries have been added to the data base file. All that remains is to correct the storage location for the new entries by editing the Loc. (location) categories, since this is the only entry that is different for the ten new records.

GROUPING AND TOTALING RECORDS

There are two questions that are often asked about a collection: How much is it worth? and how many of each type of thing is in the collection? For example, how many cards for a given team are in the baseball card collection? AppleWorks' Data Base can answer these questions in a report using combinations of the **Grouping** and **Totaling** commands.

Let's set up a report to answer the first question:

What You Type	Why You Type It
⌘-P	To start the report.
2 <RETURN>	To select **Create a new "Tables" format.**
Value <RETURN>	To name the report.
⌘-RIGHT-ARROW 8 times	To expand the Player category width by eight characters.
<RIGHT-ARROW>	To move to the **Team** category.
⌘-RIGHT-ARROW 8 times	To expand the Team category.
<RIGHT-ARROW>	To move to the **Card #** category.
⌘-LEFT-ARROW 6 times	To reduce the Card # category width by six characters.
<RIGHT-ARROW>	To move to the **Year** category.
⌘-LEFT-ARROW 8 times	To reduce the Year category.
<RIGHT-ARROW>	To move to the **Company** category.
⌘-D	To delete the Company category.
⌘-D	To delete the Loc. (location) category.

The cursor is now in the value column and the report is formatted for printing. You have not done anything yet to obtain a value total. Continue:

What You Type	Why You Type It
⌘-T	To Add/Remove category totals in the **Value** column.
2 <RETURN>	To use two places after the decimal in the display.
<RETURN>	To accept three spaces after the category.

The value category changes to a display of all nines showing the number of decimal places you selected. The line of equal signs at the bottom of the category indicates that totals are printed on the report for this category.

Use ⌘-P to print the report on the screen.

The last page of the screen report shows the total value of the cards appearing in the list. This value is 262.80 for all of the cards. (The total reflects only those items that appear in the report. If you had used the selection rules to display only part of the collection, the total would only be for the displayed part of the collection.)

Determine the total value of the cards for each team in the collection.

You do not need to apply the selection rules several times to do this. Using **Group Totals** provides a more convenient way.

What You Type	Why You Type It
Arrows	To move the cursor to the **Team** category.
⌘-G	To provide group totals on Team.
\<RETURN\>	To answer "No" to the "Print group totals only?" question.
\<RETURN\>	To answer "No" to "New page?"
⌘-A	To arrange Teams alphabetically.
\<RETURN\>	To select **A to Z** order for the arrangement.
⌘-P \<RETURN\> \<RETURN\>	To print the report on the screen again.

There is now a blank line separating each team. The subtotals show the value of the cards belonging to each team. A portion of the report is shown in Figure 10-5.

```
PLAYER                  TEAM                  CARD # YEAR      VALUE
--------------------    --------------------  ------ ----  ----------
.
.       ◄──────────────── The three dots indicate that part of the list is missing.
.
.
CEPEDA, ORLANDO         ATHLETICS             545    1973        1.45
FINGERS, ROLLIE         ATHLETICS             84     1973        1.15
HENDERSON, RICK         ATHLETICS             482    1980        6.50
HENDERSON, RICK         ATHLETICS             482    1980        6.50
                                                                15.60

UPSHAW, WILLIE          BLUE JAYS             341    1979        2.00
UPSHAW, WILLIE          BLUE JAYS             341    1979        2.00
UPSHAW, WILLIE          BLUE JAYS             341    1979        2.00
                                                                 6.00

.
.
.
WILSON, WILLIE          ROYALS                409    1979        2.00
WILSON, WILLIE          ROYALS                409    1979        2.00
                                                                 4.00

HOWARD, FRANK           TIGERS                560    1973        1.45
MORRIS, JACK            TIGERS                251    1979        1.00
                                                                 2.45

                                                               262.80*
```

FIGURE 10-5.   A Report Grouped on Team.

The report shows that the Athletics' cards are worth a total of 15.60, the Blue Jays' cards are worth 6.00, and so on. The total value of the collection is still 262.80. The total does not change when group subtotals are included in the report.

If you are interested only in the total value of the cards for each team, it is not necessary to print out any information other than the team name and the subtotal. Here's how to obtain this summary:

WHAT YOU TYPE	WHY YOU TYPE IT
Arrows	To move to the **Team** category.
⌘-G	To remove group totals from the Team category.
⌘-G	To re-insert group totals for the **Team** category.
Y	To print group totals only on the report.

Print the report on the screen.

Figure 10-6 is a portion of the printout.

```
  PLAYER                  TEAM                 CARD #  YEAR     VALUE
  --------------------    --------------------  ------  ----  ----------
    .
    .
    .
                          ATHLETICS                              15.60

                          BLUE JAYS                               6.00
    .
    .
    .
                             ROYALS                                4.00

                             TIGERS                                2.45

                                                                262.80*
```

FIGURE 10-6.   Report with Group Totals Only.

Now only the summary information is displayed for each team's group of cards. Again, the grand total is unaffected since all of the cards are included in the report.

How many cards for each team, player, year or company are there? This is the second question we want to answer, and it is a little more difficult. If we had included a category called Count and had entered a 1 into the Count category for each card, then you could answer the question by totaling the 1's by groups just as you totaled the dollar amounts. You do not, however, have a Count category.

It is possible to include a Count category on a report without adding the it to the file. It is also possible to have the computer automatically insert the 1 into the category. This automatic category is a calculated category. The only necessary condition for a calculated count category is that at least one of the categories in the file contain values to use in the calculation. Calculations are made using the column letter, numbers, and the four calculation symbols + - * and / for addition, subtraction, multiplication and division (parentheses can not be used in the calculation formula.)

Let's review what we're trying to do. We want a count of the cards for each team. This means that we need a category that contains a count number (1) for each card in the file. Printing a group total for the count category will give the desired total for each team. We do not want to add another category to the file for this, we just want to add the category to the report.

Describing the process is much harder than doing it. Here are the exact steps to follow:

You should start at the Report Format screen of the Value report.

WHAT YOU TYPE	WHY YOU TYPE IT
Right-Arrow	To move to the **LEN** line. (LEN appears vertically on the line to which you need to move the cursor.
⌘-K	To insert a "calculated category."
⌘-Y	To delete the default name.
Count <RETURN>	To name the category "Count".
E/E <RETURN>	Divide the number in the value column by itself (=1).
0 <RETURN>	To select 0 decimal places.
3 <RETURN>	To select 3 blank spaces after the category.
⌘-T	To total the category.
<RETURN> <RETURN>	To accept the default values for the total.
<LEFT-ARROW>	To move to the **Team** category.
⌘-G	To remove groups from this category.
⌘-G	To reset groups for the Team category.
<RETURN>	To display all records.
<RETURN>	To not go to a new page at a category change.

The last time you set groups for the Team category, you selected the option to display the totals only. The only way to show all the records again for the category is to remove and reset the group.

Reduce the widths of the Player and Card # categories by 5 and 2 characters respectively so that the report fits on the screen.
Print the report on the screen.

Figure 10-7 shows a section of the report.

As you can see, each of the calculated values in the Count column is 1. The subtotals for each group answer our question about the number of cards in the collection for each team.

✓ CHECKPOINT

How can you alter the report you just printed so that only the group totals are shown on the report?

```
  PLAYER              TEAM                 CARD # YEAR VALUE COUNT
  ------------------- -------------------- ------ ---- ----- ------
    .
    .
    .
  CEPEDA, ORLANDO ATHLETICS               545   1973   1.45    1
  FINGERS, ROLLIE ATHLETICS                84   1973   1.15    1
  HENDERSON, RICK ATHLETICS               482   1980   6.50    1
  HENDERSON, RICK ATHLETICS               482   1980   6.50    1
                                                      15.60    4

  UPSHAW, WILLIE   BLUE JAYS              341   1979   2.00    1
  UPSHAW, WILLIE   BLUE JAYS              341   1979   2.00    1
  UPSHAW, WILLIE   BLUE JAYS              341   1979   2.00    1
                                                       6.00    3
    .
    .
    .
  WILSON, WILLIE   ROYALS                 409   1979   2.00    1
  WILSON, WILLIE   ROYALS                 409   1979   2.00    1
                                                       4.00    2

  HOWARD, FRANK    TIGERS                 560   1973   1.45    1
  MORRIS, JACK     TIGERS                 251   1979   1.00    1
                                                       2.45    2

                                                    262.80*  66*
```

FIGURE 10-7. A Report Showing a Calculated Category.

Here are some other examples illustrating the use of the calculated category.

1. Calculate a 6% tax on the price of an item.

```
        Price     Tax
--- -G------  -H--------
        9999999.99       Two decimal places were indicated.
        .06*G            .06*G is 6% of the price in column G.
```

2. Calculate a 6% tax on the price of an item and compute the total amount to charge for the item.

```
        Price     Tax          Total With Tax
--- -G------  -H--------   -I------------
        9999999.99  9999999.99        Two decimal places.
        .06*G       G+H               Price plus tax.
```

Example 2 shows that the results of one calculated category, Tax, can be used in another calculated category, Total With Tax.

3. Calculate the average of the values in two columns.

```
        Value 1          Value 2          Average
--- -G------  . . .  -K------  . . .  -I------------
                                       9999999.999
                                       G+K/2
```

Calculated fields in the Data Base do not have to be next to the values they use. The value columns must have letters identifying the columns or else they cannot be used in the formulas (if you have more than 26 categories in a report, no letters appear for the columns beyond the 26th). You cannot use parentheses in the formula; if you do, the calculation result is lost and number signs (#) are displayed in the field. Number signs are also displayed if the calculation cannot be performed (if it requires division by zero, for example) or if the number is larger than the column width. (This is the same thing that happens when a number does not fit into a column in the spreadsheet.) Arithmetic is done from left to right only; calculations can only be done across the row. (You cannot, for example, average a column as you do in the spreadsheet.) Only three categories can be totaled at one time on a report. Calculated fields are handy, but the calculations provided are not nearly as powerful or as flexible as those in the spreadsheet.

PRINTER OPTIONS

Each of the baseball cards in the collection is stored in its own protective jacket. As a final project with this file, you'll print a label for each jacket to identify its contents.

Labels come in several sizes. The most common is approximately 1 inch by 3 inches and is used for addressing envelopes. You'll set the report for this is the size label . You must change the printer options th inform AppleWorks of the nonstandard size of the material that you are printing on.

Setup a new label report called Labels.

```
File: BEST CARDS            REPORT FORMAT           Escape: Report Menu
Report: Labels
Selection: All Records


=====================================================================
LOC.     YEAR            CARD #
PLAYER                   VALUE
TEAM
COMPANY



----------------------------------Each record will print  6 lines----------------



-------------------------------------------------------------------------
Use options shown on Help Screen                      ⌂ -? for Help
```

FIGURE 10-8. Label Record Layout.

```
File: BEST CARDS            PRINTER OPTIONS        Escape: Report Format
Report: Labels
=====================================================================

-------Left and right margins--------      ------Top and bottom margins-------
PW: Platen Width         3.5 inches    PL: Paper Length          1.0 inches
LM: Left Margin          0.0 inches    TM: Top Margin            0.0 inches
RM: Right Margin         0.0 inches    BM: Bottom Margin         0.0 inches
CI: Chars per Inch       12            LI: Lines per Inch        6

    Line width           3.5 inches        Printing length       1.0 inches
    Char per line (est)  42                Lines per page        6

           -------------------Formatting options------------------
    SC:  Send Special Codes to printer                  No
    PD:  Print a Dash when an entry is blank            No
    PH:  Print report Header at top of each page        No
    OL:  Omit Line when all entries on line are blank   Yes
    KS:  Keep number of lines the Same within each record Yes


-----------------------------------------------------------------------
Type a two letter option code                         48K Avail.
```

FIGURE 10-9. Printer Options for 1-by-3.5 inch Labels.

A suggestion for this report appears in Figure 10-8. Use six lines per record as shown in the figure. (The printer prints six lines per inch, so a one inch label should be set for exactly six lines. If you set the format for fewer lines, you may have trouble lining up your labels when you print them.)

Now change the printer options to match the label form for the report. The paper length and platen width need to be changed to 1.0 and 3.5 inches respectively. No header should be printed, and each record must print the same number of lines so that records do not print across the margin between two labels. Figure 10-9 shows what the Printer Options menu looks like after the changes have been made.

Print the report on plain paper. If you have entered the printer options correctly, exactly eleven labels will print on each page of the report.

REVIEW QUESTIONS

1. What are the minimum and maximum number of records the **find** command can locate at a time?

2. If you use the find command to find **AT** in the following records, which records would appear in the display and why?

Time	Name	Action	Thing
morning	Matt	made	a mortise
evening	Ellen	evaluated	enterprise
all day	Dean	discounted	a dormer
at twilight	Toni	tested	a tarpaulin
one hour	Helen	hammered	a hatch

3. How do you exit the find command and display all records?

4. What selection rule would display only the "4 Players" and "Dwight Gooden" cards in the Best Cards file? What find command would display the same seven records?

5. Explain how you would use the record selection ules or the find command to delete from the Best Cards file records of all cards that are not from the Topps card company.

6. You arrange the Best Card file alphabetically by player and then print the report Value which prints the total value of the cards by team. What happens to the report when the file is arranged this way rather than by team? Why?

EXERCISES

10.1 Open the file "Video Movies" (Use "Video 10K set" if you have a 64K machine) found on the Student Data Disk. Save a copy of the file on your data disk.

   a. Set the rules so that only the tapes that are not movies are displayed. Print a hard copy of your display. (Note that the rule "Type is not equal to movie" does not work.)
   b. Display all of the dramas in the collection. Print a hard copy of your display.
   c. Add a category to the file called Star Rating. Rate each tape as 5 star (great), 4 star, 3 star, 2 star, 1 star or 0 stars. Delete all of the 0 star items from the file. Print a report with the 5–star tapes grouped together followed by the 4–star tapes, 3–star tapes, 2–star, and 1–star. Each group of tapes should be in alphabetical order.
   d. What other categories would you add to the file? Why?

10.2 Open the file "Original YrBk" on the Student Data Disk. Save a copy of the file on your data disk.

   a. Create a tables style report that prints the total charged and paid.
   b. Print the report by homeroom. Show subtotals and totals in both the Charged and Paid columns.
   c. Add a calculated category to the report to print the amount due for any student who has not paid in full. (Students who have paid in full would show an amount due of $0.00.)
   d. Print the report again. Show subtotals by homeroom for Charges, Paid, and Amount Due.

10.3 Create a data base of your own design. Print a report for the file which includes column totals and calculated categories.

APPLICATION

F

THE PLAY'S
THE THING

THE SCENARIO

Your knowledge of data bases has spread throughout the school. Your good friend is in the drama club and has lined up your first job - - helping the drama coach, who must keep track of hundreds of plays, set up a data base. You make an appointment to meet the coach.

You discover that the coach, Dr. Actu, has several students who are familiar with AppleWorks. They have already built a data base and a spreadsheet to keep track of ticket sales. The coach's major problem, however, is keeping track of plays for the drama class and for the school productions.

As part of the drama class, students need to present scenes from plays that they have chosen. They present some scenes alone and others in groups with two or three other students. They can find scenes for class presentations by searching through a file cabinet full of plays, but none of them do this on a regular basis. They rely on the suggestions of their coach, who can not always find exactly what they want. Even if they do search through the file cabinet, they still need to spend a lot of time finding something that fits their particular group. For example, they may need to find a scene for one male and two females, or one for three males, or one for two males and a female, and so forth. They may want only a drama, a comedy, a melodrama, a period piece, or a musical. If the play is one of the school productions, they also need to know how many sets are used, how long the play is, where to buy the scripts for each cast member, and how much the royalty fee is.

305

The coach would like a data base to make it easier and faster to finding this information. Additionally, she would like all of her students to be able to use AppleWorks to find the information that they need.

Dr. Actu shows you the kind of information that needs to be stored in the data base.

Title	
Author	
Publisher	
Year	
# Males	(the number of males in the play)
# Females	(the number of females in the play)
Type	(musical, comedy, drama, etc.)
# Acts	(the number of acts)
Length	(the running time of the play in minutes)
# Sets	(the number of set in the play)
Royalty	(the royalty cost for production)
Notes	(comments about special features of the play; there should be room for three line of notes)

YOUR TASK

Your task is to set up a data base called Plays with about five sample entries. You must also create a short user manual for the drama students. The manual should contain information about how to start AppleWorks, how to get the Plays data base onto the desktop, how to arrange it in a variety of ways and how to find information in the data base.

Print out both the data base and the user manual.

UNIT

11 ADVANCED SPREADSHEET APPLICATIONS

LEARNING OBJECTIVES

After completing this unit, you should be able to ...

a. recognize and use the other AppleWorks spreadsheet functions.

b. determine the result of function calculations.

c. use spreadsheet protection and know why it is used.

d. use a lookup table and know when you might use it.

e. use @INT to create your own round-off function.

f. use @SUM to keep a running total.

In the last spreadsheet unit you developed a large spreadsheet with detailed help from the textbook. In this section, you will be given information about the pieces of a spreadsheet. You should then be able to use these pieces to construct a spreadsheet on your own. When you understand the pieces that build a worksheet, you understand the whole worksheet.

ADDITIONAL SPREADSHEET FUNCTIONS

Some new spreadsheet functions are listed here along with sample formulas illustrating their use. Additional uses of these functions are illustrated throughout this unit.

The following terms are used inside of the parentheses in the functions below:

Value　　　A single number or a formula or a mathematical expression that has a single number result.

Range　　　A series of adjacent cells identified with ellipsis marks (...), for example, B1...B20 or A9...K9.

List　　　Single values or ranges separated by commas, for example, A1,B5,C4...C12 is a list of two values and one range; A1...A20,B1..B20 is a list of two ranges. (A1...B20 is the same list as A1...A20,B1...B20.)

Built-in Arithmetic Functions:

FUNCTION	RESULT PRODUCED
@ABS(value)	The **absolute value** of the value. For example, @ABS(3) is 3 and @ABS(-3) is 3. The absolute value of a number is also called the magnitude of the number or the number without its sign.
@AVG(list)	The **mean** (average) of the values in the list.
@COUNT(list)	The number of value entries in the list. Blanks and labels are not value entries and are not included in the count.
@INT(value)	The **integer** portion of the value. For example, @INT(12.73) is 12. The integer is the number without its decimal. The INT function does not round off a number.
@MIN(list)	The smallest value in the list.
@MAX(list)	The largest value in the list.
@SQRT(value)	The **square root** of the value. For example, @SQRT(9) is 3. Values must be positive numbers.
@SUM(list)	The **sum** (total) of all of the values in the list.

The following formulas illustrate the use of these Arithmetic functions:

1. The lowest value in a range of values in cells D5 through N5:

    @MIN(D5...N5)

2. The single highest value in a set of values in cells D5 through N5 or in cells Q5 through W5:

@MAX(D5...N5,Q5...W5)

3. Average of the values in cells D5 to N5, dropping the lowest value:

@SUM(D5...N5,-@MIN(D5...N5))/(@COUNT(D5...N5)-1)

4. Count the highest value twice in the average of the values in cells D5 to N5:

@SUM(D5...N5,@MAX(D5...N5))/(@COUNT(D5...N5)+1)

5. Determine the standard deviation of a set of values. (The standard deviation is a statistical measure of the spread of a set of numbers. The smaller the standard deviation, the closer the numbers are to the mean (average). This formula is for the population standard deviation.)

The scores are in cells J1 through J15, the mean of the scores (determined by the formula @AVG(J1...J15)) is in cell J17, the squares of each score (determined by formulas +J1*J1, +J2*J2, +J3*J3, etc) are in cells K1 through K15, and the formula for standard deviation in cell K17 is:

@SQRT(@SUM(K1...K15)/@COUNT(K1...K15)-(J17*J17))

6. Round off the value in cell A1:

To the nearest 100:	@INT(A1/100+.5)*100
To the nearest 10:	@INT(A1/10+.5)*10
To the nearest unit:	@INT(A1/1+.5)*1 or @INT(A1+.5)
To the nearest tenth:	@INT(A1/0.1+.5)*0.1
To the nearest hundredth:	@INT(A1/0.01+.5)*0.01

Search Functions:

FUNCTION	RESULT PRODUCED
@CHOOSE(value, list)	The value in the list indexed by the value given in the function. For example, @CHOOSE(3,80,85,90,95) is 90, because 90 is the third value in the list.
@LOOKUP(value,range)	The value in a second range adjacent to the largest entry less than or equal to the value given in the function. In other words, the computer finds the largest entry less than or equal to the value given, then provides the value in the cell adjacent to the one found.

The Logical Function:

FUNCTION	RESULT PRODUCED

@IF(logical relation, value1, value2) Value1 if the logical relation is TRUE or value2 if the logical relation is FALSE.

Logical relations are created with the symbols:

<	less than
>	greater than
=	equal
<=	less than or equal to
>=	greater than or equal to
<>	not equal to

Other Functions:

FUNCTION	RESULT PRODUCED
@ERROR	Displays ERROR.
@NA	Displays NA ("Not Available").

THE LOGICAL FUNCTION

The @IF is used to determine which of two values or which of two calculations is to be used in a given cell. A payroll overtime calculation is a good example for demonstrating the @IF function. In most businesses, if a person works over forty hours, that person receives one-and-a-half-times their regular rate of pay for each of the hours worked over forty hours in addition to their regular pay for the 40 hours, so one set of calculations is needed when an employee works regular hours and another when that person works overtime.

Suppose you hold a job where you are normally paid $6.00 per hour and you earn $9.00 (1.5 times $6.00) each hour that you work overtime. Let's do some calculations for a few weeks' worth of work.

```
Week 1 - You work 30 hours
     Your pay is:   30 hours times $6.00 per hour   =    $180.00 regular.
     plus            0 hours times $9.00 per hour   =       0.00 overtime.
                                                         _____
                    Your total pay is                     $180.00

Week 2 - You work 40 hours
     Your pay is:   40 hours times $6.00 per hour   =    $240.00 regular.
     plus            0 hours times $9.00 per hour   =       0.00 overtime.
                                                         _____
                    Your total pay is                     $240.00
```

```
Week 3 - You work 41 hours
     Your pay is:    40 hours times $6.00 per hour  =    $240.00 regular.
     plus             1 hour  times $9.00 per hour  =       9.00 overtime.
                                                           _____
                     Your total pay is                    $249.00

Week 4 - You work 50 hours
     Your pay is:    40 hours times $6.00 per hour  =    $240.00 regular.
     plus            10 hours times $9.00 per hour  =      90.00 overtime.
                                                           _____
                     Your total pay is                    $330.00
```

Look at the calculations for regular pay. If you work less than 40 hours in a week as in week 1, your pay is the number of hours times the pay rate. If you work exactly 40 hours as in week 2, the calculation for regular pay is the same, the number of hours times the rate of pay per hour. If the hours are over 40 as in weeks 3 and 4, you are paid 40 times $6 for your regular pay.

So, for you, the regular pay is either the number of hours you work times 6.00 or the regular pay is 40 times 6.00. Which calculation you use depends upon the number of hours that you work, 40 hours or less, or more than 40 hours. In a more formal statement of the same information you might say: determine if the logical relation "hours greater than forty" is true; if it is true, regular pay = 40 times $6; if it is false, regular pay = hours worked times $6. Using the @IF statement to again say the same thing, you would write:

@IF (hours>40, 40 * rate, hours * rate)

Cell names would be substituted for hours and rate when the formula is used in the spreadsheet.

Now consider the overtime calculations. If the hours you work for the week are 40 or less as in weeks 1 and 2, the overtime pay is 0 times the overtime rate or just 0. If the hours are over forty as in weeks 3 and 4, calculate the overtime pay as one-and-a-half times the regular rate times the number of hours over forty. In a more formal way, determine if the logical relation "hours greater than 40" is true; if it is true, overtime = 1.5 times $6 times hours over forty; if it is false, overtime = 0.

@IF (hours > 40, 1.5 * rate * (hours - 40), 0)

Notice that the hours over forty are calculated by subtracting 40 from the number of hours worked and that this calculation is valid only if the number of hours worked is really over forty. For example, if you work 42 hours, the number of overtime hours is 42-40 or 2. (If you work less than 40 hours, the result of this calculation would be a negative number; the @IF function does not do the overtime calculation in this case.)

Let's put the work we have done into a spreadsheet.

> Create a new spreadsheet from scratch and call it Pay.
> Enter the flowing values and formulas in cells A1 to A5.

CELL	VALUE/FORMULA	RESULT PRODUCED
A1	6	The rate of pay per hour.
A2	40	The number of hours worked.
A3	@IF(A2>40,40*A1,A1*A2)	The regular pay.
A4	@IF(A2>40,1.5*A1*(A2-40),0)	The overtime pay.
A5	+A3+A4	The total pay.

Change the number of hours in cell A2 to 30, then to 41, and finally to 50 to verify that the formulas produce the same results as the preceding examples.

EXERCISE 11.1

Produce a payroll calculation spreadsheet. A sample worksheet appears in Figure 11-1. The hours for each new week are inserted when they are recieved. The formulas for regular pay, overtime pay, and total pay are then copied from adjacent cells.

Notice that the rate of pay appears in only one location. How can you implement this idea? Do you think that this is a good idea? Why or why not?

```
File:    Pay                                    Page   1
Name:  Mike  Short

Rate              $6.00
===========================================================
Week #                    1       2       3       4
===========================================================
Hours                 30.00   40.00   41.00   50.00
Regular Pay          $180.00 $240.00 $240.00 $240.00
Overtime Pay           $0.00   $0.00   $9.00  $90.00
                     ---------------------------------------
Total Pay            $180.00 $240.00 $249.00 $330.00
```

FIGURE 11-1. Sample Payroll

LOOKUP TABLES

The Internal Revenue Service has produced several examples of lookup tables, many of which pertain to payroll. The tables are used to determine one piece of information when another piece of information is known. A hypothetical withholding table is shown below. Let's examine what it means and how it is used.

Annual Salary			Withholding Factor
0	to	2,390	0.000
2,390	to	3,540	.010
3,540	to	4,580	.035
4,580	to	6,760	.070
6,760	to	8,850	.080
8,850	to	11,240	.100
11,240	to	13,430	.110
13,430	to	15,610	.120
15,610	to	18,940	.130
18,940	to	24,460	.150
24,460	to	29,970	.175
29,970	to	35,490	.200
35,490	to	43,190	.220
43,190	to	57,550	.250
57,550	to	85,130	.290
85,130	to	110,000	.350
110,000	and	up	.400

The table gives you information about withholding when you know a person's annual salary. For example, a person who earns $5,200 per year has a withholding factor of 0.070 and a person who has an annual salary of $52,000 has a withholding factor of 0.250.

If an annual salary falls exactly on a number in the table, the rule is to use the higher withholding factor. For example, $15,610 has a withholding factor of 0.130. With this understanding, it is really not necessary to include the second column of numbers, since the second number in one row is the same as the very first number in the next row. Our table with one less column would then look like this.

Annual Salary	Withholding Factor
0	0.000
2,390	.010
3,540	.035
4,580	.070
6,760	.080
8,850	.100
11,240	.110
13,430	.120
15,610	.130
18,940	.150
24,460	.175
29,970	.200
35,490	.220
43,190	.250

57,550	.290
85,130	.350
110,000	.400

To use the table to find the withholding factor for $5,200, you would reason as follows: 5,200 is higher than 4,580 but not higher than 6,760, so the withholding factor that I need is 0.070.

✓   **CHECKPOINT**

What is the withholding factor for a $35,000 annual salary? A $13,430 annual salary? A $26,231.96 annual salary?

Now that you understand how to determine a withholding factor for a given annual salary, a legitimate question might be, What is the withholding factor used for? The answer is that it is used to estimate federal tax and to determine how much money should be deducted from your paycheck toward those taxes. Here are some examples of the calculations needed:

Earnings of $100.00 per week
 Annual earnings are 52 weeks times $100 per week or $5,200.
 The withholding factor is 0.070.
 Taxes withheld are 0.070 times $100 or $7.00 per week.

Earnings of $240.00 per week
 Annual earnings are 52 weeks times $240 per week or $12,480.
 The withholding factor is 0.110.
 Taxes withheld are 0.110 times $240 or $26.40 per week.

Experiment with the lookup table in a spreadsheet.

Move to an unused area in the pay spreadsheet you created in exercise 11.1, say column H.
Enter the figures from the first column in the list above into cells H2 to H18.
Enter the figures in the second column in cells I2 to I18.
Move to any empty cell, say J18.
Type: @LOOKUP(5200,H2...H18)   and press <RETURN>.

The value .07 appears in the cell. This is the withholding factor for an annual salary of $5,200.
 In the same cell, type: @LOOKUP(12480,H2...H18)   and press <RETURN>.

The value .11 appears in the cell. The withholding factor for $12,480 is 0.11

In the same cell. type: @LOOKUP(12480,H2...H18)*240   and press <RETURN>.

The value 26.4 ($26.40) appears. This is the withholding tax for earnings of $240.00 per week. The computer multiplied 0.11 by $240.

Now let the computer do all of the work, including finding the annual salary from the weekly earnings:

Type: @LOOKUP(52*240,H2...H18)*240 and press <RETURN>.

Again the value 26.4 appears in the cell.

EXERCISE 11.2

Add a withholding calculation to the payroll spreadsheet you developed in Exercise 11.1. Also include a calculation for FICA (Social Security) deductions, which are 7.05% times the net pay (7.05% is 0.0705 times the pay). Display the final amount left for take-home pay after FICA and federal withholding have been subtracted. A sample worksheet is shown in Figure 11-2 for illustration and reference. You do not need to duplicate this example; but using the values in the example will help you determine if your calculations are correct. Print a hard copy of the screen showing the formulas that you used to generate this spreadsheet. Print a report showing 4 weeks of earnings at 7.50 per hour. The hours for the 4 weeks should be 33, 40, 52, and 79.

ROUND-OFF ERRORS

You may notice that the take-home pay is sometimes off by a penny. Even though you asked AppleWorks to round off the dollar display to two decimal places, it keeps track of all of the fractions of a cent in your answers. Occasionally, the results of a calculation with all of the extra fractions of a cent produce a one-cent error such as you see for week 4 in Figure 11-2.

To correct the penny errors, round off the calculation with the @INT function. The formula to round off the FICA value in cell F13 to the nearest cent (hundredth) is:

    @INT(B13*F11*100+.5)/100

The round-off formula for the calculation in cell F14 is:

    @INT(@LOOKUP(52*C11,H2...H18)*C11*100+.5)/100

In both cases the edit command (Open-Apple-U) is used to insert @INT(at the beginning of the existing formula and to add *100+.5)/100 at the end of the formula. Rounding off values in each cell prevents strange penny disappearances in other cells. Formulas for rounding off to hundreds, tens, units, and tenths are listed near the beginning of this unit.

```
File: Pay                  REVIEW/ADD/CHANGE              Escape: Main Menu
==========A==========B========C========D========E========F========G====
  1|Name: Mike Short
  2|
  3|Rate              $6.00
  4|=====================================================================
  5|Week #                    1         2         3         4
  6|=====================================================================
  7|Hours                 30.00     40.00     41.00     50.00
  8|Regular Pay         $180.00   $240.00   $240.00   $240.00
  9|Overtime Pay          $0.00     $0.00     $9.00    $90.00
 10|                    ------------------------------------------
 11|Net Pay             $180.00   $240.00   $249.00   $330.00
 12|
 13|FICA          7.05%  $12.69    $16.92    $17.55    $23.26
 14|Witholding           $18.00    $26.40    $27.39    $42.90
 15|
 16|Take Home Pay       $149.31   $196.68   $204.06   $263.83
 17|
 18|
-------------------------------------------------------------------------
C14: (Value, Layout-D2) @LOOKUP(52*C11,H2...H18)*C11

Type entry or use Ꮹ commands                          Ꮹ-? for Help
```

FIGURE 11-2.   Payroll with Federal Deductions.

PROTECTION

When you finish your payroll worksheet and are satisfied that it is correct and error free, you may wish to **protect** the formula cells from inadvertent change. For example, if you or someone using your spreadsheet were to type something in a formula cell, whatever was typed would replace the current contents of the cell. This action would make the spreadsheet invalid. For example, if you type 1000 into cell F8 your regular earning would be $1,000 no matter how many hours (or how few) were entered into cell F7.

To avoid potential problems, most spreadsheet users protect cells that have formulas in them once their worksheet is correct and in final form. You can do this for the worksheet shown in Figure 11-2 is as follows:

WHAT YOU TYPE	WHY YOU TYPE IT
Arrows	To move the cell locator to cell A1.
Ꮹ-L	To change the layout.
R	To select **Rows**.

⌘-9	To highlight all rows.
<RETURN>	To complete the selection.
P	To select **Protection.**
N	To allow nothing to be entered into any cell.
Arrows	To move to cell C7
⌘-L	To change layout.
B	To select **Block.**
<RIGHT-ARROW> 3 times	To highlight cells C7 to F7.
<RETURN>	To complete the selection.
P	To select **Protection.**
V	To allow only **Values** to be entered into these cells.

The only cells containing information that can be changed now are the hour cells, C7 to F7. Indeed, they can only be changed by entering values. Try it. Move to any cell that contains information and type a letter. The computer beeps and ignores your keystroke.

Notice that the display at the bottom of the screen includes protection information for a cell, for example,

```
C7: (Value, Layout-C2, Protection-V) 30
```

indicates that the protection allows only values (V) to be entered, while

```
C11: (Value, Layout-D2, Protection-N) +C8+C9
```

indicates that the protection allows nothing (N) to be entered into the cell. `Protection-L` in the display indicates that only labels may be entered. If there is no protection indication, then anything may be typed into the cell.

To turn off protection for the entire worksheet, you would use Open-Apple-V and select Protection followed by No. You would then turn the protection back on (for those cells that have been marked for protection with Open-Apple-L) by using Open-Apple-V and selecting Protection followed by Yes.

The Open-Apple-V setting for protection is like a master control. If it is set to yes (protection is on), nothing can be typed into a cell with "Protection -N" indicated; if it is set to no (protection is off), anything can be entered into any cell no matter what the protection indicator for the cell reads.

RUNNING TOTALS

You will occasionally need to keep a running total of the values in a column or row of the spreadsheet. For example, a running total of the weekly earnings in the payroll example would show how much money an employee had earned so far this year as well as how much he or she had earned by the end of the first week, the second week, and so on. If you are keeping track of automobile expenses, a running total would indicate the approximate odometer reading and would also let you check on maintenance needs such as a lube and oil that are performed every 3,000 miles or so (you would see when the mileage reached a multiple of 3000.)

```
=====A=========B=========         Formula Used In Column B       }
    Value     Running Total
     10         10    (10)                  @SUM(A2...A2)
     20         30    (10+20)               @SUM(A2...A3)
     30         60    (10+20+30)            @SUM(A2...A4)
     40        100    (10+20+30+40)         @SUM(A2...A5)
     45        145    (10+20+30+40+45)      @SUM(A2...A6)
     55        200    (10+20+30+40+45+55)   @SUM(A2...A7)

     -----------------
    200
```

FIGURE 11-3. Formulas for Keeping a Running Total.

Keeping a running total can be an easy task with a creative use of the copy function. Figure 11-3 shows an example of a running total.

To generate a running total formula, enter the summation formula in the first cell to contain the running total and then copy the formula to the other cells with "No change" for the first cell reference and "Relative" for the second cell reference.

REVIEW QUESTIONS

1. What value should be in cell A1 so that the result of the calculation in cell A2 is the value shown.

NUMBER IN A1	FORMULA IN A2	VALUE DISPLAYED IN A2
1 (example)	@CHOOSE(A1,-8,17,42,9)	-8
a.	@CHOOSE(A1,-8,17,42,9)	42
b.	@ABS(A1)	42
c.	@SQRT(A1)	2
d.	@INT(A1)	2
e.	@INT(A1/10+.5)*10	40

2. A worksheet contains the values and formulas shown in Figure 11-4.

```
================A================B====================
 1|            10                  5
 2|            15                 45
 3|            25                 67
 4|            30                 98
 5|            45                112
 6|-------------------------------------------------
 7|@COUNT(A1...A5)
 8|@SUM(A1...A5)
 9|@MAX(A1...A5)
10|@MIN(A1...A5)
11|@AVG(A1...A5)
12|@LOOKUP(1,A1...A5)
13|@LOOKUP(31,A1...A5)
14|@LOOKUP(409.34,A1...A5)
15|@CHOOSE(2,A1,A2,A3,A4,A5)
16|@SQRT(A3)
17|@IF(A1>=5,-10,-20)
18|@IF(A1>=50,-10,-20)
```

FIGURE 11-4.   Question 2 Data.

Determine the values that appear in cells A7 to A18.   (Do not use the computer.)

3. Use the pattern in the round-off formulas shown at the beginning of this unit to determine new round-off formulas for the nearest thousand and the nearest thousandth.

EXERCISES

11.3 Develop a spreadsheet to keep statistics on the players in your favorite sport. The players can be from a professional team, a school team or a back-yard team of friends. Check the newspaper or with a coach to determine what information is kept for each player for each game. Keep averages for the players for several games.

11.4 Help a faculty member develop a spreadsheet to keep class grades. Be sure to explain how you can get the computer to drop the lowest grade from the average of a set of grades automatically. (See the @MIN example at the beginning of this unit.)

11.5   You have just purchased a used car. You paid $200 cash and have a loan for the balance of $1,800. The loan payments are $87.28 per month for 24 months. (A 15% loan has an interest charge of 294.72, so the payments total $2,094.72.) Insurance costs you $1,300 per year if you are male, $800 per year if you are female. You sell the car for $1,200 at the end of the two years. If you drive the car approximately 900 miles per month, get an average of 22 miles per gallon of gas, use unleaded gas ($1.23 per gallon), change the oil and lubricate every 3,000 miles ($26.00 for lube and oil), and tune up once a year ($70.00), how much does the car cost you for the two years you own it? What is the average cost per week? Per month? Use a spreadsheet to answer these questions.

11.6   (a continuation of exercise 11.5.) Use the spreadsheet you developed to determine the cost per mile of running the car. If you took a summer job both years (for three months only) that required you to use your car for an additional 1,000 miles per month, what happens to the cost per mile? The average cost per week?

APPLICATION

G MATHEMATICAL PROBLEMS

Your instructor will assign one or more of the following problems to you. The first two problems are examples that might be used in a first year Algebra class. The third problem is an example you might find in any math class and the last two problems deal with topics found in Algebra II.

1. LINE GRAPHS

Line graph equations or linear equations are those of the form $y = mx + b$, where m and b are real numbers. A specific linear equation is $y = 3x - 2$. Linear equations are so named since each has a graph in the coordinate plane that is a straight line. One method for finding the line that represents a given equation is to pick several values for x and then calculate the corresponding y value for each x value. For example, if 2 is chosen for x, then $y = 3x - 2$; $y = 3(2) - 2$; $y = 6 - 2$; $y = 4$. Thus the x, y pair where $x = 2$ and $y = 4$ or simply (2,4) is a graph point on the line. When several x, y pairs or points have been found, they are plotted on a coordinate system and connected to form a line. Figure G-1 shows a table of x, y pairs for the equation above.

The numbers in the X column are generated from cell X2 to X11 by formula. All of the numbers in the Y column are generated by a formula similar to the one shown in cell Y1. The numbers were entered into the X and Y columns of the spreadsheet since they represented x,y values.

```
========X========Y======
   1|         -5          -17
   2|         -4          -14
   3|         -3          -11
   4|         -2           -8
   5|         -1           -5
   6|          0           -2
   7|          1            1
   8|          2            4
   9|          3            7
  10|          4           10
  11|          5           13
    |
   ------------------------
Y1:  (Value)  3*X1-2
```

FIGURE G-1.   Table of X,Y Pairs for Y=3X-2.

YOUR TASK

Create spreadsheets to generate *x, y* tables for the following linear equations (make one spreadsheet for each equation). Use the copy command to enter the formulas in the X and Y columns. Print out the table for each formula as a report and as a hard copy of the screen showing the formulas that you used to generate the table.

   a. $y = 3x - 2$
   b. $y = -3x - 2$
   c. $y = 3x + 2$
   d. $y = -3x + 2$
   e. $y = 1.25x + 4.5$
   f. $y = -1.125x + .375$

2. EQUATIONS

Equations of the type $Ax + B = Cx + D$ can be solved for *x* by calculating the formula:

$$x = \frac{D - B}{A - C} \qquad \text{where A is not the same as C.}$$

The equation $2x + 3 = 1x + 5$ has the solution:

$$x = \frac{5 - 3}{2 - 1}$$

$$= \frac{2}{1}$$

$$= 2$$

YOUR TASK

Construct a spreadsheet to solve equations similar to the one shown above. For each problem in the problem set below, enter the values of A, B, C, and D in columns A, B, C, and D of the spreadsheet (one problem per row). Enter the formula for calculating x into column F. Use the copy command to repeat the formula for each problem. Print out the information in the spreadsheet and print out the formulas in the spreadsheet. Hand in this information to your teacher.

	THE PROBLEM	A	B	C	D
a.	$5x+8=4x+10$	5	8	4	10
b.	$3x-4=8x+11$	3	-4	8	11
c.	$2.6x-3.1=4.2x-18$	2.6	-3.1	4.2	-18
d.	$-0.05x+1.25=0.01x-0.55$	-0.05	1.25	0.01	-0.55
e.	$2/3x+7/12=1/2x+3/4$	2/3	7/12	1/2	3/4
f.	$29x=15x+28$	29	0	15	28
g.	$2x+7=x+7$	2	7	1	7

3. AVOIDING ERROR

There are two primary calculations that cause the message ERROR to be displayed in a cell. The first is attempting to divide by zero (this cannot be done by mathematicians either); the second is attempting to take the square root of a negative number. The result of division by zero is undefined, the square root of a negative number is called an imaginary number by mathematicians; imaginary numbers can not be directly calculated on most microcomputers.

Figure G-2 illustrates the use of the @IF function to avoid the ERROR message in cell E3. If the denominator of the fraction in the calculation is 0, the message NA (not available) is displayed. If the denominator of the fraction is not 0, the calculation is performed.

Notice that protection is used in cell E3 to prevent accidental erasure of the formula in this cell. Protection is used in the other cells as well. Cells C2 and C4 are protected to allow value entries only; the cells that contain labels are protected so that nothing can be entered to overwrite them.

```
========A========B========C========D========E====
  1|
  2|Numerator      ===>         4           Quotient
  3|                        ---------            NA
  4|Denominator    ===>         0
  5|

--------------------------------------------------------
 E3:  (Value, Protect-N) @IF(C4=0,@NA,C2/C4)
```

FIGURE G-2.   Formula for Division Without ERROR Message.

YOUR TASK

Create a formula to calculate the positive (principle) square root of any value entered into cell C1. Your formula should display NA if the number entered is less than zero. Use protection so that the formula and the labels that you use cannot be accidentally overwritten. Figure G-3 is an example of how your display might look.

```
========A========B========C====
  1|Number         ===>         4
  2|Square Root                 2
  3|
  4|Number         ===>        -3
  5|Square Root                NA
```

FIGURE G-3.   Square Root Calculation Without ERROR Message.

```
========A========B========C========D========E========F========G====
  1|Number         ===>         9
  2|Square Root             + or -          3      + or -          0i
  3|
  4|Number         ===>       -25
  5|Square Root             + or -          0      + or -          5i

---------------------------------------------------------------------
 C4:  (Value, Protect-V) -25
```

FIGURE G-4.   Imaginary Square Root Calculation Display.

ALTERNATIVE TASK

Create formulas to calculate the real or imaginary square root of any real number. Your display might look like the one in Figure G-4. The figure shows the square root in imaginary form, so the square root of 9 is displayed as ±3±0i and the square root of -25 is displayed as ±0±5i (the ±0 or ±0i is used to generalize the answer since the same formulas are used to find both real and imaginary roots).

4. QUADRATIC FORMULAS

Mathematics students are asked at some time in their careers to solve second degree equations of the form $Ax^2+Bx+C=0$. One method for solving such equations calculates the values of x from the quadratic formulas:

$$x = \frac{-B \pm \sqrt{B^2 - 4AC}}{2A}$$

The symbol ± is read as "plus or minus." The equation produces two values for x; one when the plus (+) is used after the first value for B and the other when the minus (-) is used. To produce two distinct values for x, the value of B^2-4AC must be greater than zero. If the value of B^2-4AC is 0, the two solutions for x are the same; i.e. there is one solution. If the value of B^2-4AC is a negative number, then there is no real number solution to the problem. Since B^2-4AC determines the number of solutions that a quadratic has, it is called the determinant.

YOUR TASK

Create a spreadsheet to solve the quadratic equations given below. If there is no solution for an equation, the values of x should appear as NA. Figure G-5 is an example of a screen layout you might use. Use protection to allow values only to be entered into cells A6, B6, and C6; all other spreadsheet cells that contain information should be protected so that nothing can be entered to change their contents.

Print out four hard copies of the screen. On the first, show problem 1 with the cell locator positioned at cell A6. On the second, show problem 2 with the cell locator positioned at cell D9 (as illustrated in Figure G-4). On the third, show problem 3 with the cell locator positioned on cell D11, and on the last, show problem 4 with the cell locator on cell D13.

Problems:
1. $2x^2+14x+12=0$ Solutions $x = -1$ or $x = -6$
2. $1x^2-5x+6=0$ Solutions $x = 3$ or $x = 2$
3. $3x^2-7x-4=0$ Solutions $x = 2.808143$ or $x = -.4748096$
4. $1x^2-1x+1=0$ Solutions $x = NA$ or $x = NA$

```
========A========B========C========D====
  1|SOLUTION OF QUADRATIC EQUATIONS
  2|
  3|Enter the values of A, B and C for
  4|        A x^2 + B x   +   C = 0
  5|
  6|        1           -5          6
  7|        A^          B^          C^
  8|
  9|            Determinant                1
 10|
 11|                            x =        3
 12|                            or
 13|                            x =        2
 14|
 --------------------------------------------
 D9: (Value, Protect-N) +B6^2-(4*A6*C6)
```

FIGURE G-5.   Spreadsheet for the Solution of Quadratic Equations.

ALTERNATIVE TASK

Solve the quadratic equations listed above over the complex number system. Display all of the solutions as complex numbers of the form $a+bi$ where a, b are real numbers. Do enough problems with imaginary roots to convince a senior mathematics teacher that your method of solution is correct. Print out the four screens as described in the section above.

5. BASES

A method for converting a base 10 number into a number in another base is as follows:

1. Divide the base 10 number by the base to which you wish to convert.
2. Write down the remainder and the quotient.
3. Divide the quotient by the base.
4. Write down the remainder and the quotient.
   Repeat steps 3 and 4 until the quotient is 0..
5. Write down the remainders, last to first. This is the number in the new base.

Here is a specific example. Convert 25 from base 10 to base 2.

Step	Problem	Quotient	Remainder
1	25/2		
2		12	1
3	12/2		
4		6	0

```
3       6/2
4                       3               0
3       3/2
4                       1               1
3       1/2
4                       0               1
5                                       11012 = 2510
```

$1101_2 = 25_{10}$

```
┌─────────────────────────────────────────────────────────────────────┐
│                                                                       │
│  File: BASE                       REVIEW/ADD/CHANGE                    │
│  ========A========B===========C===========D====EFGHIJKLMNOP==Q===R==  │
│    1|Number Base 10:                 25<===                           │
│    2|Convert to base:                 2<===       000000011001 Base  2 │
│    3|Quotient Remainder                                               │
│    4|        12          1             1's                            │
│    5|         6          0             2's                            │
│    6|         3          0             4's                            │
│    7|         1          1             8's                            │
│    8|         0          1            16's                            │
│    9|         0          0            32's                            │
│   10|         0          0            64's                            │
│   11|         0          0           128's                            │
│   12|         0          0           256's                            │
│   13|         0          0           512's                            │
│   14|         0          0          1024's                            │
│   15|         0          0          2048's                            │
│   16|                                                                 │
│   17|                                                                 │
│   18|                                                                 │
│  ------------------------------------------------------------------   │
│  B7:  (Value, Protect-N) +C2*((A6/C2)-@INT(A6/C2))                    │
│                                                                       │
└─────────────────────────────────────────────────────────────────────┘
```

FIGURE G-6.   Base Conversion Spreadsheet.

A spreadsheet version of this procedure is shown in Figure G-6. The formula for the quotient is obtained by rounding off the results of the division to the nearest whole number using the @INT function. The formula for the remainder is shown in the figure. It works by first finding the remainder in decimal form and then multiplying the decimal form by the base to obtain the whole number remainder. For example, using the formula and information shown in the figure:

```
A6/C2 is 3/2 = 1.5
@INT(A6/C2) is @INT(1.5) =1
(A6/C2)-@INT(A6/C2) is 1.5 - 1 = .5
+C2*((A6/C2)-@INT(A6/C2)) is 2*(.5) = 1    (The result in B7.)
```

C2 is constant in every formula in the column and A6 is relative (above and to the left of B7). The remainders are copied into cells E2 to P2, which have been reduced in width to display only one digit. Calculation is done by column to avoid forward referencing.

If you use a base higher than 10, the number in row 2 may show # signs for some of the digits. For example, 127_{10} displays as 00000000007# base 16. The remainder column shows that the # sign is used to represent 15 (F). You need to supply the missing digit in these cases. ($127_{10} = 7F_{16}$.)

YOUR TASK

Create a spreadsheet to convert numbers in base 10 to any other base where the base is greater than 1. All of the value cells in the spreadsheet should contain formulas with the exception of cells C1, C2, and C4. Print out a hard copy of the number 3128 converted to base 2, base 3, base 8, base 12, and base 16. The cursor positions on these five printouts should be cells C2, A4, B4, B15, and C15, respectively, to illustrate your formulas.

12 INTEGRATION AND ORGANIZATION

LEARNING OBJECTIVES

After completing this unit, you should be able to ...

a. work with 1 to 12 files on the Desktop at one time.

b. move or copy information from one application to another application of the same type.

c. move or copy information from one application to another application of a different type.

d. delete a file from the disk.

e. handle a full disk or a full Desktop.

f. store files logically on several disks.

MORE THAN ONE FILE ON THE DESKTOP

There will be occasions when you work on more than one file at a time. You may be writing a report based on information that was compiled in a data base or tabulated and calculated in a spreadsheet. You may wish to take a quote from a research paper that you have typed and saved and include it in another paper. You may have written a piece for the school's literary journal and wish to examine your work and that of others electronically. You might even wish to combine several of these journal works into one document.

Let's add three files to the Desktop from the Student Data Disk.

Start from AppleWorks Main Menu.

WHAT YOU TYPE	WHY YOU TYPE IT
<RETURN>	To select **Add files to the Desktop**.
<RETURN>	To select **The current disk**.
Down-arrow	Until you highlight **Sayings**.
<RIGHT-ARROW>	To select this file as one of the files to load. An arrow appears in the left column pointing to the file name.

The display shows an arrow pointing to the Sayings file.

WHAT YOU TYPE	WHY YOU TYPE IT
<DOWN-ARROW>	To move the highlight bar down to the next file name. Note that the arrow remains pointing at Sayings.
Down-arrow	Until you highlight the file name **Suggestions**.
<RIGHT-ARROW>	Another arrow points to Suggestions.

Now arrows point to two file names. Both of these files have been selected for loading.

WHAT YOU TYPE	WHY YOU TYPE IT
Down-arrow	Until the file **Original YrBk** is highlighted.
<RIGHT-ARROW>	To select this file for loading as well. Another arrow points to this file.
<RETURN>	To load all of the selected files (three in this case) onto the Desktop.

After the files are loaded, give the ⌃-Q command. A Desktop Index window appears in the middle of the display as shown in Figure 12.1.

All three files are on the computer's Desktop, even though you can only observe one file at a time. Once the files are on the Desktop, you do not need to load them from the disk again until you either quit AppleWorks or remove the file from the Desktop using the Main Menu item 4. As long as the file is on the Desktop, you can display it quickly using the ⌘-Q command. (Remember this command lets you change quickly from one file to another.) Try using this command to switch from one file to another on your own.

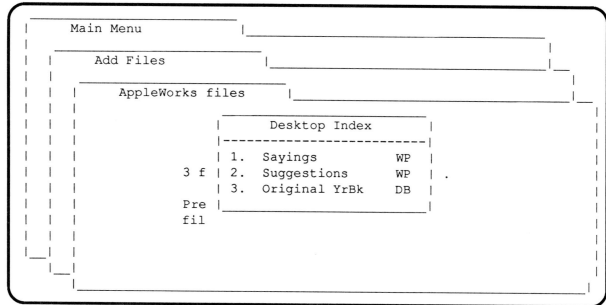

FIGURE 12-1.   The Desktop Index.

✓ **CHECKPOINT**

When you use Open-Apple-Q to move from one file to another and then back to the first, where do you find the cursor in the first file?

1. At the beginning of the file.   2. At the end of the file
3. At some random point in the file.   4. Where it was when you left the file.

TRANSFERRING INFORMATION

The strongest feature of AppleWorks is the integration of its three applications. Information from one application can be transferred to another application electronically so that duplicate typing is virtually eliminated. You have used this feature in several previous sections of this text to save yourself time and effort.

The sections that follow review or introduce all possible combinations of transferring data from one application to the same or another application.

WORD PROCESSOR TO WORD PROCESSOR

Copying information from a Word Processor file to another Word Processor file is the least restricted and easiest of all of the information exchanges. It involves just a few basic steps:

1. Display the file that information will be copied from.
2. Give the copy or move command and copy or move the desired information to the clipboard, following the instructions given in the command. (The clipboard is a special area on the Desktop for storing information. The clipboard was discussed in Unit 7) Remember, copy leaves a duplicate of the information in the original file; move does not.
3. Display the file that the information is to be copied to.
4. Move the cursor to the insertion point in the file.
5. Give the copy or move command and copy or move the clipboard information into the file at the cursor position.

Here is a specific example.

WHAT YOU TYPE	WHY YOU TYPE IT
⌂-Q (and other keys)	Display the file **Suggestions**. (The other keys should be familiar to you now and no longer need to be spelled out.)
Arrows	To move the cursor to the beginning of the line in the first paragraph.
⌂-C	To start the copy command.
T	To select **To clipboard (cut).**
Down-arrow	To highlight the first two paragraphs for the cut.
<RETURN>	To complete the copy of the information to the clipboard.
⌂-Q (and other keys)	Display the file **Sayings** on the screen.

Use any key combination that you desire to move the cursor to the first blank line after the line **AppleWorks is really great** (You could also use the find command to locate a point in the text.)

Type the following additional line:

It can be used to move information such as the paragraphs below from one word processor document to another.

WHAT YOU TYPE	WHY YOU TYPE IT
⌂-C	To start the copy command.
F	To copy information from the clipboard into the document that appears in the display.

Both the information that you typed from the keyboard and the information that you copied through the clipboard are now permanent parts of the Sayings file.

DATA BASE TO WORD PROCESSOR

Information that is transferred to the Word Processor from the Data Base is first printed to the clipboard and then inserted into the Word Processor document using either the copy or move command in the Word Processor . You select what is printed to the clipboard just as you select any other information for printing. You can print the information in either a "labels" or a "tables" style report for even greater flexibility.

Here's how to transfer Data Base information to the Word Processor. First, let's look at a general overview of the steps in the process:

1. Display the file that originates the information.
2. Arrange the information as if you were preparing to print a report.
3. Print the report to the clipboard rather than to your printer.
4. Display the Word Processor document that is to receive the information.
5. Copy the information from the clipboard into the Word Processor document.

Let's try a specific example:

WHAT YOU TYPE	WHY YOU TYPE IT
⌂-Q (and other keys)	To display the file **Original YrBk** on your screen.
⌂-P <DOWN-ARROW>	To start the report printing process.
<RETURN>	To make a new "tables" report.
To WP <RETURN>	To name the report.

Modify the report so that the information to be printed appears on your computer display as it is shown in Figure 12-2. The modifications only involve making some of the column widths narrower.

WHAT YOU TYPE	WHY YOU TYPE IT
⌂-P	To print the report.
Arrows <RETURN>	To select **The clipboard (for the Word Processor).**
Other information as requested in your display.	

A few moments after you have entered the date and pressed Return, the following message appears on the display:

```
The report is now on the clipboard,
and can be moved or copied into Word
Processor documents.
```

You then copy the information into your Word Processor document just as you did in the preceding example. As long as the report is no wider than 60 characters, no adjustments are necessary in the document to which the report is copied. In the next section, the Spreadsheet example addresses the problem of wide reports.

```
File: Original YrBk              REPORT FORMAT              Escape: Report  Menu
Report: To WP
Selection: All records




================================================================================
--> or <--   Move cursor                    ⌂-J  Right justify this category
   >  ⌂  <     Switch category positions     ⌂-K  Define a calculated category
--> ⌂ <--    Change column width             ⌂-N  Change report name and/or title
⌂-A  Arrange (sort) on this category         ⌂-O  Printer options
⌂-D  Delete this category                    ⌂-P  Print the report
⌂-G  Add/remove group totals                 ⌂-R  Change record selection rules
⌂-I  Insert a prev. deleted category         ⌂-T  Add/remove category totals
--------------------------------------------------------------------------------


Last Name First Name Home Room Date Ordered Charge Paid L
-A------- -B-------- -C------- -D---------- -E---- -F-- e
Cuber     Andrea     21        Nov 87       20     20   n
Fallon    Lisa       21        Nov 87       20     10   5
Fallon    Julie      21        Nov 87       20     0    6


--------------------------------------------------------------------------------
Use options shown above to change report format              49K Avail.
```

FIGURE 12-2.   Data Base Report Ready For Transfer.

SPREADSHEET TO WORD PROCESSOR

Spreadsheet information is transferred to the Word Processor in much the same way that Data Base information is transferred.

1. Create a report for the spreadsheet file using "All", "Rows", "Columns", or "Block".
2. Print the report to the clipboard.
3. Display the Word Processor file the information is to be copied to.
4. Copy the information from the clipboard into the Word Processor document.

The flexible width of the reports generated by the Spreadsheet and the Data Base can sometimes cause problems with this process. The following example illustrates how to transfer from the Spreadsheet to the Word Processor and also how to compensate for a document that does not fit.

    <ESCAPE>   To the Main Menu.

Add the file Pizza onto your Desktop from the Student Data Disk. (You now have four files on your Desktop.)

WHAT YOU TYPE	WHY YOU TYPE IT
🍏-P	To print the file.
RETURN	To select the entire file for the report.

Notice that the print screen tells you that the report is 66 characters wide, too wide for the normal Word Processor setting. The normal setting leaves 6 inches between the margins, at ten characters per inch, only 60 characters are printed on a line.

WHAT YOU TYPE	WHY YOU TYPE IT
Down-arrow	To select **The clipboard (for the Word Processor).**
Today's Date <RETURN>	To enter the date.

The following message appears in the display:

```
The report is now on the clipboard,
and can be moved or copied into Word
Processor documents.
```

Now move to the Word Processor document and copy the information from the clipboard:

WHAT YOU TYPE	WHY YOU TYPE IT
<ESCAPE> twice	To return to the Main Menu.
<RETURN>	To **Add files to the Desktop.**
3 <RETURN>	To make a new file for the Word Processor.
<RETURN>	To select **From Scratch.**
FromSpreadsheet	To name the file.
<RETURN>	To display a blank Word Processor document.
🍏-C	To start the copy command.
F	To copy the Pizza information from the clipboard.

As you can see from your screen or from Figure 12-3, the file looks like a mess, but it is easy to transform it to a more presentable form.

```
┌─────────────────────────────────────────────────────────────────────────┐
│ File: FromSpreadsheet          REVIEW/ADD/CHANGE        Escape: Main Menu  │
│ ==== |==== |==== |==== |==== |==== |==== |==== |==== |==== |==== |==== |==== |==== |==== |=== │
│ File:   Pizza                                                             │
│            Page  1                                                        │
│                                                                           │
│      June  6, 1988                                                        │
│                                                                           │
│               CUSTOMER     BEGIN        END                               │
│ DOLLAR                                                                    │
│    DATE        NAME       ODOMETER    ODOMETER    MILEAGE                 │
│ AMOUNT                                                                    │
│ ------------------------------------------------------------             │
│ ------                                                                    │
│    Tue  6/1  Burd         19,230      19,241         11                   │
│ $2.31                                                                     │
│              Owens        19,241      19,249          8                   │
│ $1.68                                                                     │
│              Smith        19,249      19,266         17                   │
│ $3.57                                                                     │
│              Sauer        19,266      19,268          2                   │
│ $.42                                                                      │
│              Pepper       19,268      19,275          7                   │
│ ------------------------------------------------------------------        │
│ Type entry or use ⌘ commands           Line 1  Column  1    ⌘ -? for Help │
└─────────────────────────────────────────────────────────────────────────┘
```

FIGURE 12-3. Newly Copied Spreadsheet Information.

WHAT YOU TYPE	WHY YOU TYPE IT
⌘-1	To move the cursor to the top of the file.
⌘-O	To display the printer options.
RM <RETURN>	To set the right margin.
0.5 <RETURN>	The right margin value is now 0.5 in.
LM <RETURN>	To set the left margin.
0.5 <RETURN>	The left margin value is now 0.5 in.

By moving the margins out 1/2 inch on each side, the extra six characters are easily accommodated. The table columns realign and appear as they originally did in the spreadsheet.

You would have to move the margins out to the end of the page (LM 0, RM 0) to fit each of the two title lines on one line. Alternatively, you could delete spaces between the title and the word "Page" and delete the same number of spaces before the date. If the title and date are not needed, you could delete them from the Word Processor document or use the printer options in the Spreadsheet to stop them from printing.

There are, of course, other methods of adjusting the document for the extra characters. For example, instead of changing the margins you could change from 10 characters per inch to 12, or you could change the number of characters per inch and change the margin settings. If necessary, you could reduce the size of the columns in the spreadsheet before you print it to the clipboard.

How you edit a document is entirely up to you now. One caution, do not use proportional printing with column information similar to the information that you have just transferred from the Data Base or the Spreadsheet.. You cannot get the columns to line up using proportional printing.

There is another method that can be used to transfer information from either a Spreadsheet or a Data Base to the Word Processor. You first print the Data Base or Spreadsheet information to an **ASCII** file on the disk. (ASCII means American Standard Code for Information Interchange. It is one of several standard ways that information is stored in computer files.) After you have saved the information in an ASCII file, you read it into a new word processor file. You can then transfer it into any other file by using the clipboard.

There are two major differences when you transfer data with an ASCII file: (1) you must create a new Word Processor file to receive the ASCII information, and (2) when you have completed the transfer of files using the ASCII method, you find that there is a formatting problem that is far more involved than the problem in the preceding example. The transfered information is listed in one long column rather than in several columns as it originally appeared in the Spreadsheet or Data Base. This method of transfer to the Word Processor is therefore impractical.

Transferring with ASCII files seems like a long complicated way to do things, but sometimes, as you'll discover in one of the following sections, it is the only way to transfer information from one application to another.

WORD PROCESSOR TO DATA BASE

Transferring information from the Word Processor to the Data Base is accomplished by using ASCII files which we discussed in the preceding section. The information in the original Word Processor file must be organized in a very precise way: it must be listed in one column with the categories in the order in which they are to appear in the file and there can be no gaps or blank lines between records. Any missing category information must show as a blank line, for example, to transfer four records with three categories per record, the word processing file must be as shown in Figure 12-4.

The general steps for a Word Processor to Data Base transfer are:

1. Generate a Word Processor document that contains the records in the file in a single list like the one shown in Figure 12-4.
2. Print the file to an ASCII file on the disk.
3. Create a new Data Base file from the ASCII file.
4. Rename the categories in the Data Base file to reflect the contents.

```
File: WP to DB                    REVIEW/ADD/CHANGE
=====|====|====|====|====|====|====|====|====|===
Record 1 Category 1▓
Record 1 Category 2▓
Record 1 Category 3▓
Record 2 Category 1▓
Record 2 Category 2▓
Record 2 Category 3▓
Record 3 Category 1▓
Record 3 Category 2▓
Record 3 Category 3▓
Record 4 Category 1▓
Record 4 Category 2▓
Record 4 Category 3▓
```

FIGURE 12-4.   Word Processor File Ready For Transfer to Data Base.

Here are the steps for a specific transfer of four records with three categories per record.   The categories are Course Name, Instructor, and Room.

Create a Word Processor file identical to the one in Figure 12-5.

```
File: WP to DB   REVIEW/ADD/CHANGE
=====|====|====|====|====|====|====|====|====|==
English ▓
Mrs. Rannestad▓
512 ▓
Math ▓
Mr. Lyon ▓
209 ▓
History ▓
Mr. Sweeney ▓
607 ▓
Science ▓
Mrs. Purcell▓
408 ▓
```

FIGURE 12-5.   Word Processor File of Four Records.

WHAT YOU TYPE	WHY YOU TYPE IT
⌘-P	To start the print process.

<RETURN>	To print from the beginning.
Down-arrow <RETURN>	To select **A text (ASCII) file on disk.**
/AWD/X <RETURN>	To enter the pathname for your file. /AWD/ is the name you used to create your data disk in unit 2. X is the name of the ASCII file that is stored on the disk.

The disk light comes on for a moment as the file is saved and then the Review/Add/Change Word Processor screen reappears. You now need to create a Data Base file from the ASCII file.

WHAT YOU TYPE	WHY YOU TYPE IT
<ESCAPE>	To return to the Main Menu.
<RETURN>	To select **Add files to the Desktop.**
4 <RETURN>	Select **Make a new file for the Data Base.**
2 <RETURN>	Select **Make a new file from a text (ASCII) file.**
3 <RETURN>	To indicate 3 categories.
/AWD/X	To enter the pathname.
To DB from WP RETURN	To enter a name for the new Data Base file.

Your screen now shows the Data Base file in Figure 12-6.

```
File: To DB from WP              REVIEW/ADD/CHANGE


Selection: All records



Category 01      Category 02      Category 03
=================================================
English          Mrs. Rannestad   512
Math             Mr. Lyon         209
History          Mr. Sweeney      607
Science          Mrs. Purcell     408
```

FIGURE 12-6. Data Base File Created From an ASCII File.

Finally, use the ⌂-N command to change the names of the categories to Course Name, Instructor and Room.

This procedure can be used to convert a text file generated by any AppleWorks application to a Data Base file. The ASCII file must be correctly organized as illustrated in Figure 12-4 for the transfer to work correctly. Category information lines should not be longer than 75 characters; if they are, the characters after the 75th character are lost in the transfer.

DATA BASE TO DATA BASE

There are several ways to transfer information from one data base file to another. One way is to use the clipboard. The clipboard allows you to copy information from any Data Base file to any other Data Base file. Information copied to the clipboard and then to another Data Base file is always copied in the category order that was originally defined for the file the information is copied from. The file that you copy or move the information from should have the same number of categories as the file you are copying information to. If this is not the case, one of the following conditions will occur:

(1) If the "from" file has a greater number of categories than the "to" file, the extra categories are not transferred. Which categories are not transferred is determined by the original category order, not the layout order. For example, if the "from" file has five categories, A, B, C, D and E, and the "to" file has only three categories, X, Y and Z, the information in A is transferred to X, the information in B is transferred to Y, and the information in C is transferred to Z. Information in categories D and E is not transferred. Changing the order of the layout in either file does not change the order of the transfer.

(2) If the "from" file has fewer categories than the "to" file, the extra categories are left blank. For example, if the "from" file has the categories A and B and the "to" file has categories X, Y and Z, the information in category A is transferred to category X, the information in category B is transferred to Y and category Z is left blank. Changing the order of the layout does not change the order of the transfer.

The second way to transfer information from one data base file to another is to print the information from the first data base file into an ASCII file and then create a new Data Base file from the ASCII file. Since you control which categories are printed into the ASCII file and the order in which they are printed, you can create a new Data Base file that contains some or all of the original categories in the same or a different order. Care must be taken to answer the question How many categories in the new file? correctly. If you answer the question incorrectly, the information appears in a jumble and the Data Base file needs to be created again. (The ASCII file is probably ok when this happens; just delete the Data Base file you created and create it again.)

Printing the ASCII file is very similar to printing any Data Base file; the only difference is that the printer is an ASCII file on the disk. Creating a Data Base file from an ASCII file was discussed in the section "Word Processor to Data Base."

A third way to make a data base to data bsae transfer is to print the records in the original file to a **DIF** file and then create a new Data Base file from the DIF file. DIF stands for Data Interchange Format, another standard way of storing information. It is usually used to store information that is kept in tabular form, the form used in a data base or a spreadsheet.

Here is a general outline for a DIF transfer:

1. Print the information to be transferred into a DIF file on the disk.
2. Create a new Data Base file from the DIF file.

Specifically:

WHAT YOU TYPE	WHY YOU TYPE IT
Ú-Q (and other keys.)	Display the file **To DB from WP** on your monitor.
Ú-P	To start the print process.
<RETURN>	To select **Create a new "tables" format.**
To DIF <RETURN>	To name the report "To DIF".
Ú-D	To delete the first category and transfer only the instructor's name and the room number. (The choice of categories is arbitrary for this example.)
Ú->	To change the order of the categories to Room, Instructor.
Ú-P	To print the report.
Arrows <RETURN>	To highlight and select **A DIF (TM) file on disk.**
/AWD/X RETURN	To enter the pathname of the DIF file.
Y	To reuse the space that is no longer needed by the old X file.

The DIF file is created on your data disk and the Report Format screen reappears. You now need to create a new Data Base file from the DIF file.

WHAT YOU TYPE	WHY YOU TYPE IT
Ú-Q <ESCAPE>	To return to the Main Menu.
<RETURN>	To select **Add files to the Desktop.**
4 <RETURN>	Select **Make a new file for the Data Base.**
4 <RETURN>	Select **Make a new file from a DIF (TM) file.**
/AWD/X <RETURN>	To enter the pathname of the DIF file.
To DB from DB <RETURN>	To enter the name of the new Data Base file.
Ú-N <RETURN>	To change the category names.
Ú-Y	To remove the first category name, **Category 1.**
Room <RETURN>	To enter the correct category name.
Ú-Y	To remove the second category name, **Category 2.**
Instructor <RETURN>	To enter the correct category name.

AppleWorks created this file with 30 categories. All of the remaining categories after the first two are blank. They can be removed from the file quickly by moving to Category 3 and then holding down the Ú-D combination until they are all eliminated. (There are times when you want to leave additional blank categories in a file so that future changes can be made without loss of reports or custom screens; this is not one of those times.)

SPREADSHEET TO DATA BASE

There are two routes that can be used to transfer Spreadsheet files to Data Base files: print the Spreadsheet file to either an ASCII file or to a DIF file and then create a new file for the Data Base from either the ASCII or DIF file that was created. No matter which method is used, the formulas in the Spreadsheet are not transferred; only the values in the cells at the time the ASCII or DIF file is created are transferred.

The general approach for transfer from a Spreadsheet to a Data Base file is:

1. Print the information from the Spreadsheet to either a DIF or an ASCII file.
2. Create a new Data Base file from either the DIF or ASCII file.
3. Rename the categories in the Data Base file.

```
File: SS to DB                    REVIEW/ADD/CHANGE
========A========B========C========D========E===
   1|A        B        C        D
   2|E        F        G        H
   3|I        J        K        L
    .
    .
    .
  17|
  18|
-------------------------------------------------
A1: (Label) A
```

FIGURE 12-7.   Spreadsheet Ready for Transfer.

The Spreadsheet can create a DIF file in two very different ways: by reading each column item across each row from top to bottom or by reading each row item down each column from left to right. Consider the Spreadsheet in Figure 12-7.

If a DIF file is created by column from the Spreadsheet in Figure 12-7, the order of the cell or item information in the DIF file is:

A B C D E F G H I J K L.

If the DIF file is created by row, the order of the item information in the DIF file is:

A E I B F J C G K D H L.

Since the Data Base is always created by reading the DIF file from first to last item, two different Data Bases can be created from the file illustrated. One is a file of three records with four categories per record; the other is a file of four records with three categories per record. Figures 12-8 and 12-9 show these two files.

```
File: From DIF Column              REVIEW/ADD/CHANGE

Selection: All records

Category  1        Category  2        Category  3        Category  4
====================================================================
A                  B                  C                  D
E                  F                  G                  H
I                  J                  K                  L
```

FIGURE 12-8.   Data Base file from DIF Created by Column.

```
File: From DIF Row                 REVIEW/ADD/CHANGE

Selection: All records

Category  1        Category  2        Category  3
=================================================
A                  E                  I
B                  F                  J
C                  G                  K
D                  H                  L
```

FIGURE 12-9.   Data Base file from DIF Created by Row.

It may help you keep the order differences straight if you think of the column order as preserving the original columns and the row order as the ordering that converts each row into a column. ASCII files are stored in the same order as column DIF files.

WORD PROCESSOR TO SPREADSHEET

As the saying goes, "you can't get there from here." If you really need to make this type of transfer, you can print the Word Processor file to an ASCII file, create a Data Base from the ASCII file, print the Data Base file to a DIF file, and finally, use the DIF file to create a Spreadsheet file.

DATA BASE TO SPREADSHEET

This is a very straight-forward transfer. Print a DIF file from the Data Base file, and then create a new Spreadsheet file from this DIF file. Alter the layout of the Spreadsheet file to your needs.

SPREADSHEET TO SPREADSHEET

There are two possibilities for this type of transfer. One method is to copy or move the information from the original file to the clipboard, display the second file and copy or move the information from the clipboard into the second file. This method allows you to transfer full rows of information only. If there is information in the row that you do not want in the new file, you can blank it from the new file when the transfer is complete.

Alternatively, you can print the information from the original file to a DIF file and then create a new Spreadsheet from the DIF file.

WHAT TO DO WITH A FULL FILE OR A FULL DESKTOP

As you become more proficient with AppleWorks, your collection of files grows. At some point you will be confronted with one of the following error messages:

```
WARNING.  Desktop is full.  Action not completed.

Word Processing files are limited to 2,250 lines.

AppleWorks Data Base files are
limited to 1,350 records.
```

First, you need to know that chances are very good that you did not lose any information. If you did, AppleWorks usually informs you that you did. For example you might see a second error message such as:

```
Some cells were lost from row 437.
```

The first step to take when any of these error messages appears is to save your file over the *oldest* copy of the file. This generally means that you would save the file on your backup disk. Until you are completely convinced that you did not lose any part of your work, you should not save the Desktop copy over your latest disk copy. Once you have saved the file, check the Desktop version. If it is complete, make a backup by saving your file a second time (if your first save was to the backup disk, this save should be to your primary disk). (WARNING: If you are using version 1.1 or 1.2 of AppleWorks, DO NOT save a spreadsheet file after you see any message about lost information. A programming error in these earlier versions makes it impossible to re-load the file.)

Once you have saved the file, assess the problem and make an appropriate correction.

MESSAGE	ACTION
WARNING. Desktop is full. Action not completed.	If there is more than one file on the Desktop, save the extra files and remove them from the Desktop. If there is only one file on the Desktop, the file must be split into two files (see the following instructions) before you can continue.

It is possible that you have a very large amount of information taking up room on the clipboard. Try copying the smallest piece of data you can onto the clipboard. If the amount of work that you have to do to finish your file is less than what you had stored on the clipboard, you may be able to finish your work without any additional difficulty.

`Word Processing files are`   The Word Processing file must be split into two parts.
`limited to 2,250 lines.`   (See the following instructions.)

`AppleWorks Data Base files`   The Data Base file must be split into two parts.
`are limited to 1,350 records.` (See the following instructions.)

An easy way to split a Data Base or Word Processing file is:

1. Decide where the file is to be split. For example, in a Word Processor file it should be at the end of a page, unit or section. In a Data Base file, it might be split by alphabet or date etc. Arrange the Data base file, if necessary, so the split is physically between one part and the other.
2. Save the file and back it up.
3. Rename the file by appending Part 2, P2, or 2 to the original name.
4. Delete all of the information in the Part 2 file from the split point to the **beginning** of the file. Remember, you have already saved this information and backed it up.
5. Save the Part 2 file and back it up.
6. Remove the Part 2 file from the Desktop.
7. Load the original file back onto the Desktop.
8. Delete all of the information in the original file from the split point to the **end** of the file.
9. Rename the file by appending Part 1 or P1 or 1 to the original name and save this part of the file.

Your file is now in two parts. When you print the file, the first part should end at the bottom of a page and the second part should start at the top of a new page, so the printout will appear to come from one continuous file. You can move information from one portion of the file to the other so that the report does this.

WHAT TO DO WITH A FULL DISK

When your disk is full, you need to either get a new disk or delete some of the files that you no longer need. If you are saving a new file and you get the message: **Insufficient room for your file on this disk,** these are your only choices. If you are replacing an old file with new information, you have a third choice that you can use if the first two choices are not possible.

If you have a new disk, format it using the procedure discussed in unit 2 and save your file. You do not lose information from the Desktop when you format a new disk using AppleWorks formatter. If you do not have a new disk, you might consider asking a friend for temporary use of some disk space and save your file on his or her disk until you are able to obtain a new disk.

If the first option is not possible, you must make room for your file by deleting an old file from your disk. To delete files from a disk, select 5. "Other Activities" from the Main Menu. Next, select 4. "Delete files from disk" from the Other Activities menu. The disk catalog then shows all of the files on the disk including non-AppleWorks files such as the DIF and ASCII files you created. Select the files to be deleted by using the arrow keys. Press Return and the files are verified for deletion one by one.

The third choice which is available to you only if you are resaving a file, is to delete the old file before you save. This action usually leaves sufficient room to save the updated version of the file. Here's why: When AppleWorks resaves a file, it saves the new version of the file on the disk completely before it deletes the old version. This method allows you to press Escape to abort the save; it also allows two copies of the file to exist temporarily on the disk at the same time. There must be enough free space on the disk to hold the file, even if you are replacing an old file.

If you use the third method, remember, you have only the Desktop copy of the file until you save. You are very vulnerable to a file loss until you have the file safely copied onto a disk.

ORGANIZING SEVERAL DISKS

As your use of AppleWorks increases, you should consider a logical method of storing your files on disks. When you first start, saving all of your files on one disk is convenient and practical. However, as your files increase in number, keeping track of which disk contains a given file can be a burden.

Floppy disks are relatively inexpensive, so it is not unreasonable to assume that an individual may have several data disks. A simple example of disk organization might be:

Disk #1	Business course files.
Disk #2	Social Science papers, data files, and reports.
Disk #3	Math projects on the Spreadsheet.
Disk #4	English papers and reports.
Disk #5	Personal and hobby files.

The best system that you can use to organize your files on several disks is the one you devise for yourself. Use a careful description of the contents of the disk on the disk label if there is enough room on the label. If you are organized, you should seldom, if ever, need to search through several disks to find an old file that you need.

USING FILES GENERATED BY OTHER SOFTWARE

The more you use AppleWorks, the more you'll want to use it. You may find that you want to convert files that you created with other programs to AppleWorks files. This process is called importing.

Two types of files can be easily imported into Appleworks, VisiCalc (R) and Quick File (TM) files. Quick Files are read directly from a Quick File data disk and are automatically converted to AppleWorks as they are read. VisiCalc files are read from a VisiCalc data disk.

Other software's files can be imported into AppleWorks if the software can produce either a DIF or an ASCII (text) version of the file. (If these files are generated in DOS 3.3, Apple's old Disk Operating System, they can be converted to ProDOS, AppleWorks' operating system, with the utility disk that comes with the computer.) The ASCII or DIF files are then used to create new AppleWorks files using the steps outlined earlier in this unit. The details on how to generate ASCII or DIF files can be found in the manuals that come with the software. Information on converting files from DOS to ProDOS can be found in the manual that comes with the the ProDOS program disk.

APPLICATION

LIVING IN THE USA

What is it that makes living in the United States of America so good for so many people? What is it that makes it best for you? Is it being in a state with a high population or a low population, a growing state with a lot of migration to the state; a state with a younger population (median age less than 30) or an older population, a state with a high per capita income, a state where a large number of the population graduates from high school, or is it some combination of these factors?

The Student Data Disk contains census information about all of our states in a data base file called Census Info. Figure H-1 shows one record from that file. Take a moment to examine the categories in the figure.

```
=====================================================================
LOCATION: -                              1980 BIRTH RATE/1000: 15.9
STATE NAME: United States of America     1980 DEATH RATE/1000: 8.8
POPULATION 1982: 231,534,000             80 INFANT DEATH RATE: 12.6
POPULATION 1980: 226,546,000             BLACK POP 1980: 26,495,000
# POP CHANGE 80/82: 4,988,000            HISPANIC POP 80: 14,609,000
% POP CHANGE 80/82: 2.2                  MEDIAN AGE 1980: 30
POPULATION 1970: 203,302,000             % POP. 65+ 1982: 11.6
POP RANK 1960: -                         % H.S. GRADS 25+ 80: 66.3
POP RANK 1982: -                         $ PER.CAP.INCOME 82: 11,107
PROJECTED POP 1990: 249,203,000          % UNEMPLOYMENT 1983: 9.8
AREA SQ.MILES: 3,618,800                 % VOTING 1980: 53.2
AREA RANK: -                             SEATS-HOUSE OF REP.: 435
POP/SQ.MI.1982: 65                       ABBREV.: U.S.A.
POP/SQ.MI.RANK: -                        CLIMATE: -
EST NET MIGRATION: 1,257,000             STRUCTURE OF LAND: -
---------------------------------------------------------------------
```

FIGURE H-1. Census Info Record.

Here is an explanation of each of the category names used in this application:

CATEGORY NAME	MEANING
LOCATION	Geographic Region of the country.
STATE NAME	
POPULATION 1982	Resident population July 1982.[1]
POPULATION 1980	Population April 1, 1980.[1]
# POP CHANGE 80/82	Number of population change April 1, 1980, to July 1, 1982. A negative number indicates a decrease in the population.[1]
% POP CHANGE 80/82	Percent of population change April 1, 1980, to July 1, 1982. A negative percent indicates a decrease in the population.[1]
POPULATION 1970	Resident population, April 1, 1970.[2]
POP RANK 1960	Rank order of population size in 1960. The state with the highest population is 1; the state with the lowest population is 50.
POP RANK 1982	Rank order of population size in 1982. The state with the highest population is 1.
PROJECTED POP 1990	Resident population projected to July 1, 1990.[3]
AREA SQ.MILES	Total area in square miles.[4]
AREA RANK	Total area rank order.[4] The largest state is number 1.
POP/SQ.MI.1982	Number of persons per square mile of land area in 1982.[4]
POP/SQ.MI.RANK	Rank order of persons per square mile of land area.[4] The state with the greatest number of people per square mile is ranked 1.
EST NET MIGRATION	Estimated new migration April 1982 to July 1982.1 A negative number indicates migration from the state; no sign before the number indicates migration to the state.
1980 BIRTH RATE/1000	Crude birth rate, 1980.[5]
1980 DEATH RATE/1000	Crude death rate, 1980.[5]
80 INFANT DEATH RATE/1000	Infant mortality rate, 1980.[5]
BLACK POP 1980	Black Population, 1980.[6]
HISPANIC POP 80	Hispanic Population, 1980.[6]
MEDIAN AGE 1980	An estimate of the average age of the residents.[6]
% POP. 65+ 1982	Percentage of the population aged 65 and over, 1982.[7]
% H.S. GRADS 25+ 80	Percentage of the population aged 25 and over that have completed high school.[8]
$ PER.CAP.INCOME	Estimated 1982 per capita income.[9]
% UNEMPLOYMENT 1983	Percentage unemployment rate, May 1983.[10]
% VOTING 1980	Percentage of the eligible voters voting in the 1980 presidential election.[11]

SEATS-HOUSE OF REP.	Seats allocated for the Federal House of Representatives.
ABBREV.	Abbreviation of state name.
CLIMATE	Notes on climate. Examples: warm all year, short summer, dry. (There is no data in the file for this category.)
STRUCTURE OF LAND	Notes on the structure of the land forms in the state. Examples: mountains, plains, several lakes. (There is no data in the file for this category.)

As you know, you can organize and arrange the file in several ways. For example, arrange the file by number of high school graduates over the age of 25 in 1980 (H.S. GRADS 25+ 80). The higher the number (in percent) the higher the number of graduates in that state. Arrange the file by order of the percentage of the voters in each state that voted in the 1980 election. The higher the percentage, the greater the proportion of people in the state who exercised their democratic right. Arrange the states by median ("average") age; the lower the age, the younger the population.

Arrange the states by population per square mile (POP/SQ.MI.1982) to see how many people, on the average, live in each square mile in the state. You can determine which states have the least people per square mile and which states have the most.

YOUR TASK

Select four categories that you consider important for a good life in the United States. For example, you might pick low population per square mile, high per capita income, low infant death rate and high employment (low unemployment). Write a report using the Word Processor explaining why these categories are important to you. Include in your report a listing of the seven states that meet your criteria for each of the four categories that you have selected. (Transfer the information by creating a report in the Data Base and then printing the report to the clipboard for the Word Processor.)

Research the states that appear on your four lists for a fifth category that you consider important for a good life in the United States. Add this information to your copy of the data base. Climate and structure of the land have been included in the list of category names as suggestions for categories to research. If you do not wish to consider these categories, delete them from the list of category names and add your own. Include one of these categories in your report. Conclude your report with a list of five to seven states that best suit you.

Use the Spreadsheet to help you analyze your findings and to pick the states that are best for you. For example, you might devise a scoring system for each category and for each state in the category. The state with the highest score should win your heart.

Summarize your findings in your report. Include an illustration of the spreadsheet analysis that you created by transferring the Spreadsheet file to the Word Processor.

FOOTNOTES FOR THIS APPLICATION

1. Resident population totals (which exclude armed forces overseas) are from U.S.Bureau of the Census, Current Population Reports, Series P-25, No. 927, "Provisional Estimates of the Population of States: July 1, 1981, and 1982." The 1980 Census counts given are final figures published in the 1980 Census (Vol. 1, Chapter A).

2. Data are from the 1980 Census, Vol 1, PC80-1-A1, Number of Inhabitants, United States Summary.

3. Data from U.S. Bureau of the Census, Current Population Reports, Series P-25, No. 937, "Provisional Projections of the Population of States, by Age and Sex: 1980 to 2000."

4. Total area includes 3,539,289 sq. miles of land and 79,481 square miles of water.

5. The crude birth rate is the annual number of births per 1,000 population as given in the National Center of Health Statistics' Monthly Vital Statistics Report.

6. Data from the 1980 Census of Population, Vol. 1, PC80-1-B1, General Population Characteristics, United States Summary.

7. Data are from U.S.Bureau of the Census, Current Population Reports, Series P-25, No. 930, "Estimates of the Population of States, by Age: July 1, 1981, and 1982."

8. Provisional sample estimates from the 1980 Census, Supplementary Report, PHC80-S1-1.

9. Estimates prepared by the Bureau of Economic Analysis and given in U.S. Dept. Commerce News, BEA 83-47, Sept. 6, 1983.

10. These rates are not seasonally adjusted and are published in U.S. Dept. of Labor News, Bureau of Labor Statistics, USDL 83-304.

11. Data from the U.S Bureau of the Census, State and Metropolitan Area Data Book, 1982, Table C.

APPENDIX

A GETTING STARTED ON YOUR MICROCOMPUTER

This appendix covers introductory information on the use of Apple IIe or compatible computers. It is provided to give students unfamiliar with the computer a basic level of competence for using the software provided in this book. This appendix can also serve as a review for students returning to the Apple computer after a time away from it, and it can be used for a quick overview of the Apple by those who are familiar with other computers.

PART 1: THE KEYBOARD

The Apple IIe has 53 keys. An illustration of the keyboard appears in Figure A-1.

Figure A-1. The Apple IIe Keyboard.

Several of the keys have symbols or words other than characters. To minimize confusion, the following conventions are used in **Understanding and Using AppleWorks**. When you are asked to press a single key identified by a word, the word is written out in capital letters using a special type

A-1

style and is enclosed in angle brackets. For example, if you must press the Tab key, the text shows: <TAB>. Here is a list of the special keys and how they appear in the text when you are asked to press them. The table lists the special keys across each row starting with the top row. The keys are usually listed in a table under the heading WHAT YOU TYPE. Do not type these keys now.

WHAT THE TEXT SHOWS	NOTES ABOUT THE KEY
<ESCAPE>	The key is in the upper left corner of the keyboard. On some computers it is marked ESC and on others Esc. This key usually cancels the last command you entered.
<DELETE>	When you press and release this key, the character to the left of the blinking cursor is usually erased.
<TAB>	This is the left most key in the second row down. This key usually moves the cursor to the right a fixed number of positions.
<RETURN>	This key usually signals the end of an operation.
<CAPS LOCK>	Press this key once and it stays down; press it again and it stays up. When this key is up, the letter keys typed alone type lowercase; the shift key is used to change the letter keys to uppercase and the shift key is used to type the upper symbol on two symbol keys. When this key is down, the letter keys typed alone type uppercase; the shift key does not change the letters (they stay uppercase) and it must still be used to type the upper symbol on two symbol keys. This key is sometimes called a toggle key since it toggles (switches) the capital letters on or off.
<LEFT-ARROW>	This is also called a cursor movement key. On this key there is a picture of an arrow pointing to the left.
<RIGHT-ARROW>	Another cursor movement key. Its symbol is an arrow pointing to the right.
<DOWN-ARROW>	The third cursor movement key.
<UP-ARROW>	The last cursor movement key.

MULTIPLE KEY COMBINATIONS

The shift key is used in combination with other keys to change the information that the second key sends to the computer. For example, with the Caps Lock key in the up position, pressing L produces l; holding SHIFT while pressing L produces L; holding CONTROL while pressing L starts underlining in the Word Processor and holding ⌃ while pressing L changes the layout format in either the Data Base or the Spreadsheet.

Multiple key combinations are shown in the text in the same special type used for the single keys. The key symbols are separated by a dash which you do not type. For example, if you are asked to use the combination that consists of the Open-Apple key and the Tab key pressed together, the text would read ⌃-TAB. Angle brackets are not used with multiple key combinations.

It is important to note that there is a very specific order that must be followed when using a multiple key combinations. The Control, Shift or Apple key must be pressed first and held down while the second key is pressed and released. For example, to enter the command ⌘-L, press and hold the ⌘ key while you press and quickly release the L key and then release the ⌘ key. If the keys are not pressed in the correct order, you'll probably type an unwanted character into your document. Here is a list of keys that are pressed in combination with other keys.

COMBINATION KEY	NOTES ABOUT THE KEY
SHIFT	There are two shift keys, one on either end of the fourth row down. The two shift keys do the same thing. They switch letters from lowercase to capital letters or they shift to the upper character showing on two character keys. To use a shift key, press and hold the shift key while you press and release the letter or character key.
CONTROL	The left most key in the third row down. This key does nothing when pressed alone. It is used together with other keys to give commands to AppleWorks. It is used in the same way as a shift key is used; hold the Control key down while you press and release the other key and then release the Control key.
RESET	This key does nothing when pressed alone. When pressed at the same time as the Control key, it stops AppleWorks and erases all of the work in the computer's memory. There is no way to recover work from a Control-Reset if the work has not been saved.
⌘	The Open-Apple key is used as yet a third shift key.
🍎	The Solid-Apple key is yet another shift key. Its operation appears to be identical to the Open-Apple key; however, several AppleWorks enhancement products such as spelling checkers and desktop accessories use this key to produce different results than the Open-Apple key. It is a good habit to use the Open-Apple key exclusively.

AUTO REPEAT

With the exception of the Control, Shift, Caps Lock and Apple keys, all keys go to automatic repeat mode if you hold the key down for more than a second. Automatic repeat can produce some rather strange looking results that are disturbing when they first occur. For example, holding the Escape key down while you are working in the Word Processor will cause the Main Menu and your document to rapidly flash back and forth on the screen. Holding a key down may cause the screen to fill up with the character printed on the key or may cause the beep to sound continuously. To stop the problem, take your hands off of the keyboard.

PART II: GETTING STARTED

When you sit down before your computer the first thing that you need to determine is if it is on or off. In order for the computer to be on and ready, two switches need to be turned on, one for the computer and the other for the monitor. (If you have a printer, you'll need to turn that on and prepare it, too.

We'll discuss printers later.) The computer and the monitor are independent, each works without the other, but they must work together in order for you to have a functioning computer.

Check your monitor. There is either a label on the on/off switch to indicate the position of the switch or a small light that glows when the monitor is on. Turn the monitor on by turning or pressing its switch.

Check your computer. The lower left corner of the keyboard has a green or white light that glows to indicate that the computer is turned on. If the computer is not on, reach around to the back of the computer with your left hand. The computer's power switch is about halfway up the computer about two inches in from the edge. Press the top of the switch to turn the computer on. (Some systems have a master switch located to the left of the computer. If your system has a master switch, turn it on.)

When the computer is turned on, it beeps and the red light on Disk drive 1 lights. Note which drive is lit. The red light indicates that the disk drive is operating.

RULE: Never insert or remove a disk from the disk drive when the red light is on.

All that you have determined so far is which drive is Drive 1. (Sometimes drives are not labeled or are mislabeled.)

Now turn the computer and the monitor off.

> Press the bottom of the computer's on/off switch.
> Reverse the process you used to turn on the monitor.

STARTUP PROCEDURES

IF THE COMPUTER IS TURNED OFF

1. Open the door on Drive 1 if it is not already open. On a tan door, press in on the center of the handle and it will pop up. On a black door, press in on the top of the door flap.

2. Insert the startup disk for the software that you are using in Drive 1. The label on the disk should be up; the oval opening in the disk should be away from you and toward the disk drive. The oval opening on the disk is on the edge first inserted into the disk drive.

3. When the disk is fully inserted, close the drive door.

4. If you have a printer attached to your computer, turn the printer on. Roll the paper forward so that the top of a page is just above the print head. (Ask your instructor for help with this if you're not sure how to set the paper correctly.) The power light and the select light (on-line light on some printers) should be lit. If the select light is not lit, press and release the button next to the light.

5. Turn on the monitor.

6. Turn on the computer.

7. When the red light goes out on the disk, it indicates that the program is loaded into the computer. The program's opening screen should appear on the monitor.

IF THE COMPUTER IS TURNED ON

1. Insert the startup disk for your software into Drive 1.

2. When the disk is fully inserted, close the drive door.

3. Make sure that the printer is turned on and ready.

4. Issue the warm start command. This command erases any information that is in the computer's memory. Make sure that you are not inadvertantly erasing someone else's work before you give the command.
   With your left hand, hold down both the CONTROL and the ⌘ keys.
   With your right hand, press and release RESET.
   Release the CONTROL and the ⌘ keys.

5. When the red disk drive light goes out, the program should be loaded and the program's main screen should appear in your display.

SHUTDOWN PROCEDURES

1. Make sure that you follow the proper escape or exit procedures for the software you are using. If you do not follow these procedures, you may lose some or all of your data. (In other words, you'll have to retype your work.)

2. When the disk drive's red light is off, remove the disk. Remove the disk from the second drive if you used the second drive.

3. Unless otherwise instructed, turn off the monitor, printer, and computer.

4. Straighten up the work area for the next person who will use the machine.

PART III: DISK CARE

Disks can be easily damaged if they are not treated with care. It is a good idea to make a copy of your important files on a separate disk to guard against loss (see Part IV). It is also a good idea to treat your disks with care. Follow these rules and your disks should work well for a year or more:

• Always return the disk to its protective jacket after you remove it from the computer.
• Do not keep them in books. (Their outside jackets get crushed and prevent the disk from turning freely inside.)
• Don't bend them or force them into or out of the disk drive.
• Never touch the exposed surface showing in the oval window. (Oil and grit on your hands may make the spot you touch unreadable.)

- Keep them away from magnets, including magnets in TVs, speakers, and library security devices.

PART IV: USING THE SYSTEM UTILITIES DISK

The system utilities disk that comes with the Apple II computer contains programs that let you list the contents of a disk, delete files, copy files, rename files, or duplicate the entire disk. It is most important to keep a backup of the work that you do. As the number of files that you have created increases, making a backup is best done a whole disk at a time.

DUPLICATING A DISK

Insert the System Utilities Disk into Drive 1 and start your computer system.

The current version of the disk appears in the display. (The version discussed here is 2.1.) After a few moments, a question appears asking you if you prefer an 80-column display.

WHAT YOU TYPE	WHY YOU TYPE IT
Y	To indicate that you prefer an 80-column display.

The Main Menu appears.

WHAT YOU TYPE	WHY YOU TYPE IT
Down-arrow	To highlight the program **DUPLICATE A DISK.** The highlight is indicated in this program by changing the program name from capital and lowercase letters to all capitals. "Down-arrow" is shown in lower case to indicate that the key may need to be pressed more than once.
<RETURN>	To start the program.
<RETURN>	To indicate the slot and drive of the source (original) material.
<RETURN>	To accept the default answer of slot 6. (Slot refers to the location of the disk connection inside of the computer. It is usually slot 6.)
<RETURN>	To accept the default drive for the source disk as Drive 1.
<RETURN> three times	To accept the default values for the destination (duplicate) drive.
Read the screen	To verify that the source is in slot 6, Drive 1 and the destination is in slot 6, Drive 2.
Write protect the original disk	To prevent any accidental erasure of the information on the disk. A properly working computer does not write on a disk that has the small square notch covered.
Insert the disks as indicated on the display.	
<RETURN>	To start the copy process.

The computer may inform you that you are about to destroy the contents of a disk. If you are sure that the disk you are about to copy information onto (the destination disk) does not contain any useful information, press Return. Otherwise, use another destination disk.

The computer displays the message: Formatting followed by the message Duplicating.

Press <ESCAPE>   To return to the Main Menu when you are finished.
Remove both disks.
Test the new copy   by starting the computer with the copy or by reading data from the disk with a software package such as AppleWorks. This will determine if the copying was successful.

You should feel free to explore the other utilities on the utility disk. You will not harm the utility disk if you experiment with it. Original utility disks have no notch cut into them so they are write-protected. When you are finished, select EXIT SYSTEM UTILITIES and press <RETURN>. You may turn the computer off when you see the prompt for Applesoft Basic ( ]).

APPENDIX

B ANSWERS TO CHECKPOINTS

| PAGE | | ANSWERS TO ✔ CHECKPOINTS |

The Escape key.

The message is "Use arrows to see remainder of Help."

The Delete key.

The Open-Apple key and the letter S key pressed together (⌘-S).

On the Main Menu Help Screen.

The Escape key.

The Escape key.

a. The Activity 1 File is still on your primary data disk. (Use the "add files to the Desktop" option if you want to verify this. Do not add the file to the Desktop; press <ESCAPE> twice to cancel the add operation and to return to the Main Menu.)

b. The Activity 1 File is no longer on your primary data disk; formatting the disk erases all files on the disk. If you try to load the file from the this disk, you'll find it is empty.

c. If you followed the text, your backup file did not contain your name and the blank line following your name.

d. Type your name and the blank line back into the file.

e. If you format a disk that contains information, the information is erased by the fomatting process.

f. There are two major lessons to be learned from this experience: (1) don't format a disk that contains information unless you are sure that the information is unwanted, and (2) if you lose your primary disk or the information on your primary disk, you can restore all or most of that information from an up-to-date backup.

The message Escape: "Lounge" appears in the upper right corner.

On the Desktop (in the computer's memory).

The blank line and the words "The End" are part of the Desktop copy of the document; they are not part of the disk copy.

	PAGE	ANSWERS TO ✔ CHECKPOINTS
UNIT 3	45	The two messages refer to the Escape key and the space bar. The messages are: Escape to stop printing and return to Review/Add/Change and space bar to pause (or) to continue printing.
	51	⌘-S and ⌘-E only appear on the Main Menu Help Screen.
	57	The printer options for centering and 5 characters-per-inch are not on the disk copy.
	65	You have just finished saving your file, so you do not need to save it again.
UNIT 4	76	There are two copies of the file on your disk, Original YrBk and Yearbook Sales. The only copy on the Desktop is Yearbook Sales. All three copies are identical at this time, however, as you make changes to Yearbook Sales the files will be different. The file Original YrBk remains unchanged; you have it as a backup in case you make an error changing the working copy.
	81	1. Move the cursor to the top of the file.
		2. Move the cursor to the bottom of the file.
		3. Move the cursor up one line.
		4. Move the cursor down one line.
		5. Move the cursor to the bottom of the current screen display or to the bottom of the next screen display depending on its position when you give the command.
		6. Move the cursor to the top of the current screen display or to the top of the previous screen display.
		7. Move the cursor to the next tab stop (usually 5 spaces).
		8. Move the cursor to the previous tab stop.
		9. Move the cursor right one character.
		10. Move the cursor left one character.
	83	The "Insert New Records" mode. Escape returns to Review/Add/Change mode.
	86	Removes information from the cursor position to the end of the line.
	88	Normally you would need to arrange the file twice, first alphabetically and then by home room. Since the file was already in alphabetical order, you only needed to arrange it by homeroom.
	96	There are several rules that are correct; one of them is Last Name begins with H.
	100	⌘ R, Y resets the rules to display all records.

PAGE	ANSWERS TO ✔ CHECKPOINTS

UNIT 5

109 There are 18 rows (1 to 18) and 8 columns (A to H), or 144 cells (8 times 18) visible in the display.

114
1. 7 (15 and 20 are added first, then the result (35) is divided by 5).
2. 19 (20 is divided by 5 and the result (4) is added to 15).
3. 19 (arithmetic is done in the same order as it was in problem 2).
4. 1 (5 and 15 are added and the result (20) is divided inot 20).
5. 90 (80, 90, and 100 are added and the result (270) is divided by 3).
6. 90 (100, 90, and 80 are added and the result (270) is divided by 3).
7. 1000 (10 is multiplied by itself 3 times (10 times 10 times 10)).

117 It just fills the cell (6 digits+period+comma+space = 9 characters). The lower left corner of the screen tells you that the layout is C2 (commas with two decimal places).

122 D5, E5, D8, and E8 are acceptable starting location since they are in the corners of the rectangle to be blanked.

128 The standard label format, unchanged for this spreadsheet, left justify. Ú-V changes the standard value for label formats.

130 Period starts the selection of a range of cells (copy to many), Return selects the one cell at the location of the cell locator (copy to one).

132 The 75 is an exact value, not the result of a formula, so it does not change unless another value is typed in its place.

133 D10 is 75, the value in the cell above it that its formula calls for.

138 Always save your file before you print it.

UNIT 6

160 Default is the setting used by the computer if you do not act to change it. The margins are: top 0.0, bottom 2.0, left 1.0, and right 1.0.

164 Underline Understanding and Using AppleWorks, the title of this text. No words need to be boldface.

174 The line changes to: "   d.   The last wor   d." since both d.'s are changed.

UNIT 7

197 Use Ú-" in the multiple record layout display.

198 The exact message is: Custom record layouts, made using Ú-L, will be set back to standard. All of the categories are displayed on the multiple record screen in the original order. The screen layout was set back to standard when you added the Study category.

201 Yes, first arrange the dates chronologically so the blank dates are together at the top of the list; then use Ú-" as you did before.

205 Ú-R, Y.

207 72 (6 times 12).

211 The line width is 5 (8-2-1); the character per line estimate is 60 (5 times 12).

211 To the clipboard.

	PAGE	ANSWERS TO ✔ CHECKPOINTS
UNIT 8	231	Extra information in the column, titles and dashed lines for example, is not a part of the arrangement and needs to be excluded.
	241	No.
	243	The calculation mode is manual, so no calculations are done after the copy command. Use ⌘-K to calculate the correct averages.
	244	Save your file (you might also want to back it up).
	246	Use ⌘-L since the changes are for one row only, not for all cells in the spreadsheet.
	254	Take the information from 40 cells above and 20 cells above this cells location.
UNIT 9	278	Place the cursor under the 1 in question 11 to insert the answers for question 10, under the 1 in 12 to insert answers for question 11, and at the beginning of the blank line under question 12 to insert the answers for question 12.
	280	Proportional 2, the last type style indicated before the header and footer commands were inserted.
UNIT 10	291	"4 " (4 space).
	293	4.
	300	On the Report Format Menu move to the Team category, then type :⌘–G, ⌘–G, Y.
UNIT 11	314	0.200, 0..120, and 0.175, respectively.
UNIT 12	331	4. Where it was when you left the file.

TELLING APPLEWORKS ABOUT YOUR PRINTER

This appendix discusses printers and how to get them to work with AppleWorks in a very general way. Specific information about a particular printer can only be found in the manual for that printer. Information that applies to a very broad range of printers, printer connections, AppleWorks printer settings, and printer problems can be found here. Likewise, very specific information about setting AppleWorks for a particular printer can be found in the AppleWorks manual. Only general information, some of which may not be found other manuals, is included here.

```
Disk: Disk 2 (Slot 6)          PRINTER INFORMATION        Escape: Other Activities
_____
   _____
  |    Main Menu           |_____
  |    _____                                        |
  |   |    Other Activities        |_____|__
  |   |   _____                                            |
  |   |  |    Printer Information   |_____|__
  |   |  |                                                                      |
  |   |  |                                                                      |
  |   |  |    Change standard values                                           |
  |   |  |    1.  Open-Apple-H printer   Apple DMP (Slot 1)                     |
  |   |  |                                                                      |
  |   |  |    Add or remove a printer                                          |
  |   |  |    2.  Add a printer (maximum of 3)                                 |
  |   |  |    3.  Remove a printer                                             |
  |   |  |                                                                      |
  |   |  |    Change printer specifications                                    |
  |__|  |    4.  Apple DMP (Slot 1)                                           |
      |  |    5.  Imagewriter (Slot 1)                                        |
      |__|                                                                     |
         |_____|
_____
Type number, or use arrows, then press Return                          55K Avail.
```

FIGURE C-1. Printer Information Menu.

PRINTERS

If you have an Apple Imagewriter printer or an Apple Dot Matrix Printer, AppleWorks is all set for you. If you have another printer, you'll need to give AppleWorks some information about it. Let's look at how you do this.

Start at the Main Menu.

WHAT YOU TYPE	WHY YOU TYPE IT
5 <RETURN>	To select **Other activities.**
7 <RETURN>	To select **Specify information about your printer(s).**

The **Printer Information Menu** shown in Figure C-1 appears on the screen.

If you have an **Apple Dot Matrix Printer** (DMP): Everything is set correctly for your printer. Press <ESCAPE> <u>twice</u> to return to the Main Menu.

If you have an **Apple Imagewriter Printer**: It is convenient, though not necessary, to make the Imagewriter printer the first printer on the list. To do this:

WHAT YOU TYPE	WHY YOU TYPE IT
3 <RETURN>	To select **Remove a printer.**
<RETURN>	To select and delete the DMP printer. The Imagewriter will move to the #4 position on the printer list.

Check to see that the Open-Apple-H printer is now the Imagewriter printer. If it is not, type 1 <RETURN> <RETURN> to select it.

<ESCAPE> twice	To return to the Main Menu.

If you have **another printer**: Remove the DMP printer and the Imagewriter printer from the list of printers; then add your printer. Here's how.

WHAT YOU TYPE	WHY YOU TYPE IT
3 <RETURN>	To select **Remove a printer.**
<RETURN>	To remove the DMP printer.
3 <RETURN> <RETURN>	To remove the Imagewriter printer.
2 <RETURN>	To select **Add a printer.**

Find the exact name and model of your printer either by asking your instructor or by reading the name plate found on either the front or back of the printer.

If your printer is on the list of printers displayed:

Select your printer from the list . Enter a name for your printer and press <RETURN>.

By convention, printers are usually connected to Slot 1. Press <RETURN> to select this option.

The next list of options you see on your display is shown in Figure C-2. The questions are answered correctly for many of the printers selected from the list. Assume for the moment that they are answered correctly for your printer. Proceed with the section "Interface Cards" found below.

```
Disk: Disk 2 (Slot 6)           ADD A PRINTER      Escape: Printer Information
_____

     _____
    |     Main Menu         |_____
    |    _____                                         |
    |   |    Other Activities    |_____|__
    |   |   _____                                  |
    |   |  |    Printer Information     |_____|__
    |   |  |   _____                             |
    |   |  |  |    Add a Printer         |_____|__
    |   |  |  |                                                        |
    |   |  |  |   Printer name: Your  Printer  Name  (Slot  1)         |
    |   |  |  |                                                        |
    |   |  |  |   Printer type: What  you  select  from  the  list     |
    |   |  |  |                                                        |
    |   |  |  |   1.  Needs line feed after each Return       No       |
    |   |  |  |   2.  Accepts top-of-page commands            Yes      |
    |   |  |  |   3.  Stop at end of each page                No       |
    |__|  |  |   4.  Platen width                       8.0 inches     |
       |  |  |   5.  Interface cards                                   |
      |__|  |   6.  Printer codes <== Only for Custom  Printers        |
         |__|_____|
_____
Type number, or use arrows, then press Return                    55K Avail.
```

FIGURE C-2.   Add (or Change) A Printer Menu.

If your printer is not on the list of printers displayed:

After you have selected Add a printer, continue with:

WHAT YOU TYPE	WHY YOU TYPE IT
Arrows <RETURN>	To select **Custom printer.**
a name for your printer	To enter the name of your printer. To avoid later confusion, include the model number as part of the name if you are able to fit it in the space provided.
<RETURN>	To enter the name.
<RETURN>	To indicate the slot to which your printer is connected. This is usually Slot 1. If your printer is not connected to slot 1, you'll need to enter the correct slot number before you press Return.

You need to experiment with the Yes/No answers to the first three questions displayed on the next screen. (See Figure C-2.) Assume, for the moment, that these settings are correct and continue with the section below.

INTERFACE CARDS

There are several different **interface cards** used to connect the computer to the printer. Some of the cards are designed to display a duplicate of what the printer is printing on the screen. AppleWorks was not programmed to operate this way, so a special code must be sent to the interface card to turn off the screen display. If the text appears in odd places on the screen as it is printed on the printer, or if your interface card (found inside the computer) is specifically mentioned below, change the interface card code using the following steps:

WHAT YOU TYPE	WHY YOU TYPE IT
5 <RETURN>	To select **Interface cards** from the Add/Change a Printer Menu. Note: Early versions of AppleWorks do not have this feature.
<SPACE BAR>	To proceed past the explanation paragraph.
<RETURN>	To answer "No" to the question Is this **OK?** (Is the code Control-I 80N OK?)

You now need to enter the code for your interface card. The interface card manual should give you the correct code. Three of the more popular interface cards and their codes are:

Grappler® and PKASO® cards Control-I 0N
Tymac® cards   Control-I 99N

Here is a specific example of how you would enter one of these codes. The example uses the code Control-I 0N.

WHAT YOU TYPE	WHY YOU TYPE IT
<CAPS LOCK>	To select all capital letters. The "I" and the "N" must be capital letters.
Hold down <CONTROL>	
Press and release the letter I	
Release <CONTROL>	To enter the Control-I part of the code.
0N	To enter the 0N (zero, capital N) part of the code. The screen display should now read: **Control-I 0N** (The only way to correct an error is to signal the completion of the entry and repeat the process from the beginning.)
SHIFT-6	To signal the computer that you have completed the code you type a caret (^).
Escape	To return to the Main Menu.

Test your printer selection and code by printing a word processor document such as the Lounge story described in the Unit 3.

TROUBLESHOOTING:

(See Figure C-2 to determine how to bring the questions back onto your display.)

Problem: All of the text prints on one line.

Correction: Change the answer to **Needs line feed after each Return** from No to Yes.

Problem: The text double spaces even though the word processor is set to single space.

Correction: Change the answer to **Needs line feed after each Return** from Yes to No.   (See Figure C-2.)

Problem: The paper does not scroll up one full page to the top of the next page at the end of a report, or the second page of a report does not start on a new page.

Correction: First make sure that you started the paper correctly when you printed your document. If you see a white space in the middle of your document between pages your problem is not with the settings in AppleWorks; you probably need to set the paper correctly before you start to print. Check this procedure with your instructor.
If you are sure that your paper is set correctly, change the answer to the question **Accepts top-of-page commands** to No.

Problem: Your printer takes single sheet paper and does not wait for a new sheet to be inserted after it completes the first sheet.

Correction: Change the answer to the question **Stop at the end of each page** to Yes.

Problem: Your printer stops at the end of each page and AppleWorks requests that you press a key before it continues. You do not want it to do this.

Correction: Change the answer to the question **Stop at the end of each page** to No.

Problem: You have a wide carriage printer and you always print on wide paper.

Correction: Set the **Platen width** to 13.2 inches. If you print on both wide and narrow paper, leave the platen width setting at 8.0 inches. The setting can be changed for wide printouts in the individual application files as required.

ADDITIONAL NOTES

To make full use of all of the features of your custom printer, printer codes for different character sizes, underling, boldface, etc. must be entered. Since the 200 or more printer models available to work with the Apple computer have a wide variety of codes, you need to consult your printer manual for this information. This probably requires the help of an expert and the AppleWorks Reference Manual Appendix B.

Return to the "Printer Information" menu. The Open-Apple-H printer should show the name that you entered for your printer. If it does not, select the option **Open-Apple-H printer**, press <RETURN> and select your printer (the one you just set up) for this option.

Setting up the printer is a process that only needs to be done once. You will not repeat it unless you get a new printer or need to copy the AppleWorks Program disk from the original again.

A WORD OF WISDOM

If you took considerable time to enter information for a custom printer, make a backup of your working copy of the AppleWorks Program disk. Should you lose or damage your original working program disk, you need only make a new copy from the backup. You do not need to re-enter all of the printer codes again if you save them on a backup. Appendix A explains how to copy a disk.

D COMMON APPLEWORKS ERROR MESSAGES

The following table lists some common AppleWorks error messages along with possible corrective measures.

DISK MESSAGES

MESSAGE	PROBLEM/CORRECTION
Can't write on disk at Drive#	An unsuccessful attempt was made to save information. Make sure that your file data disk is in the drive and that the drive door is closed properly. Press the space bar to continue, and try to save again with ⌘-S.
Disk has write protect tab	An attempt was made to format a write protected disk. A write-protected disk can not be formatted. Remove the tab from the disk and try again. (You may have the disk in up-side-down or in another incorrect orientation. Make sure that the disk is inserted correctly and the disk door is fully closed.)
Disk is ProDOS/SOS volume /APPLEWORKS (/APPLEWORKS may be different.)	An attempt was made to format a disk which contains information. If you are certain that the information on the disk is useless, answer yes to the question "OK to destroy contents?" by typing the letters y e s. Otherwise obtain another blank disk, label it, and put the used disk aside.
Getting errors trying to read FILE NAME on Disk # (Slot #)	An unsuccessful attempt was made to load a file. The file, disk, or disk drive may be damaged. Try loading the same file from another disk. Try loading another file from a different disk in the suspect drive (use a disk that has several backups for this). Load a backup of the file and save it on the primary.
Insufficient room for your file on this disk.	An unsuccessful attempt was made to save a file. Use another disk to save your file.

DISK MESSAGES (continued)

MESSAGE	PROBLEM/CORRECTION
Unable to find the disk	An unsuccessful attempt was made to save or load a file. The disk door is not closed properly or the disk drive is not operating properly. Remove the disk, reinsert it, and close the door. If you have two drives, try using the other drive. You need to change the drive to Drive 1 in order to do so. (Use Other Activities Menu item 1 "Change current disk drive or ProDOS prefix" to do this.)

EDITING MESSAGES

MESSAGE	PROBLEM/CORRECTION
AppleWorks Data Base files are limited to 1,350 records.	The Data Base file record limit has been reached; the file must be split into two parts.
You are about to have more than one copy of this file on the Desktop.	An attempt was made to put a file with a duplicate name onto the desktop. Answer no to the question "Do you really want to do this?"
You are limited to 12 files on the Desktop	An attempt was made to exceed the Desktop limit of 12 files. Remove some files from the Desktop or load fewer files.
You are limited to 250 lines at one time	An attempt was made to copy or move more than 250 lines of information onto the clipboard. Do the copy or move in two or more pieces.
WARNING. Desktop is full. Action not completed.	AppleWorks Desktop capacity has been reached. If there is more than one file on the Desktop, save the extra files and remove them from the Desktop. If there is only one file on the Desktop, the file must be split into two files before you can continue. It is possible that you have a very large amount of information taking up room on the clipboard. Try copying the smallest piece of data you can onto the clipboard. If the amount of work that you have to do to finish your file is less than what you had stored on the clipboard, you may be able to finish your work without any additional difficulty.
Word Processing files are limited to 2,250 lines.	The Word Processor line limit has been reached; the file must be split into two parts.

APPENDIX

E

QUICK REFERENCE

The following is a summary of the AppleWorks commands used in this book.

WORD PROCESSOR

FILE MANAGEMENT COMMANDS

⌘-N...............................Change the file name.
⌘-Q...............................Quickly change to another file.
⌘-S...............................Save the file to disk.

CURSOR MOVEMENT COMMANDS

Up or Down arrow..............Move the cursor up or down a line.
Right or Left arrow.............Move the cursor right or left a character.
⌘ Up or Down arrow.........Move the cursor up or down one screen.
⌘ Right or Left arrow.........Move the cursor right or left a word.
⌘ 1 to 9........................Move the cursor proportionally through the text.

EDITING COMMANDS

⌘-C...............................Copy text.
⌘-D...............................Delete text.
⌘-E...............................Edit/insert cursor change.
⌘-F...............................Find text.
⌘-M...............................Move text.
⌘-R...............................Replace text.
⌘-T...............................Set Tab stops.
⌘-Y...............................Clear to end of line.
⌘-Z...............................Zoom in/out on printer settings.

PRINTING COMMANDS

☺-H...........................Print a hard copy of the screen.
☺-K...........................Calculate page breaks.
☺-P...........................Print document.

PRINTING OPTIONS -

Control-B.......................Boldface begin or end.
Control-L.......................Underline begin or end.
☺-O...........................Options display.
    BB.....................Boldface begin.
    BE.....................Boldface end.
    BM....................Set bottom margin.
    CI......................Characters per inch.
    CN....................Center text lines.
    DS ....Set double spacing.
    EK....................Enter data from keyboard.
    FO....................Set page footer.
    GB....................Group begin.
    GE....................Group end.
    HE....................Set page header.
    IN ....Set indent.
    JU ....Start justify.
    LI.......................Set lines per inch.
    LM....................Set left margin.
    P1 ....Set proportional 1 type size (elite).
    P2 ....Set proportional 2 type size (pica).
    PE.....................Pause each page.
    PH....................Pause here.
    PL.....................Set page length.
    PN....................Set page number.
    PP....................Print page number.
    PW....................Set platen width.
    RM ....Set right margin.
    SK....................Skip specified number of blank lines.
    SM....................Set marker.
    SS ....Set single space.
    TM ....Set top margin.
    TS ....Set triple space.
    UB....................Underline begin.
    UE....................Underline end.
    UJ.....................Unjustified text.

Data Base

File Management Commands

⌘-N.................................Change the name of a file or category. Insert or delete
categories.

⌘-Q.................................Quickly change to another file.

⌘-S.................................Save a file, its records, custom layouts, and reports to the disk.

Entering/Editing Information Commands

Left-arrow ....Move the cursor left one character within a category.

Right-arrow......................Move the cursor right onecharacter within a category.

Up-arrow ....Move the cursor one category up the list.

Down-arrow.....................Move the cursor one category down the list.

⌘-Up-arrow....................Move the cursor up one screen.

⌘-Down-arrow.................Move the cursor down one screen.

⌘-1 to 9.........................Move the cursor proportionally through the file.

Tab................................Move the cursor down a category in single record layout.
Move a column right in multiple record layout.

⌘-Tab...........................Move the cursor up a category in single record layout. Move a
column left in multiple record layout.

Control-Y........................Delete the characters on the line to the right of the cursor.

⌘-A.................................Arrange the file in alphabetical, numerical, or chronological
order.

⌘-D.................................Delete a record(s).

⌘-E.................................Edit/Insert cursor change.

⌘-F.................................Find information in the file.

⌘-I.................................Insert record(s).

⌘-L.................................Change record layout.

   ⌘-> or <..................In the multiple record layout change mode, move the position
of a category.

   ⌘-D......................In layout change mode for multiple records, delete a category
from the display.

   ⌘-I.......................In layout change mode for multiple records, insert a previously
deleted category into the display.

⌘-M................................Move records to (cut) and from (paste) the clipboard.

⌘-R.................................Change the rules used to select records.

⌘-V.................................Set standard values for data entry.

⌘-Y.................................Same as Control-Y.

⌘-Z.................................Zoom to single or multiple record layout.

⌘-".................................In the multiple record layout, ditto the category information
from the record above.

REPORT DESIGN/PRINTING

⌘-H..............................Print a hard copy of the screen.

⌘-P..............................Proceed to Report Menu from Review/Add/Change or print a report from the report format display.

Left, Right arrows..............Cursor movement from one category to another.

⌘-Left-arrow...................Change the size of a category column in the tables format or move a category to the left in the labels format.

⌘-Right-arrow.................Change the size of a category column in the tables format or move a category to the right in the labels format.

⌘-<..............................Change the position of a category in the tables format. Display the previous record in labels format.

⌘->..............................Change the position of a category in the tables format. Display the next record in labels format.

⌘-A..............................Arrange the file in alphabetical, numerical, or chronological order.

⌘-D..............................Delete a category from the report.

⌘-G..............................Add or remove report group totals.

⌘-I...............................Insert a previously deleted category into the report. Insert a blank line in a labels format report.

⌘-N..............................Change the name or title of a report.

⌘-R..............................Change the rules used to select records printed on the report.

⌘-T..............................Add or remove report category totals.

⌘-V..............................View the category name and the category information in a labels style report.

⌘-Z..............................Zoom in or out to show records or category names in labels or tables format.

SPREADSHEET

FILE MANAGEMENT COMMANDS

⌘-N..............................Change the name of a file.

⌘-Q..............................Quickly change to another file.

⌘-S..............................Save a file to the disk.

ENTER/EDIT COMMANDS

⌘-A..............................Arrange or sort rows.

⌘-B..............................Blank information from one or more cells.

⌘-C..............................Copy labels, values, or formulas from one or more cells to one or more cells.

⚑-D..............................Delete rows or columns.

⚑-E..............................Edit/Insert cursor change.

⚑-F..............................Find a cell and move to it.

⚑-I..............................Insert rows or columns.

⚑-J..............................Jump from one window to another.

⚑-K..............................Recalculate formulas.

⚑-L..............................Change the layout of one or more cells.

⚑-M..............................Move rows or columns.

⚑-T..............................Fix titles in the display.

⚑-U..............................Edit the information in a cell.

⚑-V..............................Set standard values.

⚑-W ....Change windows in the display.

⚑-Y ....Erase to the end of the line.

⚑-Z..............................Zoom in to show the formulas in the spreadsheet.

⚑-?..............................Examine standard values for the spreadsheet.

PRINTER COMMANDS

⚑-H..............................Print a hard copy of the screen.

⚑-O..............................Display the printer options.

⚑-P..............................Print the spreadsheet.

FORMULAS

Value..............................A single number, formula, or mathematical expression.

Range..............................A series of adjacent cells.

List..............................Single values or ranges separated by commas.

@ABS(value)....................The absolute value .

@AVG(list)......................The mean (average) of the values in the list.

@CHOOSE(value, list)........The value in the list indexed by the value given in the function. For example, @CHOOSE(3,80,85,90,95) is 90. 90 is the third value in the list.

@COUNT(list)..................The number of value entries in the list. Blanks and labels are not value entries and are not included in the count.

@ERROR........................Displays ERROR.

@IF(logical relation, value1, value2).

................................Value1 if the logical relation is TRUE or value 2 if the logical
relation is FALSE.

Logical relations are created with the symbols:

<................less than

>................greater than

=................equal

<=..............less than or equal to

>=..............greater than or equal to

<>..............not equal to

@INT(value)....................The integer portion of the value.

@LOOKUP(value,range)......The value in a second range adjacent to the largest entry less
than or equal to the value given in the function.

@MIN(list)....................The smallest value in the list.

@MAX(list)....................The largest value in the list.

@NA............................Displays NA ("Not Available").

@SQRT(value).................The square root of the value.

@SUM(list)....................The sum (total) of all of the values in the list.

INDEX

Notes

Notes

Notes

Notes

Notes